Discussion of the crucified and cursed Christ is much-needed in the African context. This is because these two concepts are often considered oxymorons in most popular African theological discourse. The theological understanding of the crucified and cursed Christ is a pillar of Christian doctrine. However, it is a topic that is less discussed, even from the pulpit. This has led to various truncated theologies regarding curses and such theologies hold many believers in constant fear. Certain curse deliverance ministries have also emerged due to this truncated theology, where many believers are being exploited to deliver them from the so-called generational curses.

This work by Dr. Cheboi is a masterpiece that helps to unpack the concept of curses through the exposition of Galatians 3:1–14. He identifies the theological foundation of the crucified and cursed Christ, and carefully connects it to the contextual understanding of this key theological foundation to the Marakwet culture, though also relevant to many African cultures, so that they can relate it to God's redemptive purposes. The work is theologically written and constructed with a simplicity that every believer can understand.

Nathan H. Chiroma, PhD
Principal,
Africa College of Theology, Rwanda

Dr. Cheboi has done a careful and sensitive study of the function of the cross in relation to rituals in the Graeco-Roman world. In essence, the author contextualizes Paul's understanding of the crucifixion in the ancient curse rituals to a particular African culture and in doing so, a modernist prejudice against ritual is overcome. From a broader perspective, societies have always recognized the significance of rituals to express their innermost convictions, stabilize a community, bring chaos into order, and make communal life possible. When biblical texts are read in the context of ritual, a particular kind of hermeneutics begins to emerge. It is in this context that the Christ event, where Jesus Christ becomes the ultimate curse remover, is recognized as a ritualistic and fundamental mode of responding to the Marakwet and African societies. This is a valuable contribution to the study of Christology and rituals. I endorse it without any reservations.

Samuel K. Elolia, PhD
Professor of Christian Theology and World Christianity,
Milligan University, Tennessee, USA

Crucified and Cursed Christ

An Analysis of Galatians 3:1–14 in the Context of Curses in Biblical Times and its Relevance to Marakwet Culture

Elkanah K. Cheboi

MONOGRAPHS

© 2023 Elkanah K. Cheboi

Published 2023 by Langham Monographs
An imprint of Langham Publishing
www.langhampublishing.org

Langham Publishing and its imprints are a ministry of Langham Partnership

Langham Partnership
PO Box 296, Carlisle, Cumbria, CA3 9WZ, UK
www.langham.org

ISBNs:
978-1-83973-835-7 Print
978-1-83973-945-3 ePub
978-1-83973-946-0 PDF

Elkanah K. Cheboi has asserted his right under the Copyright, Designs and Patents Act, 1988 to be identified as the Author of this work.

All rights reserved. No part of this publication may be reproduced, stored in a retrieval system or transmitted, in any form or by any means, electronic, mechanical, photocopying, recording or otherwise, without the prior written permission of the publisher or the Copyright Licensing Agency.

Requests to reuse content from Langham Publishing are processed through PLSclear. Please visit www.plsclear.com to complete your request.

All Scripture quotations, unless otherwise indicated, are taken from the Holy Bible, New International Version®, NIV®. Copyright ©1973, 1978, 1984, 2011 by Biblica, Inc.™ Used by permission of Zondervan.

Scripture quotations marked (ESV) are from The Holy Bible, English Standard Version® (ESV®), copyright © 2001 by Crossway, a publishing ministry of Good News Publishers. Used by permission. All rights reserved.

British Library Cataloguing-in-Publication Data
A catalogue record for this book is available from the British Library

ISBN: 978-1-83973-835-7

Cover & Book Design: projectluz.com

Langham Partnership actively supports theological dialogue and an author's right to publish but does not necessarily endorse the views and opinions set forth here or in works referenced within this publication, nor can we guarantee technical and grammatical correctness. Langham Partnership does not accept any responsibility or liability to persons or property as a consequence of the reading, use or interpretation of its published content.

Contents

Abstract ix
List of Abbreviations xi
Acknowledgments xiii
Chapter 1 1
   Introduction
      Introduction to the Study 1
          Contemporary Relevance 3
          The Motivation for the Research 5
          The Problem Statement 7
          Synopsis 7
          Purpose of the Study 7
          Significance of the Study 8
          Main Research Questions 8
      Literature Review 9
          Introduction 9
          Relevant Old Testament Studies on Curses 9
          Scholarly Studies on NT World and Galatians 3:1–14 11
          Scholarly Studies on Curses in Galatians 3:13 12
      Methodology 14
          Description of Socio-rhetorical Method 14
          Socio-rhetorical Criticism in Galatians 3:1–14 15
          Rhetorical Devices in Galatians 3:1–14 17
          Intended Contribution to Biblical Scholarship 19
          Limitation 20
          Delimitation 20
          Definition of Terms 20
      Procedure 21
Chapter 2 23
   The Practice and Function of Curses in the Ancient Near East and
   Graeco-Roman World: A Focus on Judicial Use of Curses
          Introduction 23
          Curse Terminologies 25
          Power in Blessing and Cursing 26

    Prevalence of Cursing and Blessing Practices in the OT
        and NT Worlds..27
    Fear of Curses and Binding Spells in the Ancient World............28
    Effectiveness of Curses and Binding Spells 28
Functions of Curse in the NT World 30
    The Use of Curses in Sports and Competitions.............................30
    The Use of Curses in Sex, Love, and Marriage Affairs.................31
    The Use of Curses in the Business World 32
    The Use of Curses in Legal and Political Disputes 33
    The Use of Curses in Judicial Aspects: Pleas for Justice
        and Revenge..35
    The Use of Curse as a Tool of Judicial Litigation 38
    Wrongdoing as a Basis for Judicial Curses 39
    The Use of Judicial Curses to Protect Grave Disturbance 40
    The Use of Judicial Curses to Protect a Name and Writings.......42
    Appeal to the Deities or Spirits to Execute Judicial Curses.........43
The Use of Judicial Curses in Ancient Israel and Neighboring
    Communities...44
    The Cursing Practice in the Ancient Near Eastern World 44
    The Cursing Practice in Ancient Israel 45
    Curses in Treaties and Oaths Both in ANE and Israel.................47
    The Power of a Curse...49
    Interpretation of Reality Using Curse Lenses 53
Conclusion..56

Chapter 3 57
Background Information and Exegesis of Galatians 3:1–14
    Introduction 57
    Background Information 58
        Author and Recipients..58
        Date...59
        The Situation and Paul's Opponents in Galatia..............................60
        Preceding Context (Galatians 1–2) 61
        Summary of Galatians Chapter 3 62
        The Literary Structure of Galatians 3:1–14 62
        Syntactical Outline of Galatians 3:1–14..63
        Synopsis..65
    The Crucified and Cursed Christ: An Exegesis of
        Galatians 3:1–14..65
        The Problem in Galatia (3:1–5)..65

  Beginning Right But Trying to End in a
   Wrong Way (vv.3–4) 76
  Paul's Citation of the Old Testament (3:6–14) 84
 Conclusion of the Exegetical Section 127

Chapter 4 131
Comparison and Analysis
 Introduction 131
 Removal of Curses in the Ancient World 132
  Scapegoat Rituals 133
  Sacrifice Rituals 137
  Herbal Antidotes 141
  Wearing Amulets, and the Stone of Hermes 141
  Cursing Curses and Exorcism 143
  Confession 144
 The Persistent Enigma of Curses in the Ancient World 145
 The Uniqueness and Sufficiency of Christ's Death as a
  Remover of All Curses 146
  The Concept of Crucified Christ 147
  The Concept of the Cursed Christ 151
 Significant Themes on Curse and Blessing in Galatians 3:1–14 153
  "Who Has Bewitched You?" (Gal 3:1) 153
  The Phrase ὑπὸ κατάραν (Gal 3:10) 153
  Blessing (Gal 3:14) 154
  Redemption (Gal 3:13) 154
 Conclusion 155

Chapter 5 157
Application to the African Context and Contribution from the
African Context
 Introduction 157
 The Presence, Fear, and Power of Curses in Marakwet Culture 159
 Categories of Curses in Marakwet Culture 163
  Curses Motivated by Self-Interest 163
  Judicial and Revenge Prayers 164
 The Object of Judicial and Revenge Prayers 166
 Execution of a Judicial Curse 167
 Removal and Reversal of Judicial and Revenge Curses 168
 Ways of Preventing and Removing Curses in the
  Marakwet Culture 169
  Substitutionary Concept on Curses 170

    Proclaiming Jesus Christ in a Cultural Context with Belief
        in Curses 171
        Theological Implications..171
        Pastoral Implications...172
    Conclusion...174

Chapter 6 175
    Conclusions and Recommendations
        Introduction 175
        Recommendations..179

Bibliography 181

Abstract

Past christological studies have looked at the death of Christ on the cross as mainly addressing the human problem of sin. Largely, Western theological scholarship has extensively dealt with the idea of Christ's atonement of sin. However, other than addressing the problem of sin, the death of Christ equally addresses the issue of curse. In his theological reflections and formulations, the apostle Paul wrote, "Christ became a curse for us" (Gal 3:13). In Galatians 3:1–14, Paul discusses the idea of crucified and cursed Christ and its implications. The cursing and blessing practice was a widespread phenomenon in the biblical world (ancient Near East and Graeco-Roman world) and equally evident in the Bible. In this ancient cultural and religious milieu, Paul presented the death of Christ as the ultimate solution to the problem of curse. Similar to the antiquity context, many African cultures, religions, and cosmologies still uphold the practice of blessing and cursing. Commonly, in these contexts with curse practices, curses are greatly feared and are deemed disastrous to human life. This study looks at exegetical issues in Galatians 3:1–14, a pericope where Paul discusses, among other things, the law, curse, blessing, and Christ (as crucified and cursed). In addition, this work investigates the ancient Near East and especially the Graeco-Roman understanding of curses to situate Paul's statement of the cursed Christ in Galatians 3:13 within its cultural and religious context. The study establishes a relationship between the curse in Galatians 3 and Genesis 3. Also, it surveys the use and function of curses and binding spells in the New Testament world; and concludes that Paul had in mind the judicial type of curses when writing Galatians chapter 3. The study also looks at the shortcomings of the ancient ways of removing curses; and presents the crucified and cursed Christ as the ultimate curse-remover who satisfies divine justice. Finally, the study briefly explores the Marakwet[1] understanding of cursing practice and argues that the striking similarities with cursing practices in the OT and NT worlds can aid the application of Galatians 3. The study employs the sociorhetorical method to look at the rhetorical techniques in Galatians 3 and the world of the Bible.

---

1. Marakwet is one of the subtribes of Kalenjin ethnic group in Kenya. The Marakwet people live in the northern part of the Rift Valley of Kenya. It is a community whose ways of life, cultural values, and customs have not been extensively researched. The researcher comes from this community.

List of Abbreviations

ANE	Ancient Near East(ern)
BHS	Biblia Hebraica Stuttgartensia.
BIS	Bible Interpretation Series
LXX	Septuagint Text
MT	Masoretic Text (according to BHS)
NASB	New American Standard Bible
NETS	Pietersma and Wright, *New English Translation of the Septuagint*
NIV	New International Version
NT	New Testament
OT	Old Testament
UBS	Aland et al., *The Greek New Testament: A Reader's edition*

Extracanonical Literature: Apocrypha and Pseudepigrapha

Jub	*Jubilees*
Macc	*Maccabees*
Sir	*Sirach*
Apoc Ab	*Apocalypse of Abraham*
T Levi	*Testament of Levi*
T Benj	*Testament of Benjamin*

Josephus

Ant	*Antiquity of the Jews*

Philo

Abr	*On Abraham*

De Spec Leg	*On the Special Laws*
Leg Alleg	*Allegorical Interpretation*

Pseudo-Philo

Lib Ant	*Liber antiquitatum biblicarum*

Early Christian Works

Dial	*Dialogue with Trypho* [Justin Martyr]
Barn	*Epistle of Barnabas*

Ancient Authors

Plato	Euthyphro

Acknowledgments

It takes a village to raise a child. In the same vein, it takes a community to raise a scholar. My academic journey culminating in this work has been possible through personal and collective effort. I have received immense support, mentorship, and encouragement from family, friends, churches, and parachurch organizations. Unfortunately, the space here is inadequate to recognize all of them by name; nevertheless, it suffices to mention a few.

I thank God for his guidance, salvation, and calling. Indeed, it has taken God's mighty hand for me to have come this far. I want to express my gratitude to parachurch organizations and churches that supported my postgraduate studies in one way or another. I am grateful to God for organizations like Africa Inland Mission (AIM), Christian Leaders for Africa (CLA), and Mylne Trust. Their support at different times in my educational journey actualized my academic dream. The open ministry doors at AIC Top Suwerwa, AIC Kapsowar, and AIC Nkoroi cannot go unrecognized.

Moreover, I praise God for the invaluable support from my spiritual and academic mentors, the Biblical Studies cohort, and the university academic staff. The constructive criticism, guidance, focus on details, patience, and encouragement from my supervisors and examiners (Prof. Samuel Ngewa, Dr. Nathan Joshua; Prof. Mumo Kisau, Prof. Jacob Kibor) eventually bore fruits.

In closing, I immensely appreciate the continued ministry partnerships, encouragement, and prayers of Mr. Philemon Chemweno, Mr. Philemon Kimutai, Dr. Steve Lee, Dr. Yukio Flinte, and their families. May your love for God, ministry, and God's people superabound. I extend my warmest appreciation to my family: Risper Lelei, Hudson Koech, and Precious Kayanet for their love, understanding, and support during the entire period of developing this work. Finally, I thank Langham Publishing for accepting this work for publication.

Soli Deo Gloria.

CHAPTER 1

Introduction

Introduction to the Study

Several years after the death of Jesus Christ, the apostles continued to reflect upon the significance of Christ's redemptive act on the cross. They reflected on how the sacrificial death of Jesus Christ applied to the human problem of sin and curse. Their writings have historically been examined, interpreted, and applied to different contexts. Modern studies, especially by theologians from the West,[1] have focused on the death of Christ primarily as the answer to the problem of sin. As a result, the solid historical emphasis on Christ's atoning sacrifice on the cross for the forgiveness of sins has developed a robust doctrine of hamartiology and Christology. This emphasis has richly highlighted the significance of Christ's death to the human problem of sin. At the same time, the Western inclination toward the doctrine of atonement (for sin) has come with neglect of other areas in which the death of Christ applies. One of such ignored areas is the interpretation and application of Christ's death to the problem of curses. The analogies used to expound on the doctrine of atonement, like the ransom theory,[2] have mainly addressed the doctrine of sin.

---

1. Morland, *Rhetoric of Curse*, 1. In this study, Morland argues that the concept of curse has been lost in Western societies and thus theologians from the West "lack adequate categories for ascribing to curses any real importance, and this is the handicap for modern research." Therefore, theologians from non-Western contexts should take up the role of building knowledge around this area.

2. Erickson, *Christian Theology*, 723–27. The ransom theory has Scriptural basis such as in Mark 10:45 and 1 Corinthians 6:20. Basically, a ransom is the cost required in order to

By omitting other aspects (like curses) addressed by the death of Jesus Christ on the cross, some theologians have construed the death of Jesus Christ as a miscarriage of justice.[3] On the injustice inflicted on Christ, George writes, "although he was put to death by wicked men in a horrible miscarriage of justice, this happened, as we have seen, in accordance with the eternal purpose and predetermined plan of God."[4] However, was the death of Christ a miscarriage of justice? Most probably, George's argument on Christ's death as a miscarriage of justice partly has some grain of truth when viewed in light of the events preceding the crucifixion. Yet, as a curse-bearer, as it shall be argued, the death of Christ served as the satisfaction of divine justice.

The apostle Paul's statement in Galatians 3:13, Χριστὸς ἡμᾶς ἐξηγόρασεν ἐκ τῆς κατάρας τοῦ νόμου γενόμενος ὑπὲρ ἡμῶν κατάρα, can be rendered as, "Christ redeemed us from the curse of the law by becoming a curse for us."[5] According to Paul, the death of Christ not only achieved forgiveness of sins for believers but also liberation from the "curse of the law." In Galatians 3:1–14, Paul responds to the issues faced by the church in Galatia by projecting an image of the crucified and cursed Christ. Biblical scholars have differed on several issues raised by this passage that include: the use of the Old Testament Scriptures within the context, Paul's negative portrayal of the law, and interpretation of the "curse of the law," among other textual and hermeneutical issues.

Christ's death on the cross not only atoned for human sin and removed the curse upon humanity, but also satisfied divine justice (the wrath of God

---

rescue one from bondage or captivity. Erickson is of the view that this is a classical perspective that has long enjoyed dominance from the early church until the medieval time of Anselm and Abelard. The formulation of the theory is credited to the early Christian thinkers, namely, Origen and Gregory of Nyssa. The theory was later developed by authors like Augustine to refute resultant implications that God deceived Satan. Just like any other theory or analogies, ransom theory has its own limitations; but significantly the theory boldly highlights Christ's triumph over Satan and the release of humanity from bondage.

3. Stott shows that this line of thought has a basis in the way gospel writers blended legal and moral factors. Concerning the gospel writers, he argues, "They all indicate that in both Jewish and Roman courts a certain legal procedure was followed. The prisoner was arrested, charged, and cross-examined, and witnesses called. The judge then reached his verdict and pronounced the sentence. Yet the evangelists also make it clear that the prisoner was not guilty of the charges laid, that the witnesses were false, and that the sentence of death was a gross miscarriage of justice." Stott, *Cross of Christ*, 47–48.

4. George, *Galatians*, 241.

5. This Pauline statement will be given a detailed examination in the exegetical section.

upon humanity). Thus, the exploration of the meaning of the crucified and cursed Christ in Galatians 3:13, within its context, would enrich the doctrine of Christology and present Christ's death as a unique historical event relevant to the human enigma of curses.

In the Old Testament (OT) and New Testament (NT) worlds, cursing and blessing practices were prevalent. Thus, Paul's audience, comprised of Jews and Gentiles, appropriated Paul's statement within their common cultural understanding of curses and blessings. Indeed, Paul's audience must have understood with insight his language and imageries in discussing the implication of the death of Christ. Therefore, for a modern reader to understand the impact of Paul's statement on his original hearers, it is necessary to examine the biblical text and the world of the Bible.

Notably, the apostle Paul, the writer of Galatians, represented a complexity of backgrounds and identities. He was a Jew, a Roman citizen, and a Christian. It may be hard to pinpoint which background greatly influenced his thinking in this instance, but an investigation into his context will be instructive. As a Jew, he might have drawn the understanding of curses and blessings from the Jewish traditions of the Second Temple period. Still, as a Roman citizen, he might have relied on the vast Graeco-Roman blessing and cursing practices to articulate his ideas concerning the death of Christ. As shall be concluded later in this study, both Second Temple Jewish and Graeco-Roman cultures likely influenced Paul's understanding of Christ's redemptive event on the cross.

Contemporary Relevance

In the next chapter, the study builds an understanding of cursing and blessing practices in both the OT and NT worlds. It is hoped that this understanding will provide a background upon which Galatians 3:1–14 should be read, interpreted, and applied. The succeeding chapter focuses on the exegesis of Galatians 3:1–14, followed by a comparison and analysis section. Finally, the study looks at the understanding of curses in the contemporary Marakwet cultural context. Therefore, in this study, an entire chapter is devoted to the African understanding of curses and exploration of parallels with ancient cultures. Elizabeth Mburu, in her book *African Hermeneutics*, highlights that Scripture should be relevant to the readers context, and that we should not ignore the effect of culture in biblical and theological interpretation.[6] The guiding question for this last chapter is: How does the idea of the crucified and cursed Christ apply to a context where cursing and blessing are a reality? A critical examination that warrants comparison, correlation, and application is needed to arrive at a satisfactory evaluation. This study will enrich the interpretive strand of a text like Galatians 3:1–14 and open up new areas for insight and interrogation. Three reasons underlie the inclusion of the section that deals with the contemporary African setting.

First, in the hermeneutical process, the role of the reader's horizon in discovering the meaning of the text is not passive. On the one hand, the reader brings to the text some biases and presuppositions that need to be assessed critically; on the other, the reader brings invaluable input and perspectives for the interpretive journey.[7] The incorporation of an African context into the discussion highlights the critical point of the application. For clarity, the application section is not imposed on the text; instead, it builds on the exegetical findings and understanding of curses in the OT and NT cultural worlds.

Second, scholars have argued that there is a close affinity between the world of the Bible and African religion and cosmology. The rapid emergence and spread of African indigenous churches, for example, has partly been attributed to similar cultural, religious, and social themes in these two worlds.[8] Hence, discussing an African understanding of blessings and curses at the application level garners fresh insight into the theological and hermeneutical process. In this regard, the experience, knowledge, and function of curses in Marakwet culture have been explored and critically analyzed.

Third, as voiced by Longenecker, it has been acknowledged that although the statement "Christ became a curse for us" was clear to the early Christians, much of the details of Paul's affirmation of how Jesus was both Messiah and accursed remains obscure.[9] This obscurity, compounded by the scanty literature from ancient times, can be partly mitigated by critically looking at

---

6. Mburu, *African Hermeneutics*, 5, 25.

7. Tate, *Biblical Interpretation*, 219–20.

8. Mojola, "Old Testament or Hebrew Bible." In his seven-page resourceful article, Mojola convincingly argues that there is a close affinity, resemblance and points convergence between the OT worlds and African worlds. He observes that there are similarities in religious, social, and cultural practices, and institutions despite the historical, temporal, religious, cultural, geographical, and social distance.

9. Longenecker, *Galatians*, 122.

the existing African experience and understanding of curses and the extant resources on curses and blessings from antiquity. As a foundation, the study critically compares cursing aspects in African cultural contexts with the cursing practices in the OT and NT. Then, it proposes the African understanding of curses as a possible cultural parallel that sheds light on the text in a way that Western scholarship has not, given the greater cultural distance of the West from the Jewish and Graeco-Roman cultures. Mburu proposes a four-legged stool model, an approach that "recognizes the parallels between biblical cultures and worldviews and African cultures and worldviews … as bridges to promote understanding, internalization and application of the biblical text."[10] This approach shall guide the application section of this study.

Significantly, the study argues that the death of Christ on the cross reverses the curse that has affected the entire humanity. Moreover, redemption from the curse enables God's blessings to flow through Abraham (Gen 12:1–3) to both Jews and Gentiles. Thus, a proper understanding of Paul's idea of cursed Christ demands a look into the pericope (Gal 3:1–14), Pauline theology, Jewish perspectives from the Second Temple period, and Graeco-Roman contexts, and within the larger framework of biblical theology.

The Motivation for the Research

The decision to investigate curses in Galatians 3:1–14 came from my experience as a chaplain at a Mission Hospital and Nursing College in rural Kenya. On one of the nights, at the home of one missionary surgeon in the area, thieves broke into his house and stole a toolbox of surgical equipment and other valuables. It was only in the morning that the surgeon discovered that his surgical toolbox was missing. The incident angered many and created a crisis at the hospital and the surrounding community because of canceled surgical schedules and referral of emergency cases to distant hospitals. For several days, the police and members of the surrounding community tried to identify the suspects but to no avail.

Culturally, in such cases, when no one confesses or claims to have seen or heard of such a plot to steal, the Marakwet culture prescribes a curse to

---

10. Mburu, *African Hermeneutics*, 7, 65. The four-legged aspects of the stool are: parallels to the African culture, the theological context, the literary context, and the historical context. This study will look at these aspects in different sections.

locate and dispense justice to the unknown offender. Presumably, the curse will trace and affect the offender(s), their families, and any other associates (those who saw/heard or had any leading information but decided to conceal the offender). Typically, in the Marakwet culture, the meetings during the investigation process to locate an offender go up to four times before pronouncing a curse. These four stages (or meetings) are spread days apart, allowing age groups and families to interrogate their own concerning the matter. If the culprit confesses, the person is penalized, and restitution ensues. However, a curse is uttered in a case where the offender is not identified by the community. Ordinarily, a curse is pronounced in the presence of the community to show solidarity in condemning the evil, in expressing human inability to locate the offender(s), and in common desire for justice. Usually, the curse is directed to the traditional deity to take up the case, identify the offender(s) and avenge on behalf of the offended party.

During the third meeting that I attended (culturally, second to the last), the stolen goods had not yet been recovered, and the robber(s) had not been identified. At this point, one elder who stood to talk after the others warned the gathering that a curse on the unknown offender would follow in the next final meeting. Then one of the pastors we were seated with raised his hand to ask for an extension of the time frame for the culprit to own up and confess. Upon seeing the pastor, the elder chairing the meeting, who was also a member of a particular church, quickly interjected and asked the pastor to leave the matter to the elders and the traditional deity because the God of Christians is "slow in bringing justice." This incident provoked my thinking and kept me asking questions with theological implications: What made this elder think that the Christian God was slow and unconcerned with matters concerning justice? What informed this kind of thinking? Is it that we have a shallow theology that is inadequate to address felt needs? How does the Bible address the issue of curses? Does the death of Christ apply to such matters related to cursing? This incident and questions led me to Galatians 3:13, where the subject of curse is discussed with its solution.[11]

---

11. In the words of Elizabeth Mburu, this incident became the "contact point" of the African worldview and the biblical text: Mburu, *African Hermeneutics*, 2.

The Problem Statement

The practice of cursing is a predominant theme in the Bible, ancient world literature, and contemporary African cultures. The OT and NT texts make numerous references to curses, thus proving that the practice and belief in curses were real in the biblical world. Likewise, the subject of curses is still a reality in modern Africa. Sadly, the issue of curses is still a concern, both at the doctrinal and practical levels, and that is why many Christians today still struggle with the fear of curses and binding spells. African scholars' apparent silence on the subject has not provided any solution. Therefore, there is a need to study the Bible text and the historical context and conduct an in-depth analysis and interrogation of some African cultural understanding of curses to find insights for a more meaningful application of Christ's death on the cross. Undeniably, limited exploration has been done on the significance of Christ's death (crucifixion) on this central theme of curse and its relationship to justice. A study that focuses on how the death of Christ satisfies divine justice while at the same time focusing on the rich African cultural heritage of cursing and blessing is therefore desirable.

Synopsis

Paul's application of Christ's death to the universal human problem of curses is based on the biblical narrative from the Old Testament at the backdrop of the ANE cultures and Graeco-Roman world. Therefore, appreciation of the significance of Christ's crucifixion and death for removal of the curse and satisfying God's justice and a meaningful application of Galatians 3:13 demands an exegetical study, research on the OT and NT world contexts, and a critical exploration of the African experience and understanding of the role of curses as a means of justice.

Purpose of the Study

This study examines Galatians 3:13 within its context and biblical narrative against the backdrop of the Jewish and Graeco-Roman cultures, with an application that considers similar concepts and themes of curses in an African cultural context.

How will this be achieved? The study conducts an in-depth investigation on curses as a means of justice in the world of the Bible and a critical examination of the experience and understanding of curses as a means of justice in the Marakwet culture (and other African cultures) for application purposes. This approach meaningfully informs the interpretation of Galatians 3:13 and provides an insight into the significance of Christ's death on the cross. In addition, the research involves an exegetical analysis of Galatians 3:1–14 with attention to the OT references that establish the subject of curses within the redemptive history.

Significance of the Study

This study seeks to contribute to the scholarly and ecclesiastical conversation on the significance of the death of Christ on curses, a significant aspect that African theologians should handle. Specifically, the study demonstrates that the Marakwet worldview on curses (and blessings) helps biblical scholars better appreciate the meaning of Galatians 3:1–14. The study underscores the following points:

1. The curse of Galatians 3 relates to the curse stated in Genesis 3.
2. The Graeco-Roman context and, to some extent, the ancient Near East context provide a background for reading Galatians.
3. The ancient Near East and Graeco-Roman contexts display a worldview that resembles the Marakwet people's culture.
4. Interpreting Galatians 3 in view of the Marakwet culture (and other African cultures) on curses and blessings does not amount to eisegesis but sheds light on the understanding of Galatians 3 in a way that has not been explored.

The research enriches our understanding of the doctrine of Christology and soteriology. It offers valuable and comparable information to pastors, evangelists, theologians, and missiologists serving in communities where cursing practice is a reality. It points to the death of Christ as the ultimate solution to curses. The research also provides a way to interpret a biblical text to address contextual problems without falling into the danger of eisegesis.

Main Research Questions

This research answers three main questions:

1. What aspects of curses in the Jewish and Graeco-Roman culture influenced Paul's conception of Christ as a curse-bearer for humanity?

2. How do Paul's arguments and Old Testament quotations in Galatians 3:1–14 establish Christ's death as the ultimate solution to the curse faced by humankind?
3. What are some of the African cultural curse and blessing elements and practices that can help us interpret and better appreciate Christ's substitutionary role as a curse-bearer according to Galatians 3:13?

Literature Review

Introduction

This subsection, in three stages, deals with a brief review of relevant and available scholarly publications. First, it explores relevant OT studies and dissertations on curses since Paul's arguments in Galatians 3 are grounded on the redemptive history. In Galatians 3:6–14, Paul cites six OT passages that have received much scholarly attention. In this regard, relevant OT resources on the meaning and use of curses are highlighted. Second, scholarly studies within the pericope (Gal 3:1–14) are examined to ascertain various dimensions scholars have taken on this text. Galatians 3 has elicited a great deal of controversy among NT scholars. As a result, different portions of this portion of scripture have become the subject of various scholarly studies. Third, scholarly studies on Galatians 3:13 are reviewed to identify gaps and contributions that this study brings into biblical scholarship. The general purpose of this review section is to locate the primary area and focus for this study, where the present study will make a scholarly contribution.

Relevant Old Testament Studies on Curses

A critical and a more in-depth understanding of curses in the Bible and antiquity leads to a proper interpretation and appreciation of Christ's redemptive act of becoming a curse for believers and bringing blessings to the nations. It is worth noting that past studies on curses and blessings in the Old Testament have had different emphases, and especially that curses are widely mentioned in Old Testament books. In this area, three major scholarly works have been undertaken in the last century. These works have since formed three major strands in which OT scholarship on curses has taken.

First is the ground-breaking work by George Mendenhall, *Law and Covenant in Ancient Israel*, published in 1955. This work examined biblical curses within the ancient Near East (ANE) cultures by looking at the form and content of curses in treaty documents. Mendenhall discovered underlying similarities between curses and oath-taking.[12] In a significant way, this study established that curses were part of society, especially in Egypt, and that curses served various functions. Subsequently, this work opened an avenue for later scholars to study curses in the Hittite, Assyrian, and Syrian treaties and establish parallels between ancient Near Eastern treaties and biblical literature.[13]

Second, the other notable work in this area was carried out by Joseph Scharbert in 1958, who looked at the generational aspect of curses and blessings. Scharbert examined philological issues (curse terminologies) using form-critical approaches.[14] He explored five curse terminologies in the Old Testament and concluded, "While these terms can at times be synonymous, caution needs to be exercised about making hard and fast distinctions between roots."[15] Subsequent scholars continued to explore curse terminologies with different perspectives and conclusions.

Third, some significant contribution was also made by Johannes Pedersen using J. L. Austin's "speech act theory" to explain the power and function of words and curses in the Hebrew language.[16] This study considered a curse as a performative speech act, and the approach impacted the thought of subsequent Bible scholars. For example, the study by J. Scott Anderson, published in 1998, "The Nature and Function of Curses in the Narrative Literature of the Hebrew Bible", proposed that "Austin's theory of illocutionary acts seems to explain best the power and function of curses in the Hebrew Bible."[17] Anderson achieved this by investigating curses in the narrative genre of the Hebrew Bible. These three critical works laid a foundation for subsequent curse-related studies in the Hebrew Bible.

Significantly, Anderson surveys some contributions to the curse studies from the field of social anthropology. He highlights the sociological functions

---

12. Mendenhall, *Law and Covenant*, 26.
13. Anderson, "Nature and Function," 25.
14. Anderson, 25.
15. Anderson, 25.
16. Anderson, 3.
17. Anderson, 26.

of curses both in ancient and contemporary societies.[18] Relevant to this study is the function of a curse as a tool of judicial litigation; curses can serve as a judge, jury, and executioner.[19] Although he does not develop the concept, this study underscores the relationship between curses and justice; that is, curses can be used as a means of justice.

In addition, Anne Marie Kitz, in *Cursed Are You! The Phenomenology of Cursing in Cuneiform and Hebrew Texts*, published in 2014, has looked at the widespread cursing practice in the ANE society. This resourceful work looked at "curses as petitions to the divine world to render judgment and execute harm on identified, hostile forces."[20]

Another major related study was undertaken by Timothy G. Crawford, *Blessing and Curse in Syro-Palestinian Inscriptions of the Iron Age*, published in 1992. The study examines blessing and curse inscriptions in Syria-Palestine from Iron II period (1000–586 BC). It compares and contrasts the idea of blessing and cursing in the Hebrew Bible and its surrounding cultural and religious context.

Scholarly Studies on NT World and Galatians 3:1–14

Concerning the NT world, John G. Gager has given special attention to the NT background of curse and blessing in his edited book *Curse Tablets and Binding Spells from the Ancient World*, published in 1992. The work looks at the cursing practice in the ancient Graeco-Roman world and the use of curses in every walk of life. In addition, the author sampled and translated some of these curse tablets from the ancient world, covering the periods between the fifth century BC to fifth century AD. Significantly, this background study helps locate the biblical text in its ancient cultural and religious environment.

In the New Testament, scholarly research in Galatians 3:1–14 has majorly centered on curses and blessings, the doctrine of atonement, redemption, Paul's view of the law, and Paul's usage of Deuteronomistic tradition to

---

18. Some of the sociological functions of various curses he surveys includes: curse as a scapegoat mechanism; curse as a tool of social control; curse as a tool to convey social values; the curse as "private" law of the vulnerable; curse as a tool of judicial litigation; and curse as a means of defining sociopolitical boundaries. For a detailed discussion, refer to Anderson, 46–91. It has also been observed that many cultures used curses to enforce law and morality. Little, "Cursing," 183.

19. Anderson, *Nature and Function*, 64.

20. Kitz, *Cursed Are You!*, 3.

interpret the meaning of Christ's death.[21] Studies in this area, especially those related to the law, have elicited much debate and controversy.

The monograph by Jeffrey R. Wisdom, *Blessings for the Nations and the Curse of the Law: Paul's Citation of Genesis and Deuteronomy 3:8–10*, published in 2001, primarily examines Paul's citation of Genesis and Deuteronomy in Galatians 3:8–10 against the backdrop of the Old Testament and within the context of the literature of Second Temple Judaism.[22] Wisdom acknowledges that in the contemporary scholarly debate, Paul's use of Genesis in Galatians 3:8 has received little attention, although he does not further develop the argument.[23] The present study pursues this line of thought to establish the discussion of curses and the biblical background of Abrahamic blessings (Gen 12:1–3) that came as the solution to the pronouncement of the curse to humanity and ground in Genesis 3.

Scholarly investigations have also looked at Paul's use of Scripture within this pericope. As mentioned before, in Galatians 3:6–14, Paul cites six texts from the Old Testament to argue his case. Studies on these citations have looked at both textual issues and the original contexts. Andrew H. Wakefield, in his monograph titled *Where to Live: The Hermeneutical Significance of Paul's Citations from Scripture in Galatians 3:1–14*, looked at the hermeneutical significance of interrelationship of texts that Paul quotes. He uses an intertextual approach to interrogate the OT quotations and explore how the citations function and interact. In this study, he notes, "this passage revolves around the eschatological issue of *where* one lives, in the old age which includes the law, or in the new age in Christ."[24] Numerous studies on these fourteen verses have resulted in divergent views over the past century, something which still necessitates additional studies with new approaches.

Scholarly Studies on Curses in Galatians 3:13

A survey of studies in Galatians 3:13 revolves around the cross, curse, redemption, wisdom and law, and Paul's use of the Deuteronomistic tradition. In

---

21. Wisdom, *Blessing for Nations*, 1.
22. Wisdom, 17.
23. Wisdom, 3.
24. Wakefield, *Where to Live*, 189.

addition, other studies have considered the relationship between transgression, law, faith, and Paul's view on the law.[25]

C. Marvin Pate in *The Reverse of the Curse: Paul, Wisdom and the Law*, (published in 2000), makes sense of the death of Christ in light of the Deuteronomy passage. He argues,

> Paul employs the wisdom motif for the purpose of reversing the Deuteronomistic curses and blessings (Deut 27–30). Thus for the apostle to the Gentiles, God's wisdom is none other than the crucified Christ, whose death and resurrection brought the end of the Torah as the means for acquiring justification. That is to say, Paul views Christ as having removed the Deuteronomic curses by embracing divine judgment on the cross and thereby dispensing the Deuteronomic blessings to all who believe in him.[26]

Pate's research was based on the Deuteronomistic tradition. However, a broader approach is needed. The present study will argue for Genesis as a primary reference in Paul's arguments by looking at the curse in Genesis 3.

B. Hudson McLean has undertaken another major work on Galatians 3:13 in *The Cursed Christ: Mediterranean Expulsion Rituals and Pauline Soteriology*. McLean compares Paul's theology of atonement to analogous expulsion rituals and concepts in Jewish and Graeco-Roman religions.[27] Additionally, McLean argues that Galatians 3:13 should be interpreted in the same manner as 2 Corinthians 5:21,[28] which reads, "God made him who had no sin to be sin for us, so that in him we might become the righteousness of God" (NIV). Finally, he looked at Christ's death in relation to apotropaeic (scapegoat) rituals in the Mediterranean world. While building on this ground, the present study looks at the judicial construct of curses and the function of Christ's death on the cross in reversing the curse.

The brief survey of literature has demonstrated that past studies have emphasized the Bible text and ancient context. The present study investigates the concept of the cursed Christ in relation to the issue of justice, which was one of the functions of curses in the ancient world. It seeks to contribute to

---

25. McLean, *Cursed Christ*, 113.
26. Pate, *Reverse of Curse*, 1.
27. McLean, *Cursed Christ*, 13.
28. McLean, 18.

the existing gap by: first, demonstrating that Paul used the Genesis text as a primary passage in his arguments; second, showing how the crucified and cursed Christ, in his substitutionary death, satisfied God's justice; third, suggesting the African cultural background of curse and blessing practice as a cultural parallel that can shed light on the biblical text in a way scholarship in the West has not portrayed.

In summary, although a remarkable scholarly work has been done on curse passages and the world of the Bible (by looking at the ANE treaty curses, oaths, covenants, and ancient Mediterranean curse practices and texts), the experiences and understanding of curses by contemporary African cultures have not been adequately examined. Consideration and application of the understanding, use, and lived experiences of societies that have cursing practices can in a big way provide an additional dimension to the interpretation and appreciation of biblical teaching. Concerning the approach to be employed, there is a need to have a new methodological approach that considers the gains of earlier contributions of biblical scholarship and still examines the problem of curses from a broader perspective.

Methodology

This study employs sociorhetorical criticism to interrogate the biblical text and sociocultural background surrounding the text. The sociorhetorical method helps explore and analyze rhetorical devices used in the Scripture and traces Paul's arguments within the passage. Also, the approach highlights cursing and blessing perspectives from the author's cultural, religious, social, and historical context. The twofold nature of the socio-rhetorical method utilizes the gains of earlier contributions of biblical scholarship and opens new perspectives on the interpretation of Galatians 3:13 within its pericope.

Description of Socio-rhetorical Method

The socio-rhetorical approach has been defined as "a textually-based method that uses programmatic strategies to invite social, cultural, historical, psychological, aesthetic, ideological and theological information into a context of minute exegetical activity."[29] Only relevant aspects of the text and context

---

29. Robbins, "Socio-Rhetorical Criticism," 165.

are explored in this work. Each text has an origin in a particular culture and addresses a particular need. Tate observes, "While the text is an artifact of a particular culture and social location, it is also a response to that culture and social location."[30] Therefore, Paul's arguments should be interpreted in light of the problem faced by believers in Galatia and the prevailing cultural beliefs among his audience. The socio-rhetorical method assumes that "words themselves work in very complicated ways to communicate meanings that we only partially understand. It also presupposes that meanings themselves have their meanings by their relation to other meanings."[31] The terms used by Paul, such as curse, bewitching, and redemption, can be better understood by looking at their meanings within the Graeco-Roman context's social, cultural, and religious landscape. Robbins states that the goal of this method is "to bring skills we use on a daily basis into an environment of interpretation that is both intricately sensitive to detail and perceptively attentive to large fields of meaning in the world in which we live."[32] This approach involves situating words and terms within their surrounding contexts.

Socio-rhetorical Criticism in Galatians 3:1–14

Robbins, in his book *Exploring the Texture of Texts: A Guide to Socio-Rhetorical Interpretation,* discusses in detail five textures of the text, namely: inner texture, intertexture, social and cultural texture, ideological texture, and sacred texture.[33] He notes that no interpreter will ever employ all aspects of sociorhetorical criticism in a single text, just like in any other method.[34] Therefore, the study only highlights relevant and helpful aspects of the textures and other relevant features of sociorhetorical criticism.

Inner Texture of Galatians 3:6–13

One of the foundational ways of interrogating the biblical text before locating its meaning is examining its inner texture. The inner texture "leads the interpreter to explore repetitive, progressive, narrational, opening-middle-closing,

---

30. Tate, *Biblical Interpretation*, 340.
31. Robbins, *Exploring Texture of Texts*, 132.
32. Robbins, 2.
33. Robbins, 3.
34. Robbins, 2.

argumentative, and sensory-aesthetic texture. This texture lies clearly in the words in the text itself."[35] The approach helps the interpreter to pay close attention to observable detail and patterns in a text.

Galatians 3:1–14 is a rhetorical unit with an introduction, a body, and a conclusion. In the beginning section (3:1–5), Paul introduces the challenge faced by Galatians by using rhetorical questions. The middle section (3:5–13), introduced by the conjunction καθώς, is the main section of the pericope. It details Paul's augmentation and use of OT references. The main section climaxes in verse 13, with the statement that highlights Christ's role in the removal of "the curse of the law." The ending verse (3:14) begins with two purpose clauses (ἵνα), concluding the entire literary unit. It ties together, in one verse, the names, and themes discussed in the pericope, such as Jesus Christ, Abraham, Gentiles, redemption, faith, and Spirit.

The inner texture also looks at patterns of repetition and progression.[36] For example, in Galatians 3:1–14, some words are repeated several times, for instance: foolish (2 times), law (7 times), faith and its derivatives (10 times), curse and its derivatives (5 times), blessing and its derivatives (3 times), Abraham (5 times), and, justify/righteous (4 times). Also, in his arguments, Paul progressively develops his thought from one point to another. For instance, in verses 6–9, Paul refers to Abraham several times, but in verses 13–14, he switches the focus to Jesus Christ, the source of all blessing.

Intertexture of Galatians 3:6–13

According to Robbins, intertexture deals with the world of a text. He defines intertexture as "the interaction of the language in the text with 'outside' material and physical 'objects,' historical events, texts, customs, values, roles, institutions, and systems."[37] Intertexture has other subcategories,[38] but this study only looks at the relevant features. Concerning recitation or replication of written tradition,[39] Paul in Galatians 3:6–14 quotes from the Jewish scriptures to support his argumentation. In some cases, as shall be considered,

---

35. Robbins, 36.
36. Robbins, 37.
37. Robbins, 40.
38. The subcategories include: oral-scribal intertexture, cultural intertexture, social intertexture, and historical intertexture.
39. Robbins, *Exploring Texture of Texts*, 41.

he restates OT Scriptures, but in other instances, he modifies the text to suit his application. He also loops into his arguments Abraham, the man of faith. In the exegesis section, a detailed consideration will be devoted to these intertextual references.

It has been observed that Scriptural quotations can be employed as a rhetorical tool. Stanley, who has researched the rhetoric behind Paul's quotations, notes, "To quote from an outside text in order to lend support to an argument is a rhetorical act, and it should be studied as such. Quotations are meant to affect an audience; otherwise, there is no reason to include them in a literary work."[40] For example, Paul quotes six OT passages to support his argument in Galatians 3:6–14; these quotations are not for aesthetic purposes but are intentionally employed to convince his readers.

Furthermore, Paul purposefully reconfigures some OT texts and situations. Robbins defines reconfiguration as "recounting a situation in a manner that makes the later event 'new' in relation to a previous event. Because the event is similar to a previous event, the new event replaces or 'outshines' the previous event, making the previous event a 'foreshadowing' of the more recent one."[41] This aspect of intertexture is explicit in Paul's discussion concerning the era of the law and Spirit. It is also evident in the way he applies the issue of curses to Christ. In Galatians 3:13, he reconfigures a criminal hanged on a tree (Deut 21:23) as the crucified Messiah who becomes accursed so as to be the end of the curse. Therefore, sociorhetorical criticism will greatly help highlight these critical aspects in the hermeneutical process.

Rhetorical Devices in Galatians 3:1–14

In his epistle to Galatians, Paul uses rhetorical devices to communicate his message to his hearers.[42] Rhetoric was a common tool of communication in the ancient world. Although the majority of Paul's audience may not have

---

40. Stanley, *Arguing with Scripture*, 3.
41. Robbins, *Exploring Texture of Texts*, 50.
42. Based on the three rhetorical categories: epideictic, forensic, and deliberative; scholars have differed on the type of rhetorics Paul uses in Galatians. Some see the epistle as forensic because of Paul's defense of himself against his opponents. Kennedy, *New Testament Interpretation*, 145; Hock, "Paul and Greco-Roman Education," 214. Others see it as deliberative because Paul seeks to persuade the Galatian believers to change their course of action, for instance, see Aune, *New Testament*, 206–7. It is worth noting that these types of rhetorics are used by the author in different sections/chapters.

been well-conversant with Roman rhetorical techniques, we can safely conclude that they understood and appreciated the power and skill of rhetoric in Paul's writing.[43]

In order to better understand the pericope, the structure of the text is analyzed in rhetorical units. The author uses various stylistic devices to communicate his message like repetition of words, textual units, forms of argument, voices, and literary and rhetorical devices. In Galatians 3:1–5, Paul uses a catena of rhetorical questions to get the attention of his hearers. In Galatians 3:6–14, he employs a series of quotations from the Old Testament. The study looks at the role and use of OT quotations and prominent figures Paul employs in advancing his thesis on justification by faith.

Social and Cultural Texture of Galatians 3:1–14

Typically, texts emerge from a social and cultural background. In many cases, some of the cultural and social themes find their way into the text. Robbins writes, "Investigation of the social and cultural texture of a text includes exploring the social and cultural 'location' of the language and the type of social and cultural world the language evokes or creates."[44] It is, therefore, necessary to examine the exchange between the text and the world of the author; in some cases, an author may redefine or supply a new meaning to a particular word beyond the normal range. Again, to understand the ancient social and cultural setting, there is a need to investigate corresponding ancient texts, in this case, the ancient curse and blessing tablets and inscriptions. In the present study, chapter 2 examines relevant ancient curse texts.

In Galatians 3:1–14, some social and cultural textures are evident. The social identities highlighted by terms like foolish, bewitched, cursed, blessed, sons, and redeemed are identities that have meaning within their social context. Other themes within this pericope, like redemption, sonship, and crucifixion, are better understood by looking at the Graeco-Roman context. Robbins notes, "meanings of these social roles, identities, institutions, codes, and relationships are appropriately explored with the aid of texts,

---

43. Scholars have also argued that rhetorical elements in Paul's time had been part of the language without requiring formal knowledge of rhetorics. See Harvey, *Listening to the Text*, 217–30; Classen, *Rhetorical Criticism*, 29.

44. Robbins, *Exploring Texture of Texts*, 71.

inscriptions, archaeological data, sculpture, paintings, and so on."[45] In this research, the social identities and cultural practices like cursing are studied in the next chapter.

As acknowledged above, Paul had multiple identities; he was a Jew, Greek/Roman, and a Christian. Also, his audience was drawn from these two major backgrounds: Judaic and Hellenistic contexts. Therefore, a keen interpreter needs to probe Paul's sociocultural context to understand what it meant to be accursed and what it meant to take upon oneself a curse on behalf of others. This approach is necessary because a statement on the crucified and cursed Christ was understood within the existing cultural, social, and religious categories of cursing and blessing practices. Therefore, exploring the biblical text and Semitic and Graeco-Roman contexts using the sociorhetorical approach unearths rhetorical devices and ancient cursing practices that help an interpreter embrace a broader scope of Christ's redemptive work.

The sociorhetorical approach broadens the conversation of a text to other contextual input and makes it possible to explore meaning from different worlds and horizons. Resourcefully, the method provides categories to interrogate a passage within its social and cultural context. The approach "challenges the interpreters to explore a text in a systematic, broad manner that leads to a rich environment of interpretation and dialogue."[46] The dialogue is essential because social and cultural context plays a crucial role in determining the meaning of a text.

Intended Contribution to Biblical Scholarship

First, this study demonstrates that the curse of Galatians 3 has a relationship to the curse, as mentioned in Genesis 3. Second, this study establishes the relationship between the judicial role of curses in the ancient world and Christ's death on the cross in satisfying divine justice. Third, the ANE and Graeco-Roman cultures resemble that of the Marakwet community. Consequently, applying the insights from the text and world of the author to the contemporary African context brings insights for an enriched Christology and soteriology. Further, understanding the destructive nature of curses leads to an in-depth appreciation of the theme of (Abrahamic) blessing and the death of Christ.

---

45. Robbins, 63.
46. Robbins, 132.

Finally, the study enables biblical scholarship and the church community to read and understand Galatians 3:13 with an in-depth understanding and appreciation. The methodological approach chosen for this study allows for an interrogation of the Bible text and the social and cultural world of the Bible.

Limitation

Reference to African culture is vastly limited to the Marakwet cultural experience, use, and understanding of curses. However, there are references to other curse studies in other African cultures. Therefore, the study is not generalized to all African cultures. This limitation does not diminish the significance of the study because the findings of this study can be used to compare with what other researchers have found in different cultural contexts.

Delimitation

The study does not investigate curse or blessing terminologies in the Bible or atonement theories. Other aspects within the Jewish and Graeco-Roman worlds that relate to curses, binding spells, and magic are not explored in-depth because this study is limited to cursing practices and functions and how it relates to justice. Furthermore, the study does not delve into the study of rabbinical interpretations of the law in Judaism; the study refers to these materials only when necessary. Again, the study only focuses on Galatians 3:13 within its pericope; the entire letter of Paul to Galatians is not investigated.

Definition of Terms

Defixiones – The Greek word refers to curse tablets and binding spells from the ancient world inscribed on thin lead surfaces used to influence and control people and circumstances.[47] It is a general term referring to the ancient binding spells of different categories.

Curse – A curse is an entreaty directed to a deity or deities for evil or misfortune to befall someone or something. This study uses the following words synonymously with a curse: anathema, imprecation, and malediction.[48] In the

---

47. Versnel, "Beyond Cursing," 61.
48. Kitz, *Cursed Are You!*, 9.

ancient world, there were different categories of curses. The ultimate effect of a curse is death.

Blessing – A blessing is a plea or a wish directed to a deity or deities that good might occur to someone or something.[49] A curse seeks to cause harm and injury, but a blessing aims to bring general good in life.

Sin – The Hebrew and Greek terms that refer to sin reveal various dimensions of sin. Sin refers to the inward corruption of man and is manifested through self-centered character, affections, actions, thinking, and attitudes. It involves failing to meet set standards and a deliberate transgression of the standards established by God.[50] The curse is a consequence of sin. Biblically, sin brings curses and death (Gen 3:14).

The Fall – It refers to the fall of humanity into sin in Genesis 3, through Adam's disobedience. The fall of humanity into sin affected the human race and the entire creation (Gen 3:14–19).

Procedure

Having looked at the introduction section with the background for the research, literature review, and methodology, the following chapters develop the thesis and argumentation of the study using the sociorhetorical method.

Chapter 2 investigates the concept of curse in the ANE and Graeco-Roman contexts to locate the background behind Paul's reference to blessing and cursing. It looks at the prevalence, fear, and power of curses in antiquity. In addition, it looks at various functions of curses in the ancient world and proposes judicial prayers as a possible basis for Paul's thought in Galatians 3. Therefore, the nature and goal of the judicial curses are examined in greater detail. Additionally, the judicial function of curses in treaties and oaths is explored. The chapter also demonstrates that people in the Graeco-Roman world often interpreted reality using curse and blessing lenses. Thus, these ancient contexts provide the background upon which Galatians 3 should be read.

---

49. Crawford, *Blessing and Curse*, 231.
50. Stott, *Cross of Christ*, 89.

Chapter 3 focuses on the background information of the book of Galatians and an exegetical examination of the passage and other Scripture quotations within the passage. The chapter briefly looks at relevant background information and the message of Galatians 3.

After looking at the biblical world and the exegetical issues of the biblical text, chapter 4 deals with a critical examination and comparative analysis of the contexts and the biblical text/language. In this section, several areas of difference and similarities are highlighted. The chapter examines how Paul's context must have shaped his Christology and soteriology. Importantly, it looks at how curses were removed in the ancient world. It explores substitutionary concepts related to cursing practices. The chapter also identifies ancient themes Paul uses to communicate Christian truths effectively. It ascertains that although the ancient people had various options for removing curses, the enigma persisted. Therefore, Paul develops a solution centered on the person of Christ.

In chapter 5, the study applies insights gained from the preceding chapters to the African context. In this section, Marakwet's cultural understanding and function of curses are stated and interrogated. Also, other relevant studies concerning curses and blessings in African contexts are highlighted. In the application, a particular focus is placed on the legal use of curses. Also, areas of correlations, similarities, and differences are explored. Again, a possible understanding of Galatians 3:13 within its pericope is suggested in the light of biblical teaching, insights from the ancient world, and contemporary African culture.

Finally, chapter 6 entails a summary, conclusion, and recommendations. In this chapter, key summaries and insights from each of the preceding chapters are highlighted.

CHAPTER 2

The Practice and Function of Curses in the Ancient Near East and Graeco-Roman World: A Focus on Judicial Use of Curses

Introduction

The Galatian audience, comprising Jews and Gentiles, must have interpreted the Pauline concept of the crucified and cursed Christ using their cultural context. On the one hand, the Jewish audience must have understood Paul's concept and the statement, "Christ became a curse for us" against the backdrop of the first century AD Jewish culture and OT Scriptures. On the other hand, the Gentile believers must have understood this statement in relation to their Graeco-Roman cultural background. As mentioned before, a combination of backgrounds was evident in the life of the apostle Paul.[1] His complex identity brings a merger of contexts and meaning. Paul, formerly Saul, was a Jew (and, for that matter, a Pharisee [Gal 1:14; Phil 3:5]); a Roman citizen (Acts 16:37–39; 22:27; 25:7–12) and spoke Hebrew, Aramaic, Greek (Acts 21:40; 22:2); further, he was a follower of Jesus.

---

1. The following resources look into his complex identity as a person who combined Stoicism, Judaism, and the nascent Christian theology: Roetzel, *Paul, a Jew*, 1–8; Chilton, *Rabbi Paul*, xi; Schnelle, *Apostle Paul*, 57–86.

So, was Paul basing his interpretation of Christ's work on the cross on his Second Temple Jewish cultural tradition or the general Graeco-Roman understanding of curse and blessing? Although this is not a major concern for this paper, it suffices to mention that the diversity of his background must have greatly contributed to and enriched his application of Christ's death on the cross (crucifixion) on the phenomenon of curses. Several references to curses and cursing practice in the Old Testament must have emanated from the Jewish understanding of curses within the larger ANE cultures. Besides, Paul's Graeco-Roman context must have also played a central role in the application of the death of Christ on the theme of curses. Thus, still in antiquity, the Mediterranean world literature on curse practices is examined to gain helpful background information necessary for interpreting and understanding Galatians 3:13.

Studies into these two contexts are guided by the study's focus on understanding the relationship between curses and justice. The present chapter examines the connection between curses and justice as a prevalent theme in the ancient world. Further, the present study demonstrates that both the Jewish and Hellenistic cultures are resourceful in the interpretation of Christ's death on the cross. The chapter explores the ANE and Graeco-Roman cultures to discover Paul's foremost background of curse and blessing practices. It argues that Paul's statement "Christ became a curse for us" was rooted in Paul's Jewish and Hellenistic cultures. It points out the fact that Paul used a cultural resource to argue a theological point and apply the death of Christ to a universal human problem of curse. The research argues that Christ satisfied God's demand for justice by becoming a curse for us. Significantly, this chapter helps in appropriating Galatians 3:13 to its immediate historical and cultural context.

Besides, the study explores how the death of one man can remove curses for others in ancient contexts. It demonstrates that Paul in Galatians 3 refers to curses in a judicial sense and that this was an aspect that cut across the ANE and Graeco-Roman understanding of curses. The study looks at these two ancient contexts in two stages: the study first establishes the prevalence of curses in the OT and NT worlds, and then deals with the judicial use and function of curses in the ancient world.

Curse Terminologies

In the recent past, curse terminologies used in the Hebrew Bible and the ancient world have become major scholarly studies. Crawford, in his study, carried out a semantic survey of terms for "blessing" and "curse" in the ANE languages.[2] The study established a similarity of root words and usage of the terms for "blessing" and "curse" in the different ANE languages and biblical literature.[3] The resemblance of these root words in the Semitic languages and the Hebrew Bible demonstrates that the practice of blessing and cursing was common in the ANE world. The parallels also demonstrate that references to "curse" and "blessing" in the Hebrew Bible should be looked at in the context of the prevailing cursing and blessing practice in the Syro-Palestine region.

The terms, "blessing" and "curse" are conjointly defined and discussed because of their converse relationship. For instance, Crawford differentiates the definition of "blessing" and "curse" in the Bible: "Blessing consists of a wish for someone to receive the good things: land, numerous progeny, sufficient food, clothing, safety, etc. Curse is the wish that someone is deprived of these same things."[4] He looks at the content of blessing and curse in terms of presence and absence of what is generally considered as "good" in life. Additionally, a blessing is a "wish or petition for good to befall someone or something," and a curse is "the wish or appeal for calamity to befall someone or something."[5] There are two key common points that can be observed in these definitions. First, a blessing or a curse is essentially a prayer or an appeal; second, a blessing or a curse has a target as either someone or something. In defining blessing and curse, Jeffers highlights the means of cursing and blessing, respectively, as "a wish, expressed in words, that evil or good might befall someone."[6] A blessing or a curse is primarily expressed in words, either written or pronounced.

---

2. The words surveyed were drawn from the following languages: Akkadian, Ugaritic, Aramaic, Phoenician, Punic, Inscriptional Hebrew, Edomite, and Hebrew. This period under scrutiny was the Iron II period, the period of the United and Divided Monarchies of Israel and Judah.

3. Crawford, *Blessing and Curse*, 231.

4. Crawford, 231.

5. Joshua, "Christian Response to Curses," 146.

6. Jeffers, *Magic and Divination*, 244.

Using the speech act theory, Scott defines blessings and curses as activities of pronouncement or "performative utterances."

> They are wishes but are much more than wishes. They may also be prayers but are more than prayers. A blessing is a potent way to invoke, distribute, or celebrate the well-being that comes from divine favour. In the Old Testament, blessings primarily invoked fertility, authority and dominion, wholeness, peace, and rest. Therefore, these blessings might proceed from God to humans, from humans to other humans, and even from humans towards God.[7]

From these definitions, we can note several things. First, a curse or a blessing is generally a petition, or a wish addressed to the deity. It looks up to the supreme being for execution. Second, a blessing is associated with good things, while a curse is associated with evil. In other words, blessings bring about good things, while a curse seeks to harm or injure the target.

Power in Blessing and Cursing

In ancient times, people believed that a blessing and curse have power. A pronouncement of a blessing was deemed to bring about life, but a curse resulted in death. In the contemporary world, some scholars have attempted to explain the power behind curses using J. L. Austin's speech act theory method,[8] thus locating the special power of a curse in the choice of words used in cursing. Jeffers remarks on the origin of the power in curses, "whether it is believed that the word itself is inherently powerful or whether the power is given by the supreme God or by spirits, the fact remains that there is an acknowledged correspondence between a word and an action."[9] Austin's speech act theory overstretches the use and application of words; clearly, it is baseless and far-fetched to argue that formulaic and repeated words in curse words or inscriptions have power in and by themselves. Even in magic, sorcery, and witchcraft, the power does not necessarily lie in the actual words uttered by the magician but in invoking spiritual powers to act over the plea and bring

---

7. Anderson, *Blessing and Curse*, 26.
8. Austin, *How to Do Things*, 12–13. According to speech act theory, words are assumed to have power to cause actions.
9. Jeffers, *Magic and Divination*, 245.

it to the desired end. Therefore, as argued later, the power of a curse lies both in the unanimity of people in uttering and invoking the deity to execute the curse. Normally, people do not fear curse words simply because a human being uttered them, but because the supreme powers were invited to take up the case and ensure justice and revenge were settled. It was even more severe when the community sanctioned the pronouncement of the curse as opposed to an individual.

Prevalence of Cursing and Blessing Practices in the OT and NT Worlds

The use and practice of cursing and blessing was a prevalent phenomenon in the ancient world. Cursing and blessing practices were common in ancient Israel and surrounding communities. The scholarly work undertaken on the phenomenology of cursing establishes the prevalence of curses in all cadres of ANE societies: "Every member of society used them, from slave to king, from young to old, from men and women to the deities themselves. They crossed cultural lines and required little or no explanation, for curses were the source of great evil. In other words, curses were universal."[10] The Jewish people understood the dangerous efficacy of curses.[11]

Gager, an NT scholar who has extensively researched and written about curses and translated many curse tablets and binding spells from the ancient world, concludes that nearly 99 percent of the ancient population believed in the power of spells and curses.[12]

Graf argues that Greeks commonly followed the practice of using binding spells.[13] There is extant evidence of the use of curses even in the emperor's court. This is in reference to Tacitus (in the *Annals*) as quoted by Gager.[14] From these references, two undeniable realities should be underscored: First, in antiquity (ANE and Graeco-Roman society), curses were widespread; and second, people in the ancient world trusted in the power or effectiveness of a curse.

---

10. Kitz, *Cursed Are You!*, 3.
11. Keener, *Galatians: A Commentary*, 209.
12. Gager, *Curse Tablets*, 244.
13. Graf, *Magic in Ancient World*, 173.
14. Gager, *Curse Tablets*, 254–55.

Fear of Curses and Binding Spells in the Ancient World

The prevalence of curses and binding spells in the ancient world also brought fear among the populace. The ancient people constantly feared being victims of a curse, and binding spells. Gager quotes Pliny the Elder on his observation of the use, widespread nature, and effectiveness of spells: "There is no one who does not fear to be spellbound by curse tablets."[15] In his work *Natural History*, Pliny acknowledged the pervasive fear of curses and binding spells during his time. Thus, it is not a coincidence that the apostle Paul highlights the significance of the cross of Jesus Christ on the aspect of curses in such a context.

Gager shows how Plato, the philosopher, not only confirmed the widespread use of binding spells but also highlighted the fear it caused in the general public in classical Greek culture: "They were widespread; they were feared by most people, they were made available by professionals, they were commonly deposited in cemeteries; and they used human figurines."[16] The use of curses during this era was professionalized. Some curse professionals (*magoi*) sold curse tablets and inscriptions. Concerning those who practiced it, Plato prescribed the death penalty because of the harm it causes to the public.[17] Similarly, in Egypt, during the third and fourth century AD, Gager observes that the oracular questions (for instance, "Am I under a spell?") and prevalent use of amulets demonstrates a widespread need for protection because people were unsure if they were under a spell or not.[18] The need for protection increased the demand for specialized professionals who dispensed amulets and binding spells. From these references, the use of curses and blessings was widespread in the ancient world, and due to this reality, people lived in constant fear of being under the power of curses and binding spells.

Effectiveness of Curses and Binding Spells

Did curses have any effect? From the outset, we need to acknowledge the subjective nuances of the Enlightenment period and the modern era, which subjectively label ancient practices such as curses as false and retrogressive.

---

15. Gager, 244.
16. Gager, 250.
17. Gager, 254–55.
18. Gager, 220.

Gager recognizes that for a long time, it has been assumed that curses, spells, charms, and amulets do not work. Still, he wonders how we are to explain and understand "the persistent irrationality of those who pursued them through so many centuries."[19] He rightly argues that we must entertain the idea that "these beliefs and practices worked *in some sense*."[20] I concur that we should not summarily dismiss the ancient belief in *defixiones*;[21] instead, we should be open to considering the possibility that these curses somehow worked. In my opinion, I believe in the existence of curses even in the modern world; they exist irrespective of people's views. Due to their prevalence, the people in antiquity must have believed it worked. Offering a balanced opinion, Gager writes, "Of course, we need not assume that they worked in the same way that the participants themselves believed. But neither are we justified in imposing simplistic or literalistic preconceptions on these participants and their beliefs."[22] We are thus supposed to shed off our anachronistic tendencies to see sense in what the ancient people strongly believed.

In the Roman era, the use of *defixiones* was generally illegal, but at the same time, it flourished.[23] Their widespread nature proves that *defixiones* worked, "The reason for their pervasive presence lies in the observation that they worked, or that they were believed to work, which comes to the same thing. Their success and effectiveness also explain why they were treated as illegal or dangerous."[24] Gager further probes the idea that they were dangerous and argues that it is a threat to the establishment of the imperial powers of Rome. He writes,

> Dangerous not because they always intended harm but because they worked. Better yet, they worked in ways that could not be controlled by the legal, social, and political centers of ancient society. Indeed, at times they stood outside, perhaps in direct

---

19. Gager, 22.
20. Gager, 22 (Emphasis original).
21. These are curse tablets and binding spells normally inscribed on thin metal sheets: Gager, v; D. Jordan, as quoted by H. S. Versnel, defines *defixiones* with some emphasis on the purpose, "*Defixiones*, more commonly known as curse tablets, are inscribed pieces of lead, usually in the form of small, thin sheets, intended to influence, by supernatural means, the actions or the welfare of persons or animals against their will." Versnel, "Beyond Cursing," 61.
22. Gager, 23.
23. Gager, 24.
24. Gager, 24.

opposition to those centers. The idea that *magoi* could dispense power on matters of central importance to human life; the idea that any private person, for nothing but a small fee, could put that power to use in a wide variety of circumstances; and the idea that all of these transactions were available to individuals who stood outside and sometimes against the "legitimate" corporate structures of society – all of these ideas presented a serious threat to those who saw themselves as jealous guardians of power emanating from the center of that society, whether Greek, Roman, Antiochene, or Rabbinic. Here was power beyond their control, power in hands of freely negotiating individuals.[25]

Certainly, the effectiveness of curses posed a threat to the political establishment, and that is why it was considered illegal. It was deemed an unregulated center of power yet an effective weapon in the public's hands. It is no wonder, as earlier observed, that Plato prescribed a death penalty to those using it.

Functions of Curse in the NT World

In the NT world, curses and binding spells were used widely in various areas of life. Their use permeated every aspect of ancient life and society. In this subsection, we explore, identify, and interrogate the possible function of a curse, which formed Paul's basis of the idea of the crucified and cursed Christ. The section looks at the use of curses and *defixiones* by concerned parties in sports, public and private life, love affairs, business affairs, political affairs, and legal matters.

The Use of Curses in Sports and Competitions

In the ancient world, especially in the Graeco-Roman world, *defixiones* were regularly used in sports and in theatre competitions against rivals. Curse spells were purposefully used to hinder one's opponent from winning and increase one's chances of gaining victory.[26] For administration and effectiveness, clients consulted professional individuals to prescribe them curse spells to gain a

---

25. Gager, 24.
26. Gager, 43.

competitive advantage over their opponents. From the extant curse tablets on sports, the prescriber of the *defixiones* was supposed to ensure that the victim either became weak, failed, fell sick, not passed the starting line, veered off the course, or in horse racing, fell and broke one's limbs. A curse inscription found in Carthage, North Africa, contains the following translated invocation to a spirit directed against opponents in a horse racing match:

> Take away their victory, entangle their feet, hinder them, hobble them, so that tomorrow morning in the hippodrome they are not able to run or walk about, or win, or go out of the starting gates, or advance either on the racecourse, or circle around the turning point, but may they fall with their drivers.[27]

On any given occasion, many competitors and fans sought advantages from whichever direction in order to attain victory over their opponent(s).[28] One of such available options was consulting the curse professionals. Thus, the initiative could either come from a competitor or the game's fanatics. This category was one of the common uses of *defixiones* in the ancient world; and as can be observed, *defixiones* in this category were mainly used for selfish reasons.

The Use of Curses in Sex, Love, and Marriage Affairs

In the ancient world, it was common for people to use curses, charms, and binding spells on matters of love, sex, and marriage. Gager approximates that one-quarter of all surviving tablets concern "matters of the heart."[29] This shows how pervasive curses, binding spells and charms were used in the ancient world. For example, a lover consulted a *magoi* to win or lure lovers into a relationship or marriage. In other cases, *defixiones* were used to regain the affection of a departed lover.[30] Typically, the victim was cursed to lose memory, have an inclination of heart toward the interested lover, or have a favorable reply from a lover. The inscriptions on the tablets seek to bind the eyes, heart, and brain or memory of any competitor and ensure that the subject of the *defixiones* is loved back. Gager adds, "Various tablets specify

---

27. Gager, 61.
28. Gager, 143.
29. Gager, 78.
30. Gager, 179.

that the object of passion is to be dragged by the hair, deprived of memory and sleep, tormented by passion, and killed with madness."³¹ One of the curses that illustrate this category is a fourth century BC tablet inscription deposited in a grave; the author of the inscription hopes that Theodora will cut off relations with Charias, her lover:

> (*Side A*) I bind Theodôra in the presence of the one (female) at Persephone's side and in the presence of those who are unmarried. May she be unmarried and whenever she is about to chat with Kallias and with Charias – whenever she is about to discuss deeds and words and business . . . words, whatever he indeed says. I bind Theodôra to remain unmarried to Charias and (I bind) Charias to forget Theodôra, and (I bind) Charias to forget . . . Theodôra and sex with Theodôra.³²

The ancients employed curses in this category to deal with matters concerning erotic love but with some sense of control and manipulation.

The Use of Curses in the Business World

Just like in other areas of ancient life, *defixiones* were widely used in the business realm to manage competition and rivalry. In the Hellenistic world, workers or traders used *defixiones* to gain a competitive edge over a workmate or one's fellow businessmen. These *defixiones* had a specific target: "in addition to the occupation, the tablet binds or curses the target's labor, products, income, and workplace, there can be no doubt that the root issue was a competition between small businesses and their proprietors."³³ Cursing or binding of the fortunes of one's competitor is a common feature of this category of extant curse tablets. The curses and binding spells, invoking a deity, targeted the person, skill, and business, as illustrated by the following curse tablet:

> I bind and restrain Manês. And you, Dear Goddesses of Vengeance, restrain him; Hermes the Restrainer, restrain Manês and the affairs of Manês and cause the entire business in which Manês is engaged to become entirely contrary and backward

---

31. Gager, 81.
32. Gager, 90.
33. Gager, 152.

for Manês. I will sacrifice a thank offering to you in exchange for the good news, Goddesses of Vengeance and Hermes the Restrainer, if Manês fairs badly.[34]

Broadly, in the ancient world, success or failure in any area of life was attributed to curses and binding spells; it is well noted that "curse tablets and apotropaic defenses against them were reckoned among the several proven techniques employed by workers to enhance their chances of success and to explain their occasional failures."[35] Many workers and traders believed in them for protection and success. Curses and binding spells of this category were primarily geared toward protecting one's economic interests.

The Use of Curses in Legal and Political Disputes

This category of curses and binding spells in the ancient world is *defixiones*, that were used to manipulate the litigation process for one's benefit. Gager notes that this category of curse tablets was common from classical Athens to the late Roman Empire.[36] *Defixiones* under this category were used against judicial opponents and accusers in the legal process to guarantee a favorable outcome.[37] In lawsuits and public trials, *defixiones* were used to reverse a bad fortune in a trial, or to make the opponent tongue-tied in court. This is clearly illustrated in a lead tablet dated approximately 300 BC, that involved a pending court case between cooks and/or butchers:

> Theagenês, the butcher/cook, I bind the tongue and soul and speech that he is practicing. Purrias, I bind the hands and feet and tongue and soul and speech he is practicing. I bind the wife of Purrias, the tongue and soul. Also, Kerkion, the butcher/cook I bind and Dokimos the butcher/cook, the tongue and soul and speech that they are practicing. I bind Kineas, his tongue and soul and speech he is practicing with Theagenês. And Phereklês, I bind the tongue and soul and evidence that he gives for Theagenês. Seuthês, I bind the tongue and soul and speech that he is practicing and his feet and hands and eyes and

---

34. Gager, 156.
35. Gager, 154.
36. Gager, 117.
37. Gager, 117–18.

> mouth. Lamprias I bind the tongue and soul and speech that he is practicing, and his hands and feet and eyes and mouth. All of these I bind, I hide, I bury, I nail down. If they lay any counterclaim before the arbitrator or the court, let them seem to be of no account, either in word or in deed.[38]

Just like *defixiones* in other categories, which sought to bring the client (private individual) a fortune or competitive advantage over others, this subcategory[39] proves the widespread use of *defixiones* in the litigation process in a manner that a commissioning party sought to tilt an impending court case favorably. For example, under this category of curses, it was common for a client to bind the tongues and accusers or witnesses;[40] or make opponents incapable of appearing before the court.[41] The use of such curses made the ancients assume that they can manipulate the future judicial outcomes to their advantage.

Common to categories surveyed above is *defixiones* for personal gain; that is, to manipulate a case in court, lure a lover (back), predetermine an outcome of a sports event, and deal with business rivalries. The self-seeking clients approached the professional dispensers of *defixiones* against their targets. Again, the self-seeking nature of the above four categories of ancient curses, in my opinion, is the primary reason why modern scholars are inclined toward associating curses with magic, sorcery, and witchcraft. H. S. Versnel also raises a similar argument regarding the above curse categories: "The intended victims in all four of Faraone's categories are not being cursed because they are guilty of any crime or misdeed against *defigens* but because they are his rivals with regard to social prestige or economic position, and any attack against their social position will increase his honor."[42] The competitors are cursed not because of any wrong committed but because of their competition. Although Paul and his audience might have been aware of these diverse

---

38. Gager, 131–32.

39. Discussed under the title, "Tongue-tied in Court: Legal and Political Disputes," in Gager, 116–50.

40. Gager, 138.

41. Graf, *Magic in Ancient World*, 153.

42. Versnel, "Beyond Cursing," 61. Versnel also agrees with Schadenzauber that these four categories of curses can be rightly described as "magical tablets" or "magical curses." Versnel, 62. *Defigens* are those who commission a curse to their advantage.

functions of curses in antiquity, it is unlikely that his conceptual framework of the cursed Christ originated from these four categories.

Still, there is a distinctive category of curses in the ancient world that primarily dealt with justice and revenge. The next section and the rest of the dissertation will look at this distinctive category of curse and propose it as underlying Paul's arguments in Galatians 3:1–14.

The Use of Curses in Judicial Aspects: Pleas for Justice and Revenge

The fifth and final category of the curse tablets in the ancient world is pleas for justice and revenge (this study prefers to refer to these pleas as judicial curses). Significantly, judicial curses emanate from the need for justice and punishment for an offense by known or unknown offenders. The ancient curses expressing pleas for justice and revenge have been seen as a distinctive category[43] of curses in the ancient world. Gager says, "the most distinctive feature of this category lies in the explicit claim that the targets or enemies have somehow wronged the client."[44] Unlike other ancient categories of curses that sought to manipulate or control fortunes by the agency of the spirits and deities for self-interest, this category was solely interested in the execution of justice and revenge in response to a wrong committed.

Gager points at another distinctive, and that is, the symbolic and ritual transfer of the stolen items to a deity:

> In virtually every case concerned with stolen property, the client temporarily transfers ownership of the goods in question, sometimes even the culprits themselves, to the deity and thereby makes their recovery a matter of divine rather than merely human concern. For it is no longer just the human owner, but the gods themselves who have been deprived, offended, and dishonored.[45]

---

43. Versnel refers to this category as "judicial prayers," or "prayers for legal help." Versnel, "Beyond Cursing," 61. The key issue raised is that this category is specifically prayers/pleas or petitions. He argues that the other categories compel or instruct the *daemons* and gods to carry out their wishes. But, in the judicial prayers the author of the curse petitions his case to the deity.

44. Gager, *Curse Tablets*, 175.

45. Gager, 175–76.

Versnel translates an inscription dated between 100 BC and AD 200 that shows a handing over of the goods in question to the gods for recovery: "I consecrate to the mother of the gods the gold pieces that I have lost, all of them, so that the goddess will track them down and bring everything to light and will punish the guilty in accordance with her power and in this way will not be made a laughingstock."[46] It is noted that the main reason for the transference was to locate unidentified offenders.[47] Certainly, the involvement of the divine in human legal matters heightened fear among the ancient people. The gods and the *daemons* in the spiritual world were thought to be fair judges, all-knowing, and effective in locating the offender. Normally, spirits or deities invoked were purposefully invited to execute justice against the target who has committed a wrong.

Further, Gager notes that the overall goal of the pleas for justice and revenge was to deliver justice and settle revenge; in cases where stealing was involved, it meant seeking redress as well as punishment of the thief.[48] Judicial prayers dealt with issues that emanated from legitimate grievances over an injustice. It is worth noting that in judicial prayers, justice and revenge often intertwine: "The guilty must be punished for an irreparable damage, and the punishment serves exclusively as satisfaction for the sense of justice of the injured person; in short, it constitutes a request for revenge."[49] Thus, the quest for justice also meant the pursuit of revenge and retaliation against the culprit.

Justice is an elusive ideal in any society, but the ancient people found an effective panacea in judicial curses. With the help of spirits and deities, they uttered judicial curses with an expectation that justice would be properly executed and that revenge would be rightly administered. Imprecations of judicial character were used as petitions for divine retribution of a wrong done on an innocent person. This category virtually resonates with what Paul writes about in Galatians 3:1–14. The revenge overtones in Paul's letter to the Galatians seem to be absent, but the presence of judicial use of curses even in Paul's quotation contexts is clear. The quote from Deuteronomy contains curses that served as a punishment for breaking God's laws. In Galatians

---

46. Versnel, "Beyond Cursing," 74.
47. Gager, *Curse Tablets*, 182.
48. Gager, 175.
49. Versnel, "Beyond Cursing," 70.

3:10, Paul establishes that the entire humanity stands cursed and so subject to death, the consequence of disobedience. However, because Christ became a curse for us, his death settled the demands of divine justice, once and for all. The substitutionary death of Christ satisfied God's justice and annulled the curse, its power, and effects of death on humanity. The next subsection further discusses the aspect of Christ's annulment of the curse on humanity.

These broad categories of curses and binding spells[50] in the ancient world establish that cursing or binding was a major practice. Curses were used as a means of punishment and settling justice. However, Jeffers wrongly associates this to magical practices, as he says, "the origins or roots of blessings and curses in magical practice can be seen in their formulations, which are characterized by the features of incantation."[51] It may be challenging to distinguish blessings and curses with origin in magic, but the curse and magic were two different things. Magicians claimed the power to control whatever happens, but many curses, especially judicial curses, were dedicated to a deity for action.

From the discussions on various categories of curses, except for the pleas for justice and revenge, all other categories of ancient curses were used for self-interest against other people. In a business, it was against a fellow trader, and in sports, it was against one's competitor. Each person sought influence over a competitor or a rival. Gager observes, "All *defixiones* expressed a formalized wish to bring other persons or animals under the client's power, against their will and customarily without their knowledge. In some cases, the wish is expressed as an intention to inflict personal harm or death."[52] However, in his discussions, Gager alienates curses of plea for justice and vengeance. This is a distinctive category that should not be confused with magic or the curses that seek to manipulate and control people and situations.

---

50. Audollent has classified ancient curses and binding spells into five categories but using Latin terminologies. The categories are: *Defixiones iudicariae* (judicial spells), *defixiones amatoriae* (erotic spells), *defixiones agonistic* (agonistic spells), defixiones against slanderers and thieves, and the defixiones against economic competitors. See Graf, *Magic in Ancient World*, 120–23, 129.

51. Jeffers, *Magic and Divination*, 244.

52. Gager, *Curse Tablets*, 21.

The Use of Curse as a Tool of Judicial Litigation

From the survey above on the functions of curses in the ancient world, Paul's conceptual framework in Galatians 3:1–14 seems to fit into the judicial use of *defixiones*. Paul applies the death of Christ on the cross in a manner consistent with judicial litigation. It has been argued that curses for pleas for justice and revenge, currently represent the largest category of extant curse tablets, as Gager says,

> Until recently, pleas for justice and revenge represented a modest share of the total corpus of *defixiones*. A rough count indicates nineteen in Greek and perhaps twelve in Latin. Since 1970s, these numbers have increased dramatically, to the point where they now represent by far the largest single subcategory of all curse tablets and binding spells.[53]

The increasing number of curse tablets under this category partly illustrates the prominence of this function of curses in the ancient world. Kitz has established that even in the ANE, curses were used in connection to judicial matters:

> Curses petition the deities for rulings in a heavenly court. And frequently they were wrapped in legal terminology. In the ancient Near East, curses are a manifestation of divine, judicial power. When the deities discharge curses, they demonstrate their ascendancy over life and death. For the harm in all curses ultimately aspires to one end: death. They seek death in order to preserve life. This death is indiscriminate. No one is immune. It can be instant or slow or torturous.[54]

Therefore, through this quote and extensive studies on the ANE, Kitz explicitly establishes the connection between curses and justice in the ancient world.

While surveying findings from social anthropologists, Anderson notes that judicial curses served as judge, jury, and executioner.[55] Imprecations in this category principally dealt with matters of justice and revenge. Gager has

---

53. Gager, 178.
54. Kitz, *Cursed Are You!*, 4–5.
55. Anderson, "Nature and Function," 64.

translated a curse tablet that appeals to the highest god for vengeance and justice in relation to the untimely death of a young woman:

> I call upon and beseech the highest god, Lord of the spirits and of all flesh, against those who by deceit murdered or cast a spell on/poisoned miserable Hêraklea, untimely death, causing her to spill innocent blood in unjust fashion, so that the same happen to those who murdered or cast a spell on/poisoned her and also to their children. Lord who oversees all things and angels of God, before whom on this day every soul humbles itself, may you avenge this innocent blood and seek (justice) speedily.[56]

Gager dates this curse inscription to be from second century BC because of clear biblical allusion to biblical passages from the Septuagint. In this judicial case, the cause of death was unknown, but the relatives suspect that unknown murderers had used spells and poisons. Thus, the ancients believed that the curse was able to locate the unknown offender and ensure that justice was served.

Wrongdoing as a Basis for Judicial Curses

A judicial curse was uttered or written down to serve as a punishment for wrongdoing, for instance, in cases of stolen property. Expectedly, the victim would suffer what was deemed as the equivalent of the harm caused. The pleas for justice emanated from wrongdoing in the past that the client sought to address justly. One of the curse tablets that Gager translates shows that a judicial curse pursued the offender and other associates who jointly committed a crime, including all those who had any form of knowledge about it.[57] This applied in a case where the identity of the culprits was unknown to the owner. In such a case, where the offender was unknown, a judicial curse was randomly uttered and directed to whoever was guilty.

---

56. Gager, *Curse Tablets*, 187.
57. Gager, 188.

McLean argues that curses came from the transgression of a taboo or a "defilement" that brought disruption and chaos in society. He defines "defilement" as

> a disturbance of the system of classification which determines two distinct worlds: the inner world of society, order and culture; and the outer world of chaos, wilderness and natural forces. Defilement poses a real danger in society because it damages the border between these two worlds such that society is overtaken by chaos and its deadly natural forces.[58]

McLean claims that the defilement could manifest itself in the form of curses. The defilement that he refers to still points to the idea of wrongdoing. It disrupts the state of order (blessing) and brings in a state of chaos and destruction (curse). Fundamentally, a judicial curse was pronounced based on wrongdoing. McLean rightly notes that a curse was "a spontaneous and automatic product of transgression."[59] It was pronounced to bring a perpetrator directly under divine judgment.[60] Reiteratively, the focus of judicial curses was to bring about justice and revenge. On this, judicial curses looked into the past (for the wrong suffered) and into the future (anticipating future compensation).[61] They sought to deliver justice on past unjust situations and looked forward to righting wrongs. Judicial curses also had other functions in the ancient world, as looked at in the subsections below.

The Use of Judicial Curses to Protect Grave Disturbance

It is clear that protection was the key feature of curses. In the ancient world, it was common for people to be buried with some valuables hoping that they would require them in the next world. However, the valuables buried with the dead often attracted grave robbers. In order to deter grave robbers from effacing and plundering the burial chamber, curses and warnings were inscribed on rocks or soft limestone walls of a burial cave.[62] The inscribed curses were not without a purpose, as Kitz observes,

---

58. McLean, *Cursed Christ*, 71.
59. Robert Parker, *Miasmus: Pollution and Purification*, 191, cited in McLean, 71.
60. Robertson Smith, *Religion of the Semites*, 62, cited in McLean, 71.
61. Gager, *Curse Tablets*, 177.
62. Gager, 191.

Tomb curses defend not just the dead but also that in which the dead are buried, tomb chambers, sarcophagi, or the earth sheltering the grave. As guardians of the dead, these curses strive to maintain a blessing in the face of blatant mortality. They strive to keep alive the *memory* of one's material existence by both defending the places where human remains are interred and by announcing who is buried there. These display inscriptions are bridges between the dead and the living. Ultimately they endeavor to circumvent the curse of extinction through the preservation of *physical* remains and the burial places that house them in the mortal realm.[63]

Principally, the curses written on rock surfaces or the limestone walls sought to protect the dead and the tomb chambers from any form of destruction and robbery.

Crawford has observed that the grave robbers were perhaps from the lower socioeconomic class and could therefore not read the inscribed curses.[64] However, illiteracy could not absolve the plunderers because they lived in a context where they understood that judicial curses were inscribed on tombs. Therefore, it might as well be concluded that these robbers knowingly disrespected the dead and burial chambers due to their unfavorable socioeconomic conditions.

In an effort to ward off grave plunderers, some inscriptions in the tombs warned the plunderer that there were no valuables stored in the sarcophagus. In 1870, a tomb inscription was discovered in the village of Siloam ("Siloam Tomb") containing a curse prohibiting the tomb's disturbance. Avigad has translated the inscription thus: "This is [the sepulcher of . . .] yahu who is over the house. There is no silver and no gold here, but [his bones] and the bones of his slave-wife with him. Cursed be the man who will open this."[65] Also, there are extant inscriptions dated fifth century BC (Phoenician Eshmunazar), eleventh century BC (Phoenician Ahiram), and seventh (The Aramaic Nerab 2 inscription) century BC that contain prohibition against disturbing the tomb

---

63. Kitz, *Cursed Are You!*, 274.
64. Crawford, *Blessing and Curse*, 120.
65. Crawford, 98.

and the claim that there were no valuables (silver or bronze) buried therein.[66] Thus, generally, judicial curses were prescribed against whoever would disturb the dead in their resting places. The judicial curse was believed to take effect the moment a plunderer looted the tomb.

It is worth noting that some tombs had inscriptions that issued an incentive to those who protected the grave. This is explicit in the Nerab inscription below that was found in 1891 at the small village of Nerab located seven kilometers south east of Aleppo.

> Sin-zer-ibni, priest of Sahar at Nerab, deceased. This is his picture and his grave. Whoever you are who drag this picture and grave away from its place, may Sahar and Shamash and Nikkal and Nusk pluck your name and your place out of life, and an evil death make you die; and may they cause your seed to perish! But if you guard this picture and grave, in the future may yours be guarded.[67]

The curse inscription addressed the would-be violator anonymously "whoever you (are)." Apart from giving an incentive to the one who would guard the grave, the curse inscription also described the prohibited action, and the punishment wished upon him, and curse against the family of the violator of the inscription.

The Use of Judicial Curses to Protect a Name and Writings

People of the ancient world valued leaving behind a rich legacy in the form of a good name. Therefore, they took measures to protect and perpetuate their names and popularity. Judicial curses became helpful in safeguarding one's name. Crawford writes, "The concern that a successor would renovate a building without giving due credit to the original builder is found frequently in the Neo-Assyrian inscriptions and was dealt with by curses against the guilty or blessings for the obedient."[68] In addition, preservation of one's name was valued in architectural works; Crawford translates a curse tablet that

---

66. Crawford, 99.
67. Crawford, 205.
68. Crawford, 169.

placed a curse on anyone who removes one's name from temple furnishings. The inscription reads,

> Whoever removes my name from the furnishings of the temple of Hadad my lord, may my lord Hadad not accept his bread and his water from his hand. May my lady Sawl not accept his bread and his water from his hand. And may he sow, but not harvest. May he sow 1000 measures of barley but take only a fraction thereof. Though 100 ewes suckle one lamb, let it not be satisfied. Though 100 cows suckle one calf, let it not be satisfied. Though 100 women suckle one infant, let it not be satisfied. May 100 women bake bread in one oven but not be able to fill it. Would that his men pick up barley from the rubbish heap to eat. May death, the rod of Nergal, never cease from his land.[69]

Further, there is evidence of curses uttered to protect the copyright of one's work. According to Gager, "Book curses, directed by scribes against those who might modify, deface, or destroy their precious writings may reach back as far as 3800 BC and the practice of attaching such curses to the colophons of medieval manuscripts of all sorts was widespread among both Jewish and Christian copyists."[70] Gager gives an example of the closing section of the book of Revelation (22:18–19), which contains a warning, "I warn everyone who hears the words of the prophecy of this book: if anyone adds to them, God will add to him the plagues described in this book, and if anyone takes away from the words of the book of this prophecy, God will take away his share in the tree of life and in the holy city, which are described in this book." (ESV).

The use of judicial curses in protecting tombs, the dead, names, and writings demonstrate that judicial curses were an effective category of curses. This category of curses was uttered based on wrongdoing.

Appeal to the Deities or Spirits to Execute Judicial Curses

A common feature of the ancient curse tablets was the invocation of a deity, *daimones,* and spirits to execute the curse. Kitz vividly expresses the chief function of these deities:

---

69. Crawford, 170–71.
70. Gager, *Curse Tablets*, 28.

Thus, a major component of their role as adjudicators would be to determine the worthiness of a curse. If the petition was justified, then they would utter a judgment and permit the actualization of the condemnation. It would have effect. If the curse was unjustified, then the deities would ignore the malediction. It would remain inactive and eventually fade from all living memory.[71]

Therefore, after the human appeal was made, the effectiveness of an imprecation uttered solely depended on the approval of a higher being or powers.

Why were judicial prayers/curses directed outside the human realm? In seeking to understand the reason for this characteristic, Graf argues that the gods were invited to deal with the unpredictability of the future beyond human reach.[72] Graf's argument is less convincing, as he cites the unpredictable nature of the future as the reason *defixiones* were directed outside of humanity. However, the appeal to the deities must have come in humble acknowledgment of human limitation in locating unknown offenders. In judicial cases, it was needful to call on to a deity, especially in cases of an unknown offender, because the deity or spirits were deemed effective in tracking down the offender(s) and bringing about justice and vengeance. Also, the deities or spirits could enter into the human sphere and help in areas of human limitation.

The Use of Judicial Curses in Ancient Israel and Neighboring Communities

The Cursing Practice in the Ancient Near Eastern World

In his book *Blessing and Curse in Syro-Palestinian Inscriptions of the Iron Age*, Timothy Crawford extensively investigated blessing and cursing practices in Syro-Palestinian epigraphic materials contemporary with the Israelite monarchy (northern and southern kingdoms). In exploring the ANE and Hebrew Bible words for cursing and blessing, he discovered a shared paradigm in the use of words. The inscriptions excavated from the Syria-Palestine region further showed that histories and practices in this geographical area were

---

71. Kitz, *Cursed Are You!*, 134.
72. Graf, *Magic in Ancient World*, 129.

intertwined, and communications between them were widespread.[73] Thus, Israel lived within a cultural context where curse words and practices cut across its geographical borders.

In a separate study, Kitz notes that the extant Sumerian, Akkadian, Hebrew, and Hittite texts contain two types of curses: conditional and unconditional curses. She distinguishes the two types of ancient curses: "the unconditional curse solicits the divine realm to harm a particular target without provision. The conditional curse entreats the deities to injure the target only if certain provisions are not honored."[74] The unconditional curses are reactionary, while the conditional is proactive. The conditional curses featured extensively in treaty documents, and were used to safeguard agreements between two or more parties.

The Cursing Practice in Ancient Israel

The Hebrew Bible was written within the ANE context, where cursing was widely practiced. It is therefore expected that the Hebrew Bible would reflect this common cultural practice. The Bible begins with God blessing his creation (Gen 1–2), but in Genesis 3, the fall of humanity brought sin, death, and curse. The curse affected the serpent, humanity, and their environment (the earth). The pronouncement of the curse came as a result of the disobedience and rebellion of humans against God (Gen 2:17). In the subsequent Bible chapters and books, the universal problem of sin and curse is not fully addressed until Genesis 12, when God calls Abraham and promises to make him a blessing. That is why Paul, in Galatians 3:8, argues that the Scriptures foresaw the justification of the Gentiles and so announced the gospel in advance to Abraham. The pronouncement of God's plan to spread his blessings to all humanity looked into the future salvation history, a period that was inaugurated by the incarnation and death of Christ, and the coming of the Holy Spirit.

Disobedience of God's Commands as a Basis for Judicial Curses

In ancient Israel, curses were associated with divine judgment. They resulted from breaking God's covenant and disobedience to his laws (Lev 26:3–39;

---

73. Crawford, *Blessing and Curse*, 3.
74. Kitz, *Cursed Are You!*, 75.

Deut 27–30). On the other hand, blessings flowed when people obeyed God and kept their part of the covenant with God (Deut 28:1–14). On several occasions, the prophets interpreted key historical events and suffering of the nation of Israel as being a divine punishment. For instance, the exile experience was directly linked to disobedience to God's commands (Deut 29:24–28; Ezra 9:6–15; Jer 22:9; Ezek 5:6; 11:12; Dan 9:4–19). Thielman notes that, unlike blessings which were generalized in terms of abundance and prosperity, curses were specifically tied to the future history of Israel.[75] Israel as a nation would face dire consequences for their sins when they violated God's laws.

Curses were understood by the Israelites to be a judgment of God upon them for disobedience to his laws and covenant. The curses, therefore, functioned as a tool of litigation. There are several instances where judicial curses were uttered and were thought to have powers to pursue (un)known offenders. For example, in Zechariah 5:1–4, we read,

> Again I lifted my eyes and saw, and behold, a flying scroll! And he said to me, "What do you see?" I answered, "I see a flying scroll. Its length is twenty cubits, and its width ten cubits." Then he said to me, "This is the curse that goes out over the face of the whole land. For everyone who steals shall be cleaned out according to what is on one side, and everyone who swears falsely shall be cleaned out according to what is on the other side. I will send it out, declares the Lord of hosts, and it shall enter the house of the thief, and the house of him who swears falsely by my name. And it shall remain in his house and consume it, both timber and stones."

Anderson comments that such curses uttered against unknown offenders ". . . added a randomizing element wherein the curse's activation supposedly had equal probability to its dormancy. Then, when misfortune did arise, it was a clear evidence of the guilt of the suffering party."[76] Thus, the curse was deemed effective to locate the offender and deliver justice and revenge.

---

75. Thielman, *Paul & the Law*, 127.
76. Anderson, "Nature and Function," 65.

Yahweh as the Focus of Judicial Prayers in Israel

In Israel, judicial curses were rarely used; but when employed, they were distinctively directed to Yahweh for implementation. Crawford affirms,

> In the ancient Near East, curse (especially in the incantation literature) had very definite magical connections which were sometimes only thinly covered by religious ideas. However, in Israelite society the use of curses is closely regulated. This is seen in that the curses are put in the form of prayers to Yahweh. Also, the thrust in ancient Israel was that Yahweh was guardian of curse; the curse was a means to see that God's will, divine judgment, etc., were done.[77]

Yahweh as a fair Judge was invoked to intervene and deliver on judicial matters among humankind:

> Another intrinsic feature of curses is divine judgment. As solicitations they inherently entreat the heavenly realm with the hope that the deities will review what is perceived by the speaker to be an unjust situation and act accordingly. Frequently, these maledictions address circumstances that are beyond human control leaving the court of the divine realm the only recourse open to the speaker.[78]

In this case, Yahweh became the refuge for those seeking justice (1 Sam 24:15). In Israel and the wider ANE culture, judicial curses were also found in treaties, oaths, and covenants.

Curses in Treaties and Oaths Both in ANE and Israel

There are extant inscriptions from ANE featuring treaties and oaths containing curses. These curses were primarily employed to safeguard faithfulness and punish those who broke the treaty terms and obligations.[79] The curse served as a judge, bringing fairness and justice to the parties in the treaty.

The practice of taking oaths was a common phenomenon in the ancient world. An oath was understood as "a solemn and explicit petition to a deity

---

77. Crawford, *Blessing and Curse*, 22.
78. Kitz, *Cursed Are You!*, 68–69.
79. Crawford, *Blessing and Curse*, 102.

or deities potentially to inflict harm on the oath-taker. It was used to endorse the binding nature of a statement or the terms of an arrangement between two parties."[80] There was the involvement of the divine world into the human realm. In definition, oaths and vows overlap in meaning, but Kitz makes a helpful distinction:

> The fundamental difference between an oath and a vow is the curse. An oath has a curse; a vow does not. An oath automatically solicits the divine world. A vow, on the other hand, involves the deities but the principle on which the solicitation is based rests on the axiom of reciprocity. A vow negotiates with the divine realm. An oath does not; it only petitions harm should the oath not be honored.[81]

So, breaking an oath resulted in a curse, but the faithful keeping of the terms of the agreement actualized the mentioned promise.

The practice of using curses in treaties was common in the ancient Israel society and Hebrew Bible. The Hebrew word אלה translated as "oath" appears seven times in the Bible, four of these occurrences are in the context of an oath (1 Kgs 8:31; 2 Chr 6:22; Hosea 4:2; 10:4), and the last two refer to false swearing.[82] The threat or curse included in an oath took effect when one failed to honor the obligations of the treaty. The oath came with terms and conditions that needed to be fulfilled by each party; otherwise a curse would ensue. The curse was then a penalty (implicit or explicit) upon the violator of an agreement that was confirmed with an oath.[83] The ancient oath-taking practice presumed faithfulness of either party to the treaty conditions and obligations.

An oath as a conditional curse had two purposes. First, it was used to discover the unknown perpetrator of an offense; and second, it was used to determine if a suspect was guilty (see examples in Exod 22:7–16; Num 5:12–28; Judg 17:1.[84] These two purposes establish a close link between oaths/

---

80. Kitz, *Cursed Are You!*, 37–38.

81. Kitz, 33. For further discussion on oaths and vows with examples in the Hebrew Bible, consult pages 32–63.

82. Crawford, *Blessing and Curse*, 109.

83. Crawford.

84. Jeffers, *Magic and Divination*, 248.

treaties and justice, revenge, and restitution. Thus, the theme of justice also runs through the OT covenants and treaties. The covenant God made with Abraham contained curses and blessings. The blessings would result when the terms of the covenant were adhered to. Conversely, curses would take effect once the terms of the covenant were violated. In Genesis 12, God made a covenant with Abraham in which, based on faith and obedience, he would receive land, nation, and blessings. God promised to bless all the families of the earth through Abraham. These promises given to Abraham were severally reiterated (Gen 12:1–2, 7; 13:14–18; 15:5–6, 18; 17:4–8, 16–21; 18:18; 22:17). The repetition not only served to remind them of their favored position but also served as a warning that if Abraham's descendants were to break the terms of the covenant, they would suffer the stipulated curse consequences.

Usually, in ancient times, treaties were protected by a curse. The following inscription on Sefire I tablet (line 16b–25) pronounces punishment on the violator of the treaty and anyone who damages the inscription:

> Whoever will not observe the words of the inscription which is [sic] on this stele or will say, "I will efface some of (its) words," or "I shall upset the good relations and turn (them) [to] evil," on any day on which he will d[o] so, may the gods overturn th[at m]an and his house and all that (is) in it; and may they make its lower part its upper part! May his scio[n] inherit no name.[85]

Any violations of a treaty led to dire consequences, which involved curses. Thus, although we have not delved into an extended discussion on treaties, oaths, and covenants, we can conclude that these ancient cultural and religious practices were related to judicial curses because the violator of the stipulated terms became accursed.

The Power of a Curse

In antiquity, curses were believed to be effective weapons (of justice) in the hands of any member of society. Curses were thought to bring about a wide array of destructive consequences and misfortunes to the victim. The cursed suffered some punishment and eventualities depending on the specification of the harm by the person who administered it. Thus, the fear of curses was

---

85. Crawford, *Blessing and Curse*, 193–94.

a reality in the ancient world because of what a curse was thought to bring. Undeniably, a curse to the ancient Near Easterners remained a powerful divine weapon:

> So close is the connection between curses and their heavenly derivation that curses can become deities themselves. They separate the dead from the living. They are disease, calamity, ailment, and misadventure. They are the agents of death. They are the personification of divine weapons, the instruments used in the execution of the evil embedded in every malediction. They are executioner deities, dispatched by their divine lord and master to work his will. They are ever active. They move in collectives. They pursue and chase offenders.[86]

The Bible also, written in the same world, takes the issue of curses seriously. Judicial imprecations threatened to bring punishments in several forms, as discussed below.

Death

The fear of curses emanated from the fact that binding spells and curses were deemed to bring disastrous consequence both to the individual offender and immediate family. Ultimately, death was the expected consequence. In an extant malediction from Esarhaddon's adê-agreement, the victim is cursed with a series of calamities, but Kitz rightly notes that the expected end is death. The malediction says, "May Anu, king of the gods, let illness, fatigue, malaria, sleeplessness, worries, and ill health rain upon all your homes."[87] She further comments:

> Even though each affliction has its own set of repercussions, the harm envisioned here is not really their individual consequences. It is rather the overwhelming, cumulative effect of all the ailments together. In the end, it doesn't really matter if the adversities occur sequentially or all at once, for there is only

---

86. Kitz, *Cursed Are You!*, 5.
87. Kitz, 200.

one possible conclusion to such relentless onslaught of calamities: death.[88]

Thus, the eventual and primary goal of a curse, especially the judicial curses, was death. The secondary afflictions specified are only meant to serve that particular end. In addition, some curses envisioned premature death. For example, the following curse beseeches Aššur to harm the victim with a short life: "May Aššur, king of the gods who issues decrees, decree an evil and unpleasant condition of existence for you. May he not grant you long-lasting old age and the achievement of extreme old age."[89] Whether premature or unexpected death, judicial curses ultimately envisioned death.

Again, an extant curse tablet contains the following death wish, as Kitz cites, "If anyone does any harm to the statue, may he leave orphaned children, a bereaved estate and a desolate home behind him. May he lose all his goods by fire and die at the hands of evil men."[90] The prominent wish in this tablet is a loss of life. This was what judicial curses were known for; they took away the life of an individual, family and community. Blessings brought life, but curses were life-taking. In Galatians 3:1–14, when Paul discusses the cursed Christ, he principally refers to the death of Christ on the cross (crucifixion) as relevant to the enigma of curses. A detailed connection and interpretation are made in the next chapter.

Cessation of Posterity

Closely related to the curse-goal above, curses were believed to have a disastrous effect on one's posterity. It is noted that "the greatest fear of the ancient was the end of one's race."[91] Just like today in the African society, the ancient people treasured having children and grandchildren to continue their family line. However, a curse threatened one's family's future. It systematically worked to wipe out one's offspring and lineage from existence. Therefore, to sustain the existence of a family, one had to avoid coming under the power of a malediction or a binding spell. Two of the ancient curse tablets that have survived to the modern era confirm this assertion: "Death takes away

---

88. Kitz, 200.
89. Kitz, 205.
90. Gager, *Curse Tablets*, 178.
91. Crawford, *Blessing and Curse*, 117.

the child still in (?) the womb and the child . . ." Also, one of Esarhaddon's vassal-treaties includes a curse on the continuance of life: "May the Lady of the gods, the mistress of creation, cut off birth from your land; may she make rare the cries of little children in the streets and squares."[92] Because of this eventuality, ancient people were cautious to ensure that they did not come under the life-threatening power of a curse.

Kitz notes, "The greatest degree of harm found in curses is extinction. These anathemas are designed to eliminate all hope for the continuance of life."[93] It threatened the existence of a family's name and posterity. A surviving curse in the treaty drawn up between Hattusili III (ca. 1267–37) and Ulmi-Teššup of Tarhuntassa identifies several target victims: "[6b](Then) may these Thousand Gods eradicate your person, together with [7]your wife, your sons, your land, your house, your threshing floor, your orchards, fields, your meadows, your oxen, your sheep, and all your possessions."[94]

Lack of Advancement

In the ancient world, curses and binding spells were understood to have the power to hold one's progress in life. This is portrayed in the first-century lead tablet excerpt that sought to deny the target person enjoyment of life: ". . . And let the earth not be walkable, the sea not sailable; let there be no enjoyment of life, no increase of children, but may utter destruction visit them or him. As an inspector, you will wield upon them the bronze sickle, and you will cut them out (?). But I exempt the writer and the destroyer."[95] The curse inscription curtails any form of advancement or enjoyment on the part of the target person.

Overturning of Kingdom

In some inscriptions found in tombs, those who damage or destroy a sarcophagus are cursed. One of the surviving curse writings seemingly targets those in power; the person who interferes with the tomb would be deprived of peace and have his kingdom overturned:

---

92. Crawford, 132.
93. Kitz, *Cursed Are You!*, 206.
94. Kitz, 206.
95. Gager, *Curse Tablets*, 183.

> Coffin which Ittoba'al, son of Ahiram, king of Byblos, made for Ahiram, his father, when he placed him in "the house of eternity." Now, if a king among kings or a governor among governors or a commander of an army should come up against Byblos and uncover this coffin, may the scepter of his rule be torn away, may the throne of his kingdom be overturned, and may peace flee from Byblos! And as for him, may his inscription be effaced . . . ![96]

The content of this Ahiram inscription discovered during excavations at Byblos in 1923 presumes that the would-be plunderers would be from the higher echelons of power. Upon destroying the tomb, the royal person would be dethroned because of the curse.

Interpretation of Reality Using Curse Lenses

With the prevalence of curses and especially judicial curses in the ancient world, one can rightly conclude that people interpreted reality around them and events that happened in both personal and national life in terms of curses and blessings. The socioeconomic, religious, and political happenings in the ancient world were certainly interpreted using the lenses of curse and blessing. The belief and practice of cursing provided an interpretive framework that helped ancient people understand their relationship with the immaterial world. It explained the day-to-day occurrence of a failure or success.

For instance, when a disaster or misfortune struck, the ancients would, among other things, quickly associate it with a curse. Graf observes, "There are particularly two situations in which the ancients suspected magic and, more precisely, ritual binding: disease or sudden death that was medically inexplicable; and unexpected and inexplicable professional failure."[97] The ancients neatly fitted unexplained realities into the dichotomies of malevolent (curse) and benevolent (blessing) forces. It is also noted that "in the era of Hippocrates, magic always served to explain what escaped medical diagnosis; even the skeptical Pliny knows of ailments for which a magical cure might be advisable."[98]

---

96. Crawford, *Blessing and Curse*, 116.
97. Graf, *Magic in Ancient World*, 166.
98. Graf, 166.

In professional arenas, it has been observed that curses greatly influenced the worldview of the people of ancient times, with odd behaviors forming part of the identification criteria:

> Professional failure is even more revealing of what the accusation of magical binding implies in the ancient societies. The lawyer who forgets his speech for the defense, the teacher of rhetoric who no longer wants to speak, the chaste *virgo Dei* who runs about the streets, her hair flying in the wind and shouting the name of a young man: all behaving in an unexpected way contrary to what the society expects of them. Such behavior, which would be completely remiss if it were under their control, might jeopardize their privileged social position. Therefore, explanations attributing odd behavior to a binding spell implied that other people, sorcerers and demons, were responsible, and an exorcism could reestablish the former social position.[99]

This can partly help explain the basis for Paul's rhetorical question to the Galatians: "Who has bewitched you?" Although they were not in a strict sense under the power of a curse or a binding spell, the Galatians had manifested a strange behavior that left Paul wondering what had happened to his once right-believing audience.

It may be argued that the typical far-reaching wishes that a client listed on a curse tablet, provided a strong hint that failures and successes in those areas of ancient life were easily interpreted in terms of curses and binding spells. One of the *defixiones* from the ancient world entails several wishes against a competitor in chariot racing:

> I invoke you, holy angels and holy names, join forces with this restraining spell and bind, tie up, block, strike, overthrow, harm, destroy, kill, and shatter Eucherios the charioteer and all his horses tomorrow in the arena of Rome. Let the starting gates not [open] properly. Let him not compete quickly. Let him not pass. Let him not squeeze over. Let him not win. Let him not make the turn properly. Let him not receive the honors. Let him not squeeze over and overpower. Let him not come from behind

---

99. Graf, 166–67.

and pass, instead let him collapse, let him be bound, let him be broken up, and let him drag behind by your power. Both in the early races and in the latter ones. Now, Now! Quickly, Quickly![100]

On the one hand, the curse details many of the sporting aspects; on the other hand, it demonstrates that every aspect of the ancient world was a target of *defixiones*. It also demonstrates that other immaterial forces outside hard work influenced actions, reactions, and happenings. For instance, a competitor who stumbles or wins would easily be attributed (rightly or wrongly) to the power of a malediction.

Furthermore, *defixiones* claimed to influence every sphere of a person's life. Kagarow, as quoted by Gager, lists a variety of areas in which consequences of curses could be manifested:

> Death, illness (fever, consumption, blindness, dumbness, lameness, broken limbs), loss of memory, various forms of mental suffering, sleeplessness, involuntary celibacy, loss of family and house, public humiliation, defeat in war and athletic competition, failure in business, conviction in public courts, denial of an afterlife, and general lack of success.[101]

The summary not only portrays the far-reaching effects of *defixiones* to the ancient life but also the range within which effects of curses applied.

Moreover, the ancient people perceived ruined cities and deserted places as an outcome of divine curses. Kitz observes, "Any place that exhibits attributes that are culturally associated with the final effect of maledictions, death, are considered cursed. These regions include destroyed cities, ruins and the wasteland in general."[102] Kitz further elaborates:

> Once a city is ruined and abandoned, it is readily classified with "the wilderness" because it shares characteristics indicative of this sort of area. Regions where life is sparse, where crops cannot grow and animals cannot graze for lack of water and vegetation are also frequently connected with maledictions. Here, life is so

---

100. Gager, *Curse Tablets*, 74.
101. Gager, 21.
102. Kitz, *Cursed Are You!*, 247. She also translates curse texts that associate devastated cities with divine curses.

marginal that survival is made tenuous and brief, which is, of course, one of the most obvious indicators of a cursed existence.[103]

It can, therefore, be concluded that the theme of curse and blessing in antiquity formed a worldview framework in which people explained surrounding reality. When Paul discusses the issue of curses in Galatians 3, his audience understood the cultural and religious theme of curse and blessing more profoundly. Thus, a modern reader of Galatians 3 needs to study the ancient context to situate Paul's thoughts in their original context.

Conclusion

In this chapter, we have looked at the reality of curses in the ANE and Graeco-Roman worlds. It is certain that cursing practice was a common phenomenon in antiquity. Curses and binding spells were used in matters judicial, erotic, commercial, agonistic, and against thieves and slanderers. It has also been ascertained that the primary intention of curses was to administer justice. These categories of curses were based on wrong-doing; whether an unjust situation, plundering of a tomb, or violating the copyright of one's work. Judicial curses are the category that Paul builds his Christology around. Curses were placed on tombs and were activated once the offender broke or plundered the grave. Also, curses were a final resort in many cases where other avenues of justice have been exhausted. This proves that the curses were not only widespread but also powerful and effective. Undeniably, a curse was viewed as a destroyer. It was understood to be a power that could bring disastrous consequences to the cursed and their families. In the ANE world, blessings and curses were a fixed part of the religion and had a prominent place in everyday life. It was a pervasive feature in ancient Palestine and Mediterranean cultures. From the discussions of ANE and Graeco-Roman cultures, it can be emphatically concluded that in developing his Christology of the crucified and cursed Christ, Paul based his thoughts on the cultural input from the ANE and Graeco-Roman cultures. The diversity of these cultures and considerable thematic parallels provided Paul with a rich background for understanding the implication and meaning of Christ's work on the cross.

---

103. Kitz, 250.

CHAPTER 3

Background Information and Exegesis of Galatians 3:1–14

Introduction

The first part of this chapter deals with background information of the book of Galatians involving issues of dating, audience, location, and authorship. This subsection on the background information of the book of Galatians does not offer a detailed look at all the issues involved, but where necessary, it recognizes scholarly debates and contentions on the background information.

The second part of the chapter features the exegetical study of Galatians 3:13 within its pericope (Gal 3:1–14). A better understanding of Paul's statement in Galatians 3:13 requires tracking his thought and argument. In addition, the section examines Paul's use of Scripture in Galatians 3:6–14, and key textual issues in the Masoretic Text (MT),[1] Septuagint (LXX),[2] and UBS text.[3] The chapter argues that Paul's reference to the curse goes back beyond the times of the law (Deuteronomy quotation) to Genesis 3.[4] It shows that Genesis 12 was the prime thought in Paul's argument and that the

---

1. Alt et al., *Biblia Hebraica Stuttgartensia*.
2. Rahlfs, *Septuaginta*.
3. Aland et al., *Greek New Testament*.
4. Wisdom, *Blessing for Nations*, 24–36. Wisdom devotes some limited attention to the Genesis narrative. But he suggests that the Genesis reference in Paul's arguments should be further probed. Paul's tracing of the human problem to Genesis 3 (in the story of Adam) and projecting a solution in Christ is not new in the Pauline corpus. In Romans 5:19, and its context, Paul demonstrates that a trespass of one man (Adam) brought death; but God's grace

Deuteronomy passage (Deut 21:22–23) was secondary in his argument. The Genesis 12 passage is God's solution to the human problem in Genesis 3. The study highlights the significance of Christ's redemptive work in reversing the curse of Genesis 3 and bringing blessings to all nations. The sociorhetorical method helps to put into perspective Paul's ideas, rhetoric, context, and development of thought. The findings in this chapter establish the foundational framework upon which the ancient understanding of cursing and blessing practice is discussed. Also, this chapter lays a biblical foundation that determines the trajectory of the application of the Bible message.

Background Information

This section begins by looking at the relevant background information with minimal detail. In any case, it affirms the positions taken by a majority of evangelical scholars. It is the express aim of this section to situate the research within its context but not to open a floor for debate on background details.

Author and Recipients

Internal evidence reveals that Paul and other unnamed associates (1:1–2) penned the epistle to Galatians. Equally, there is general acceptance and consensus among scholars that the author of Galatians is the apostle Paul.[5] According to Galatians 1:2, the recipients of the letter are the churches in Galatia.

However, an attempt to interpret the ambiguous phrase ταῖς ἐκκλησίαις τῆς Γαλατίας, (to the churches of Galatia) (1:2), has yielded two views: northern and southern Galatian theories. Originally, Galatia was the name of a district in north-central Asia Minor which had been occupied by Celtic groups migrating from Gaul during Roman rule.[6] Later, the Roman government established a province that included the district of Galatia and retained the name (Galatia) for the entire province, part of modern-day Turkey.[7] The

---

and gift came through one man (Jesus Christ). A similar pattern of reflection is evident in Galatians 3, on the issue of curses.

5. For instance, Lightfoot, *Saint Paul's Epistle*, 57–62; Betz, *Galatians*, 1; Keener, *Galatians*, 4.

6. Silva, *Interpreting Galatians*, 129.

7. Ngewa, *Galatians*, 2.

north Galatian theory holds that Paul's audience was in the district. In contrast, the south Galatian theory holds that Paul's audience was situated within the larger province that bordered the Black Sea and the Mediterranean Sea.[8] The proponents for the northern view use Acts 16:6 and 18:23 (mentioning specific locations like Phrygia) to further their case, but there is no other biblical evidence of Paul ministering in the northern area.[9] It is worth noting that the north Galatian theory was the universal view of the early church,[10] although it is now an unpopular view.

On the other hand, the south Galatia hypothesis uses Paul's missionary journey (Acts 13 and 14) as its basis. F. F. Bruce, a scholar who has widely researched these two theories, concludes, if the epistle was addressed to the churches of Pisidia, Antioch, Iconium, Lystra and Derbe, then "we have important historical, geographical, literary and epigraphic data which will provide material for its better understanding."[11] He convincingly demonstrates that Paul's audience lived in the larger province of Galatia.

Date

Internal evidence indicates that Paul wrote the letter after an earlier visit (3:1, 3). Establishing the date for the letter largely depends on the theory one takes. On the northern Galatian destination, the earliest possible time would be after Paul's second missionary journey, around AD 51–52; that is, taking Acts 16:6 to refer to north Galatia.[12] Whereas for the southern destination, the date could be as early as AD 49, after Paul's first missionary journey (Acts 13–14).[13] Concerning the south Galatian theory, Silva notes, "the arguments in favor of the North Galatian theory are much too weak, and thus a South Galatian location is to be preferred, but that the similarities between Acts 15 and Galatians 2 argue strongly in favor of a late date for the epistle."[14] The southern view makes much sense because Paul's letter deals with issues that

---

8. Ngewa, 2.
9. Ngewa, 2.
10. Cole, *Epistle of Paul*, 16.
11. Bruce, *Epistle to Galatians*, 18. This position is also supported by Ngewa, *Galatians*, 3.
12. George, *Galatians*, 46.
13. For discussion on this, see Schnabel, *Early Christian Missions*, 988–92; Wenham, "Acts and Pauline Corpus," 234–43.
14. Silva, *Interpreting Galatians*, 131–32.

the Jerusalem Council later dealt with in AD 50. As such, the letter appears to have been written before the Jerusalem Council (AD 49, in Acts 15), because in the epistle, Paul does not refer to the deliberations of the Jerusalem Council.[15] Expectedly, if the Council had already been held, apostle Paul would have quoted the Council's verdict.

The Situation and Paul's Opponents in Galatia

In his letter to Galatians, Paul addresses some serious challenges that the church was facing. He must have received, with sadness, news that Galatian believers were being lured into a false gospel, a different gospel from what he had formerly preached. Those who had previously received his message of justification by faith were now quickly turning away from the One who called them (1:6).

The false teachers in Galatia threatened the very foundations that Paul had labored to establish. In his letter, Paul refers to these false teachers as οἱ ταράσσοντες (the troublemakers, Gal 1:7; 5:10) or οἱ ἀναστατοῦντες (the agitators, Gal 5:12). Dunn believes that these opponents were Judaists of Jewish descent.[16] However, there is also a strong possibility that they could be Christian Jews who came to Galatia as "apostles" or "missionaries" preaching their gospel after Paul had planted the church.[17] This assumption hinges on the undue emphasis Judaizers placed on the law of Moses as a pathway to faith in Christ. It is also possible that these opponents taught the Galatians that having faith in Jesus was not enough; that they needed to complete their faith (3:3) by embracing the Mosaic law and Judaism requirements.[18] The concept of downplaying the work of Christ was a serious anomaly that the Galatians were plunging themselves into.

---

15. Carson and Moo, *Introduction to New Testament*, 464. Even with this stand, we need not be dogmatic since there are respectable scholars in each camp and they have plausible arguments for their positions. For instance, Keener, in his work *Galatians*, surveys both views and argues in preference of the northern view. Keener, *Galatians*, 4–11.

16. Dunn, *Epistle to Galatians*, 9. Also see Hurd, "Reflections Concerning 'Paul's Opponents,'" 144–45.

17. Dunn, 10; It is possible that they were Jewish Jesus followers but lacked direct support from the movement leaders in Jerusalem. See Cousar, *Galatians, Interpretation*, 5; Shreiner, *Galatians*, 49–51.

18. Thielman, *Paul & the Law*, 123.

In summary, the troublemakers in Galatia sought to impose the Jewish law where Paul emphasized justification by faith.[19] These false teachers stood subject to God's judgment and curse because they perverted the truth (1:8). Given how Paul defends his apostleship (1:12–2:10), it is evident that his apostolic credentials were in question. The most distinguishing feature of the false gospel was the insistence on circumcision (5:2, 6; 6:15).[20] These false teachers had used circumcision as a legal obligation that is essential for salvation. To them, a Gentile should first be a Jew before becoming a Christian; but according to Paul's teaching, the Gentiles only needed to have faith in Christ to receive justification (Gal 2:16; 3:25). On this, Paul was persuaded that the new teaching did not originate from God (5:8). Since the source was not God, then the end was clearly not desirable. Indeed, by choosing to follow the false teachers, the Gentile believers were resorting to the way of curse and death; on the contrary, by choosing to rely on God for their salvation, they would receive the Spirit, life, and blessings.

Preceding Context (Galatians 1–2)

Paul's letter to Galatians addresses pertinent issues that were affecting first-century believers and the church in Galatia. The first part of Galatians chapter 1 (vv. 1–10) expresses Paul's astonishment at the behavior of the Galatians abandoning the true gospel: "I am astonished that you are so quickly deserting the one who called you by the grace of Christ and are turning to a different gospel" (1:6). Paul notes in disbelief the rapid turning away of the very people he had formerly preached to. They abandoned the true gospel and were now resorting to a gospel that was "really no gospel at all" (1:7). In the second part of chapter 1, up to the first section of chapter 2 (1: 11–2:10), Paul defends the basis for his apostleship, noting that he was not among the initial twelve. Seemingly, false teachers in Galatia had questioned Paul's credibility and legitimacy as an apostle. Although we cannot presume that every bit of the letter was a polemical response to the issues raised by the false teachers, the defense is at the beginning. The second part of Galatians 2 (vv. 11–21) generally deals with justification by faith in Jesus Christ as opposed

---

19. Bruce, *Epistle to Galatians*, 19.
20. Bruce, 27. Circumcision was a key aspect of Jewish identity, and is mentioned several times in the letter (Gal 2:3–5; 2:12–13).

to the observance of the law. This section, primarily a narrative, reveals the spiritual state of the church in Galatia as people who struggled on the very foundations of faith. It also affirms Paul's credibility by looking at his past conversion experience and the present life in Christ. Finally, it highlights the centrality of the gospel message and Paul's conversion and calling as the basis of his apostleship.

Summary of Galatians Chapter 3

In Galatians 3, Paul continues with the discussion on the observance of the law and justification by faith. He presents his arguments using rhetorical questions, OT Scripture, and references to salvation history. He argues that the gospel he preached was the same gospel that was first preached to Abraham. In the first half of chapter 3 (vv. 1–14), Paul looks at the experience of believers in Galatia (both Jews and Gentiles) in relation to the work of Christ on the cross. He argues that the crucified Christ took away the curse by "becoming a curse for us." He gives special attention and significance to the work of Christ on the cross. Undoubtedly, some of the issues Paul addresses must have arisen from the controversies of the false teachers, Judaizers. The perversion of the truth by Judaizers gave Paul an ample opportunity to set forth the unchanging truth of the gospel.

The Literary Structure of Galatians 3:1–14

In this literary unit, Paul utilizes rhetorical questions and quotations from the OT Scriptures. There is a variation in his tone in the passage, for example, in verses 1–5, Paul sounds harsh, but that changes in verse 6 into a deliberative tone when he invites his audience alongside himself to consider some OT Scriptures and the patriarch Abraham. Further, in this section, there are various figures of speech employed. Concerning the literary style used, Paul's flow of thought presents a challenge to most interpreters. Betz has observed that what makes this chapter hard to analyze and organize is the frequent interruption of the arguments presented by dialogue, examples, proverbs, and quotations.[21] Nevertheless, Paul's statement in Galatians 3:13 remains the climax verse of the pericope.

---

21. Betz, *Galatians*, 129.

Syntactical Outline of Galatians 3:1–14

1: Ὦ ἀνόητοι Γαλάται, (You foolish Galatians!)
   τίς ὑμᾶς ἐβάσκανεν, (Who has bewitched you,)
      οἷς κατ' ὀφθαλμοὺς Ἰησοῦς Χριστὸς προεγράφη ἐσταυρωμένος; (before whose eyes Jesus Christ was evidently set forth as crucified?)
2: τοῦτο μόνον θέλω μαθεῖν ἀφ' ὑμῶν, (This is the only thing I desire to learn from you):
   τὸ πνεῦμα ἐλάβετε (Did you receive the Spirit)
      ἐξ ἔργων νόμου (by the works of the law)
      ἢ ἐξ ἀκοῆς πίστεως; (or by believing what you heard?)
3: οὕτως ἀνόητοί ἐστε; (Are you so foolish?)
   ἐναρξάμενοι πνεύματι (after beginning by the Spirit),
   νῦν σαρκὶ ἐπιτελεῖσθε; (are you now trying to finish by the flesh?)
4: τοσαῦτα ἐπάθετε εἰκῇ (Did you suffer so many things in vain),
   εἴ γε καὶ εἰκῇ. (if indeed it was in vain?)
5: ὁ οὖν (Then does the one)
   ἐπιχορηγῶν ὑμῖν τὸ πνεῦμα καὶ (who gives you the Spirit and)
   ἐνεργῶν δυνάμεις ἐν ὑμῖν (works miracles among you),
      ἐξ ἔργων νόμου ἢ ([do it] by the works of the law or)
      ἐξ ἀκοῆς πίστεως; (by believing what you heard?)
6: καθὼς Ἀβραὰμ ((It is) just as Abraham)
   ἐπίστευσεν τῷ θεῷ, ("believed God)
   καὶ ἐλογίσθη αὐτῷ εἰς δικαιοσύνην (and it was credited to him as righteousness.")
7: Γινώσκετε ἄρα ὅτι (Therefore, realize that)
   οἱ ἐκ πίστεως, (those who have faith)
   οὗτοι υἱοί εἰσιν Ἀβραάμ (are sons of Abraham.)
8: προϊδοῦσα δὲ ἡ γραφὴ (And the Scripture, foreseeing)
   ὅτι ἐκ πίστεως δικαιοῖ τὰ ἔθνη ὁ θεός (that God would justify the Gentiles by faith),
      προευηγγελίσατο τῷ Ἀβραὰμ ὅτι (preached the gospel in advance to Abraham that)
         Ἐνευλογηθήσονται ἐν σοὶ πάντα τὰ ἔθνη. ("All the nations will be blessed in you.")
9: ὥστε οἱ ἐκ πίστεως (So then those who are of faith)

εὐλογοῦνται (are blessed)
   σὺν τῷ πιστῷ (with the man of faith),
   Ἀβραάμ (Abraham).

10: ὅσοι γὰρ (For as many as)
   ἐξ ἔργων νόμου εἰσὶν (are of the works of (the) law)
   ὑπὸ κατάραν εἰσίν γέγραπται γὰρ ὅτι (are under a curse; for it is written that),
     Ἐπικατάρατος πᾶς ("Cursed is everyone)
       ὃς οὐκ ἐμμένει (who does not abide)
         πᾶσιν τοῖς γεγραμμένοις (by all things written)
         ἐν τῷ βιβλίῳ τοῦ νόμου (in the book of the law),
         τοῦ ποιῆσαι αὐτά. (to do them.")

11: ὅτι δὲ ἐν νόμῳ οὐδεὶς δικαιοῦται παρὰ τῷ θεῷ δῆλον, (And clearly no one is justified by the law before God; for),
   ὅτι Ὁ δίκαιος ἐκ πίστεως ζήσεται ("The righteous will live by faith.")

     12: ὁ δὲ νόμος οὐκ ἔστιν ἐκ πίστεως, ἀλλ' (And the law is not of faith, but)
   Ὁ ποιήσας αὐτὰ ζήσεται ἐν αὐτοῖς ("he who does these things will live by them.")

13: Χριστὸς ἡμᾶς ἐξηγόρασεν (Christ redeemed us)
   ἐκ τῆς κατάρας τοῦ νόμου (from the curse of the law),
     γενόμενος ὑπὲρ ἡμῶν κατάρα, ὅτι γέγραπται, (by becoming a curse for us, for it is written),
   Ἐπικατάρατος πᾶς ("Cursed is everyone)
   ὁ κρεμάμενος ἐπὶ ξύλου, (who hangs on a tree.")

14: (He redeemed us)
   ἵνα (in order that)
     ἐν Χριστῷ Ἰησοῦ (in Jesus Christ),
       ἡ εὐλογία τοῦ Ἀβραὰμ γένηται (the blessings of Abraham might come)
       εἰς τὰ ἔθνη (to the Gentiles),
   ἵνα (so that)
     διὰ τῆς πίστεως (through faith)
       τὴν ἐπαγγελίαν τοῦ πνεύματος λάβωμεν (we might receive the promise of the Spirit).

Synopsis

Paul highlights the significance of the work of Christ on the cross in the backdrop of false teachers who were discrediting the message of the true gospel that Paul had initially taught. The false teachers emphasized the centrality of observance of the law and placed much confidence in the flesh, yet Paul, with other apostles, stressed the importance of faith in Jesus and the Spirit's work in the lives of believers. The path that the Judaizers followed ultimately led to curses (death), but the path trodden by Paul (and other apostles) leads to blessings (life) as an endpoint. Paul presents the crucified and cursed Christ as the one who redeems and takes away the curses by becoming a curse for us.

The Crucified and Cursed Christ: An Exegesis of Galatians 3:1–14

The Problem in Galatia (3:1–5)

Paul wrote this letter to a church struggling to maintain the orthodox and apostolic message of the gospel amidst pressures to succumb to the emerging influence of false teachers and teachings. In Galatians 1:6, Paul states that Galatians were drifting from the true gospel, εἰς ἕτερον[22] εὐαγγέλιον (to a different gospel). Sadly, there was a change of the gospel message to a different gospel that was characterized by deception. Christ was no longer portrayed as crucified in Galatia, and Paul saw in this a major problem that needed to be addressed.

In addition, the inconsistent behavior of apostle Peter among the Jewish and Gentile groups (2:11–21) was an apparent leadership challenge that had to be dealt with urgently, since belief in a false gospel leads to a corresponding false living and behavior. In Galatians 3:1–5, Paul explains fundamental existential problems in the Galatian church. In these opening verses, he demonstrates that the death of Christ on the cross (the crucified Christ) obliterated all forms of legal righteousness. Significantly, the emphasis is on the death of Jesus Christ (crucifixion) and what that death achieves for believers.

---

22. The adjective ἕτερος shows that they were not turning to a gospel of the same kind, but of a different kind. By following the gospel of Judaizers, the Galatians were now turning to a false gospel.

Change of Focus: Christ No Longer Portrayed as Crucified (v.1)

Particularly, Paul's language to his audience at the beginning of chapter 3 sounds harsh. His reprimanding tone and rhetorical question use highlight the nature of the message he wanted to communicate to his hearers. Paul's tone shows that he was not happy with the Galatians who had strayed from the way of truth.

> **Galatians 3:1 Greek text:** Ὦ ἀνόητοι Γαλάται, τίς ὑμᾶς ἐβάσκανεν, οἷς κατ' ὀφθαλμοὺς Ἰησοῦς Χριστὸς προεγράφη ἐσταυρωμένος;
>
> **Translation:** You foolish Galatians! Who has bewitched you? Before your eyes, Jesus Christ was evidently set forth as crucified?

In a vocative case, Paul introduces verse one, Ὦ ἀνόητοι Γαλάται, "You foolish Galatians!" He sets forth the tone of his statement in preparation for the chastising message he wants to deliver to his audience. He identifies his audience as Γαλάται. He does not address a particular group distinctively (as Jews or Gentiles) but addresses them as a whole. Further, he quickly follows this statement with a rhetorical question: τίς ὑμᾶς ἐβάσκανεν (who has bewitched you?).

Paul's reference of the Galatians as "foolish" and "bewitched" is understandably caused by their strange change of focus. According to Galatians 1:6, they had quickly deserted the one who called them by the grace of Christ and turned to a different gospel. Hence, Paul asks, τίς ὑμᾶς ἐβάσκανεν, οἷς κατ' ὀφθαλμοὺς Ἰησοῦς Χριστὸς προεγράφη ἐσταυρωμένος; (Who has bewitched you, before your eyes, Jesus Christ was evidently set forth as crucified?). According to this verse, the Galatians had strayed from Jesus Christ, who should be their focus. They had abandoned the one whom Paul preached and by whose name they had received salvation. The different gospel message they were being persuaded to now follow was not Christ-centered. The description of the Galatians as ἀνόητος (foolish) is a strong assertion. The adjective ἀνόητος, meaning "a person without understanding,"[23] is repeated in verse 3, for emphasis. The adjective means someone who has a "lack of comprehension, not lack of intelligence."[24] Longenecker further adds that what grieved Paul was the Galatians' "failure to exercise even a modicum of

---

23. Friberg, Friberg, and Miller, *Analytical Lexicon*.
24. Dunn, *Epistle to Galatians*, 151.

spiritual discernment."²⁵ In this case, their foolishness was evidenced by their lack of spiritual discernment and sensitivity. The Galatians lacked discernment and proper understanding of the true gospel; as a result, they fell into the false teachers' trap. And by following the teachings of the Judaizers, they were now resorting to "Moses-gospel,"²⁶ which is, a gospel message with salvation founded on the observance of the Mosaic law. According to the Judaizers, a person can be saved based on strict compliance with the law of Moses.

In light of the ancient context, Witherington observes that a "fool" in the first-century cultural context disrespected social boundaries, with the effect that one disgraced oneself.²⁷ He further argues, "The issue here in part is violation of community boundaries and in Paul's view to enter the community bounded by the Mosaic Law is to exit the community bounded by allegiance to Christ."²⁸ Thus, Galatians were "foolish" because they reverted to the "Moses-gospel" especially after the initial hearing and believing of the gospel of Jesus Christ as proclaimed by Paul and his associates. In this case, Paul is justified in using strong language because these babes in Christ were committing a serious error with eternal consequences. The Galatians were on the verge of plunging into apostasy, and Paul handled this manner with the seriousness it deserved, just like when he pronounced anathemas upon those who perverted the true gospel (Gal 1:8–10).

It is worth pointing out that Paul's reproving language is deliberately used for various reasons in several other instances. For example, in Titus 3:3, talking about the pre-conversion experience, he writes, "At one time we too were foolish, disobedient, deceived and enslaved by all kinds of passions and pleasures" (NIV). He acknowledges that before the kindness and love of God appeared, believers were ἀνόητοι. Other instances in which the adjective is used include Romans 1:14 and 1 Timothy 6:9. It has also been observed that Paul's use of strong language was not uncommon among preachers of his time.²⁹ In Luke 24:25, Jesus used the adjective ἀνόητοι to refer to those who were slow of heart to believe what the prophets had spoken. Like the

---

25. Longenecker, *Galatians*, 98.
26. Garlington, *Exposition of Galatians*, 149.
27. Witherington, *Grace in Galatia*, 201.
28. Witherington, 201.
29. Betz, *Galatians*, 130.

Israelites who made themselves idols in the wilderness, the Galatians were quick to turn away from what the Lord commanded (Exod 32:8; Deut 9:16). Apostle Paul was baffled by the determination of the Galatians to abandon the true gospel that portrayed Christ as crucified.

Conversely, it is essential to underscore that Paul portrays his audience in a positive light in several other places within the same book. For example, he refers to them several times as "brothers," (1:11; 3:15, 28; 5:11, 13; 6:1), "sons of God" (3:26), "they know God and are known by God" (4:9), "my dear children" (4:19), "children of promise" (4:28), "have been set free by Christ" (5:1). Therefore, the negative portrayal of his audience in 3:1 is exceptional and purposeful because of the intensity of the matter at hand. Matters of truth are matters of life and death, and Paul uses a language that befits the situation at hand.

Subsequently, in a series of rhetorical questions, Paul wonders what had happened to the Galatians who once began in the right path but were now quickly deserting their very foundations of faith.[30] In the first rhetorical question, he asks his readers, τίς ὑμᾶς ἐβάσκανεν (Who has bewitched you?) The phrase can also be translated as "Who has cast the evil eye on you?" because originally, the verb βασκαίνω related to magic.[31] Similarly, George defines bewitching as "to give someone the evil eye, to cast a spell over."[32] The verb βασκαίνω is *hapax legomenon*, appearing nowhere else in the entire New Testament. It brings out the connotation of harming someone through a hostile look or casting a magical spell. Chrysostom, the first major Christian commentator, translated βασκαίνω as "casting of the evil eye on someone."[33] By use of a resultative aorist (ἐβάσκανεν), Paul wonders who has bewitched the Galatians!

The rhetorical phrase τίς ὑμᾶς ἐβάσκανεν; has been construed and translated differently by different scholars. It suffices to briefly mention some of the common interpretations. First is the literal approach taken by very few scholars believing that the Galatians were under a spell by sorcerers and

---

30. Rhetorical questions in 3:1–5 characterized the ancient forensic rhetorics in defenses or accusations. See Xenophone of Athens, *Anabasis* 5.8.4–5; Cicero, *Pro Sestio* 21.47.
31. Betz, *Galatians*, 131.
32. George, *Galatians*, 206–7.
33. Witherington, *Grace in Galatia*, 201.

magicians.³⁴ Second, as highlighted by Garlington, some scholars³⁵ have interpreted this in a metaphorical and idiomatic sense.³⁶ In my opinion, this approach in its exclusive sense waters down the choice of Paul's words, especially in a context where curses and binding spells were common, as earlier surveyed in this work. Third, some scholars have argued that this was how Paul aligns the false teachers with the devil and locates them with the "present evil age." Grammatically, the object of this verse is Γαλάται (also identified with the personal pronoun, direct object, ὑμᾶς) and not the devil or the false teachers; the devil could be a possible subject of the verb as we are not given the identity of the subject. This third option makes an unwarranted and unsubstantiated assumption on Paul's vocabulary. Fourth is the association of the term βασκαίνω to the "evil eye."³⁷ According to Garlington, the fourth option on "evil eye" highlights the irony of the Galatian situation. He states, "The Judaizers sought to deliver their converts *from* the curse of the law, but instead, they have delivered them *to* this very curse."³⁸ It is hasty to presume that the Judaizers' goal was to deliver the Galatians from the law's curse.

It is more reasonable to interpret βασκαίνω figuratively, but with much-needed sensitivity to the social and cultural context of the first-century world. From a figurative perspective, I concur with Samuel Ngewa, that "he [Paul] is not making any theological point about the existence of witches and witchcraft but is simply using this metaphor to express his bewilderment at the change he is seeing in the Galatians."³⁹ Hence, Paul is not implying that the Galatians had become victims of a spell, magic, or harm by an evil eye but that their unexpected behavior is reminiscent of a person under a spell. They exhibited unusual confusion, only traceable to people under the influence of an evil eye or sorcery. Longenecker also notes that βασκαίνω could mean "to confuse the mind."⁴⁰ In a context where magical power and casting of spells

---

34. This view was propagated by Schlier, *Galaterbrief*, 119, as pointed out in Witherington, *Grace in Galatia*, 201.

35. Garlington, *Exposition of Galatians*, 149.

36. A view also shared by Adeyemo et al., *Africa Bible Commentary*, 1420.

37. Garlington, *Exposition of Galatians*, 149.

38. Garlington, 149.

39. Ngewa, *Galatians*, 96. This view is also supported by Longenecker in his work, *Galatians*, 98.

40. Longenecker, *Galatians*, 98.

were common, Paul's audience must have been struck by this language into rethinking their sudden change of focus, characterized by confusion and foolishness. All in all, the Galatians had been led astray by the rhetoric of the agitators. Paul feared for their faith because, like the Corinthians, they were being led astray from their sincere and pure devotion to Christ (2 Cor 11:3).[41]

The crux of the problem was that among the Galatians, the supremacy of Christ and his work on the cross was under attack. Christ was no longer evidently set forth as crucified. Paul writes, οἷς κατ' ὀφθαλμοὺς Ἰησοῦς Χριστὸς προεγράφη ἐσταυρωμένος (before your eyes, Jesus Christ was evidently set forth as crucified). The object of Paul's kerygma was Ἰησοῦς Χριστὸς. In Paul's preaching, Jesus Christ was προεγράφη ἐσταυρωμένος (portrayed/set forth as crucified).

The compound verb προεγράφη is here construed as a constative aorist, simply referring to the past time before the Judaizers began to infiltrate with their teachings. Literally, in a temporal sense, the verb προγράφω can mean "right beforehand." Alternatively, the prefix προ can be taken as locative to mean "portray publicly/evidently," or "to display publicly as on a placard."[42] In this manner, the vivid way in which Paul presented the story of Jesus's suffering and death is highlighted. On the way Christ was publicly portrayed by Paul, Ngewa comments, "This was not just a statement about a historical event, but about the long-term implications of that event, or in other words, about its ultimate significance. Paul preached that Jesus Christ made atonement by his obedience and suffering, and had thus provided free and complete salvation received through faith in him."[43] In Paul's kerygma, Christ was the focus. Christ was the content and goal of his preaching, "Paul's doctrine had taught them about Christ in such a manner that it was as if He had been shown to them in a picture, even crucified among them. Such a representation

---

41. In 2 Corinthians 11:3, Paul φοβοῦμαι (feared) for the Corinthians because they were highly susceptible to deception, just like Eve was deceived by the craftiness of the serpent. Paul writes, φθαρῇ τὰ νοήματα ὑμῶν ἀπὸ τῆς ἁπλότητος [καὶ τῆς ἁγνότητος] τῆς εἰς τὸν Χριστόν (literally, "your minds may be corrupted from the simplicity and devotion to Christ"). The Corinthian believers faced the danger of being φθείρω (corrupted, misled, or destroyed) by the ὁ ὄφις (the serpent) just like Eve. Paul shares this experience among the Galatian believers, that in their gullibility, they were quickly falling into the deception of the enemy and abandoning the true gospel!

42. George, *Galatians*, 209.

43. Ngewa, *Galatians*, 96.

could not have been effected by any eloquence or tricks of oratory, had not that power of the Spirit been present."[44] The preaching of Christ crucified (1 Cor 1:18–2:5) radically distinguished Paul from the circumcision party. Importantly, crucifixion was the climax of Jesus's obedience and submission to the will of the Father. The clear proclamation of the death of Jesus Christ was the initial message of truth that the Galatians received and should have been contented with.

Paul had preached Jesus Christ to Galatians before they drifted in their faith. It was Paul's custom to preach the message of the crucified Christ. In 1 Corinthians 2:1–2 Paul writes, "when I came to you, I did not come with eloquence or superior wisdom as I proclaimed to you the testimony about God. For I resolved to know nothing while I was with you except Jesus Christ and him crucified." In their foolishness, the Galatians were now trying to rely on the human wisdom and eloquence of the Judaizers instead of the cross of Christ. The only way their foolishness could be corrected was by reverting to the proclamation of the crucified Christ;[45] because what was lacking in their preaching was the exaltation of the person and the work of Christ on the cross.

Jesus Christ was portrayed as crucified, ἐσταυρωμένος (literally, "having been crucified"). This is an adjectival participle (predicative function), qualifying the verb προεγράφη. As an intensive perfect, ἐσταυρωμένος focuses on the state or result of a past act of crucifixion. The stress of the perfect tense is on the crucifixion as something accomplished in the past but with present results. The use of a metonomy is explicit on the association of the two terms: "cross" and "death"; elsewhere, this is evident (1 Cor 1:17–18; 15:3; Gal 5:11; 6:12, 14; Phil 2:8; 3:18; Col 1:20; 2:14–15).[46] In 1 Corinthians 1:18, Paul calls the gospel Ο λόγος γὰρ ὁ τοῦ σταυροῦ (the word of the cross). Also, to his predominantly Jewish audience, apostle Peter proclaimed Christ crucified (Acts 2:36; 4:10). It is a message that cuts across Hebraic and Hellenistic Christianity. Bruce notes, "The gospel of Christ crucified, as Paul saw it, so completely ruled out the law as a means of getting right with God that it was scarcely credible that people who had once embraced such a gospel should

---

44. Torrance, Torrance, and Parker, *Epistles of Paul*, 47.
45. Martyn, *Galatians*, 282.
46. Longenecker, *Galatians*, 98.

ever turn to the law for salvation."[47] The root cause of the crisis in Galatia stems from the abandonment of the true gospel of justification by faith – the gospel that esteemed the person and work of Christ and the Spirit. At first, the Galatians had come to Christ after hearing and believing the message of Christ crucified.

Summary of the Verse

As highlighted above, Paul's astonishment and negative portrayal of the Galatian audience was not without reason. The Galatians had deserted the true gospel and the one who initially called them to salvation (1:6). As a result, the idea of Christ as crucified was no longer evident in their midst. The focus or center had shifted to other people (false teachers) and other things (observance of the law for salvation). True belief and conduct depend on how we understand the person and work of Christ on the cross. In light of what had happened in Galatia, Paul, out of love, was justified to use such blunt language and harsh tone. Galatians had acted unintelligently and thoughtlessly. In their unwise ways and behavior, they had become victims of a false gospel, which was no gospel at all (Gal 1:7).

In their sudden confusion, the Galatians acted like people who had been bewitched. Paul's deep concern stemmed from their change of focus in respect to the object of their faith; unlike in the past, their focus was no longer Christ crucified. Simply put, their devotion was no longer *Christo-centric*. This brought about a faith crisis. The portrayal of Christ as crucified was a vital component of their faith because it was God's ordained means of salvation. In Galatia, Paul spotted a wrong portrayal of Christ; by this, the Galatians got everything else wrong. Judaizers may have been comfortable preaching Christ without the cross, but Paul's hearers should not miss this important aspect of the cross.

Paul's argument highlights the importance of right Christology in the proclamation of the gospel and reveals the supremacy of Christ in Paul's presentation of the gospel. It is through the death of Christ that believers receive salvation, life, and blessings from God. Outside Christ, there is the false promise of salvation, life, and blessing. Therefore Paul begins Galatians 3 by challenging false conceptions of Christ and the gospel by refuting the

---

47. Bruce, *Epistle to Galatians*, 148.

false teachings of the Judaizers. The solution to the problem in Galatia lay in refocusing on the crucified Christ.

False Attribution of the Reception of the Spirit to Observance of the Law (v.2)

The second issue that the Galatians faced dealt with receiving the Spirit and observance of the law. In their confusion, Paul asks them whether they received the Spirit by observing the law or by believing the message they first heard. In this verse, Paul changes the tone of his voice to a dialogical one as he introduces the antithesis between the Spirit and the works of the law.

> **Galatians 3:2 Greek Text:** τοῦτο μόνον θέλω μαθεῖν ἀφ' ὑμῶν, ἐξ ἔργων νόμου τὸ πνεῦμα ἐλάβετε ἢ ἐξ ἀκοῆς πίστεως;
>
> **Translation:** This is the only thing I desire to learn from you: Did you receive the Spirit by the works of the law or by believing what you heard?

Paul makes his point clear, τοῦτο μόνον θέλω μαθεῖν ἀφ' ὑμῶν (This is the only thing I desire to learn from you). He uses a futuristic present (θέλω) to express his desire; and an infinitive of purpose (μαθεῖν) to state his aim, which is "to learn." One can wonder how ironical it is for Paul to desire to learn from the very people he has just called ἀνόητοι in the previous verse! Nevertheless, from the context, he does not ask the question out of ignorance. In any case, he provides two alternatives for their consideration: by the observance of the law and by believing what they heard. The rhetorical question allows Paul's readers to retrospectively ponder not only on their foolish step (v.1) but also on their faith foundations.

In the rhetorical question, Paul asks, ἐξ ἔργων νόμου τὸ πνεῦμα ἐλάβετε ἢ ἐξ ἀκοῆς πίστεως; (Did you receive the Spirit by the works of the law or by believing what you heard?). He wants the Galatians to consider the question reflectively, which involves recalling the time they first came to Christ in order to understand how they received the Holy Spirit (Gal 3:14; 4:6).

The first alternative Paul gives is whether it was ἐξ ἔργων νόμου (by observance of the law; or literally, "by the works of the law"). The preposition ἐξ (by) focuses on agency, thus highlighting how they received the Holy Spirit. The phrase τὸ πνεῦμα serves as an accusative of the direct object. Seemingly, Paul's opponents must have thrown the Galatians into confusion by attributing the reception of the Spirit to the observance of the law. However, genuine recalling of their initial conversion experience and a preview of the apostolic and orthodox heritage would shed off this erroneous belief. Deep within their hearts, the Galatians knew the answer; they only needed to recall what they first believed.

Through the reading of the preceding chapter, Galatians already knew that justification and receiving of the Spirit did not entail observance of the law. This is expressly stated in Galatians 2:16, "Know that a person is not justified by the works of the law, but by faith in Jesus Christ. So we, too, have put our faith in Christ Jesus that we may be justified by faith in Christ and not by the works of the law, because by the works of the law no-one will be justified." Thus, Galatians 2:16 answers the rhetorical question in Galatians 3:2.

Paul offers the second alternative answer to the dilemma by completing the rhetorical question: τὸ πνεῦμα ἐλάβετε ἢ ἐξ ἀκοῆς πίστεως; (or did you receive the Spirit by (the) hearing of faith?). In this verse, ἀκοῆς functions as objective while πίστεως as a genitive of means. The understanding and translation of the genitive phrase ἀκοῆς πίστεως, which has been used here by Paul for the first time in this letter, has not been without challenge among scholars. For example, the NIV translates ἀκοῆς πίστεως as, "believing what you heard" while NASB translates it as, "hearing with faith." The phrase ἀκοῆς πίστεως can also be best rendered as "the proclamation that has the power to elicit faith."[48] I have translated it as "believing what you heard." In the phrase τὸ πνεῦμα ἐλάβετε, the aorist indicative active verb ἐλάβετε, has been taken as inceptive aorist in function, looking back at the beginning of salvation experience. Galatians received the Spirit of God not based on their performances and meritorious acts but based on God's graciousness. They received the Spirit as a gift from God. In the New Testament, receiving of the Holy Spirit is another terminology for the conversion experience (Rom 8:15; 1 Cor 2:12; 2 Cor 11:4; Gal 3:14).[49] A similar observation is also made by Dunn, "for Paul and the first Christians this [receiving the Spirit] was the decisive and determinative element in the event or process of conversion and

---

48. Martyn, *Galatians*, 284. Separately, Martyn discusses with examples whether ἀκοή refers to the act of hearing (active sense) or that which is heard (passive sense). He concludes that, in this verse, Paul uses ἀκοῇ to refer to "the gospel message" spoken by God through the apostle.

49. Garlington, *Exposition of Galatians*, 151.

initiation; hence the nearest thing to a definition of 'Christian' in the NT."[50] Therefore, the Galatians are invited to reflect on the beginnings of their faith in Christ Jesus. If they are honest to themselves, they will realize that they indeed received the promise and gift of God, the Holy Spirit, as a response to their faith in Christ.

Initially, according to Paul's teachings, the Galatians knew they had received the Spirit by believing what they heard. But this changed! Although not explicit in the text, the Judaizers must have come later with a twisted message and inclination to observe the law, attributing receiving of the Holy Spirit to the observance of the law. This message, wrapped with eloquence, appealed to the Galatians! However, Paul categorically clarifies that the gift of the Holy Spirit was solely received through believing the gospel and not through the obedience of the law of Moses. George argues that the Galatians were tempted to ascribe the reception of the Holy Spirit to the observance of the law; and by this, "they have not advanced forward in the life of the Spirit but, on the contrary, lapsed into the realm of the flesh."[51] In other words, they have returned to their former state of slavery.

Summary of the Verse

Paul reminds the Galatian Christians about the sure foundation he had laid before Judaizers infiltrated into their midst with a perverted gospel. In Galatians 3:1, Paul's kerygma elevates the person of Christ and his work on the cross. He develops this idea in verse 2 by showing that the Galatians received the Spirit not by observing the law but by believing what they heard. In this verse, Paul relates soteriology to the person of the Holy Spirit. In provoking the Galatians to think retrospectively through their salvation experience, Paul is sure that they will realize the exaltation of Christ and centrality of the Spirit of God in their salvation experience. This should cause the Galatians to revert to the true gospel of the crucified Christ, as preached by Paul and other apostles. From these two opening verses of Galatians 3, it is clear that false teachers sought to destroy the foundational teachings concerning Jesus, the true gospel, salvation, and the Holy Spirit. But from the arguments, Paul has not lost hope in them.

---

50. Dunn, *Epistle to Galatians*, 153.
51. George, *Galatians*, 212.

Beginning Right But Trying to End in a Wrong Way (vv.3–4)

In a language reminiscent of the rhetorical question in verse 1, Paul points out another error that the Galatians committed. They were attempting to be perfected by the flesh! Paul noted their inconsistency because they had begun well with the Spirit but were now changing track and trying to be perfected by human effort. Again, he makes a clear distinction. They initially relied on God, but now they were relying on human efforts. In verse 4, Paul expresses his fears that after suffering so much, the Galatians stood to lose it all; because perfection through the works of the law is a futile endeavor. They were genuinely in danger, and Paul feared for them (4:11, 20; 5:4; 6:8).

> **Galatians 3:3 Greek Text:** οὕτως ἀνόητοί ἐστε; ἐναρξάμενοι πνεύματι νῦν σαρκὶ ἐπιτελεῖσθε;
>
> **Translation:** Are you so foolish? After beginning by the Spirit, are you now trying to finish by the flesh?

At the beginning of verse 3, Paul reverts to his earlier tone in verse 1 to enforce his point. In a rhetorical question, he asks, οὕτως ἀνόητοί ἐστε; (Are you so foolish?). Again, in this verse, he refers to the Galatians (using the indicative present ἐστε) as ἀνόητοί (foolish). Precisely and concisely, Paul states the problem: ἐναρξάμενοι πνεύματι νῦν σαρκὶ ἐπιτελεῖσθε (after beginning by the Spirit, are you now trying to finish by the flesh?). The Galatians had initially begun well, and they were on the path of truth, life, and freedom through the Spirit of God; but suddenly, they were led away from the truth. As a result, they were now attempting to end in a "foolish" manner because they were trying to achieve perfection by means of the flesh.

The phrase ἐναρξάμενοι πνεύματι (after beginning with the Spirit), depicts a good beginning with divine power. They rightly began with a focus on the life-giving Spirit of God. As a temporal participle, ἐναρξάμενοι is translated with "after," and is antecedent to the action of the main verb (ἐπιτελεῖσθε). Most likely the dative πνεύματι is a dative of means (by the Spirit), but it could also be possibly taken as a dative of sphere (in the Spirit) or of manner or association. Whichever of this is preferred, the key point is that the Galatians got it right at the beginning when they first heard the gospel of God from the apostle Paul. Then, suddenly, all that changed!

The phrase νῦν σαρκὶ ἐπιτελεῖσθε; (Are you now trying to finish by the flesh?) displays the determination of the Galatians to end in a manner that is not consistent with the beginning. Here I understand the dative σαρxὶ as a dative of means (by the flesh), but even if it is understood as a dative of sphere (in the flesh), or manner (how the Galatians attempted to perfect their faith), the fundamental point being made is the same. Paul's audience had experienced a drift; they began well in the Spirit but were now trying to be perfected by the flesh. As a present tense, ἐπιτελεῖσθε is taken here as a tendential present; perfection through the flesh is attempted but not achieved.

The contention here was not about perfection; certainly, Paul wanted believers to be perfected. However, in this case, they were using the wrong means to gain perfection – that is, the flesh or human effort. Bruce makes a helpful distinction, "'Flesh' here is not simply the body, in which circumcision is carried out, but human nature in its unregenerate weakness, relying on such inadequate resources as were available before the coming of faith, having no access as yet to the power of the Spirit."[52] Emphatically, Paul makes clear a point that trying to gain perfection by human efforts is both futile labor and a foolish attempt.

So, is Paul justified in the depiction of the Galatians as "foolish"? This point can be argued out in several ways. First, they were trying to achieve perfection by the flesh, something contradictory to the apostolic heritage they had received. In a manner characteristic of fools, the Galatians had contradicted themselves.[53] They were unintelligently and thoughtlessly, under the influence of the Judaizers, changing the course of their faith. Second, they were inconsistent with what they believed in. Martyn notes, "Paul portrays a development in which the end does not at all correspond to the salvific beginning."[54] By attempting to be perfected in a manner inconsistent with the beginning of their faith, the Galatians were unknowingly trying to once again come under enslavement, yet they had received freedom as sons (Gal 4:1). Third, they were pursuing what is not achievable. Perfection before God can never be gained by human effort or by the observance of the law. Nonetheless, in their futile and foolish ways, the Galatians continued in the same direction, hoping to gain perfection through human effort. According to Paul, that was an unwise step.

---

52. Bruce, *Epistle to Galatians*, 149.
53. Betz, *Galatians*, 133.
54. Martyn, *Galatians*, 284.

Fourth, their foolishness was evident in the lack of understanding of the changing times regarding the work of Christ and the coming of the Holy Spirit. Garlington distinguishes the different eras of the flesh and Spirit:

> The old aeon can be called "flesh" because the Torah ministered largely to that dimension of human nature, making the flesh, especially circumcision, high on the Judaizers' agenda. In this regard, 6:12–13 (the good showing "in the flesh") summarizes the entire message of the opponents. Thus the question of v.3 is pointedly historical in its thrust. No wonder, the Galatians are "foolish." Their quest for perfection is anachronistic: they are going in the wrong direction; they want to reverse the plan of the ages![55]

The Galatians ought to have recognized that the coming of the Holy Spirit ushered in a different era in the history of salvation. The coming of this new era abolished and rendered obsolete the former age of the law. Comparatively, the two verbs ἐνάρχομαι and ἐπιτελέω also appear together in Philippians 1:6: "Being confident of this, that he who began (ὁ ἐναρξάμενος) a good work in you will carry it on to completion (ἐπιτελέσει) until the day of Christ Jesus" (NIV). In this case, the beginning, continuing, and completion of the work of salvation are achieved in the same manner and by the same means and agent.

Summary of the Verse

Paul presents a thesis-antithesis in this verse: beginning and perfecting; the Spirit and the flesh/human effort. In Galatians 5, Paul further develops the stark contrast between the Spirit and the flesh. The two are contrary to each other. This black and white language eliminates the possibility of a middle ground. The foolishness of the Galatians was manifested in their attempt to be perfected with the flesh rather than what was received by the Spirit, in their pursuit of what was not achievable, and in the lack of understanding of the new era in the economy of salvation. Further, for Paul, to hold on to the law is to live in the flesh and not in the sphere of the Spirit. Their initial salvation experience was God-centered (Spirit-initiated), and based on that, they should have pursued the perfection of their faith by the same Spirit.

---

55. Garlington, *Exposition of Galatians*, 152.

However, they erred by employing human effort to gain perfection of their salvation. In Paul's arguments, perfection is necessary, but how it is achieved also significantly matters. Paul employs the fifth rhetorical question in the next verse to highlight the great loss the Galatians stood to experience by seeking perfection by human effort.

Galatians 3:4 Greek Text: τοσαῦτα ἐπάθετε εἰκῇ; εἴ γε καὶ εἰκῇ.

Translation: Did you suffer so many things in vain, if indeed it was in vain?

Paul questions the value and purpose of the Galatians' suffering without specifying the nature of the suffering. His readers risked losing the value of their suffering if they finished wrongly what they had rightly started. The verb ἐπάθετε is a constative aorist; the suffering seems to have lasted for some time awhile. Galatians had suffered τοσαῦτα (so much).

The verb πάσχω meaning "I suffer," and the demonstrative adjective τοσοῦτος have been translated differently by different scholars. Martyn translates πάσχω as "to experience,"[56] while he translates the correlative adjective τοσαῦτα as "such remarkable things" (Have you experienced such remarkable things in vain?). Here he refers to the Galatians' initial experience of receiving the Spirit.[57] However, some understand the term πάσχω as related to persecution on account of the gospel.[58] Although scholars have divided opinion on the meaning of this verb, it is more plausible to take the view that translates this word as "suffering." In this verse, Paul must be referring to the negative experience the Galatians faced in the past, because in verse 5, he talks about the positive experience of the Spirit's working among the Galatians.[59]

Paul argues that by attempting to be perfected through flesh or works of the law, their suffering becomes εἰκῇ (in vain). On the contrary, their suffering would have become valuable had they continued in the way of the Spirit and enjoyed the life and the freedom that the Spirit gives. Ngewa illustrates Paul's point: "There is something wrong with a farmer who endures that hardship involved in planting and caring for a crop and then cuts it down before it

---

56. Martyn, *Galatians*, 285.
57. Martyn, 285.
58. These scholars include: Chrysostom, Augustine, Luther, Lightfoot, Zahn, Duncan, and Bruce to name but a few. See Longenecker, *Galatians*, 104.
59. This view is also shared by Ngewa in his work, *Galatians*, 98.

is ripe. The whole purpose of the hard labor was to harvest and enjoy the crop; it was not just a way to get some exercise!"⁶⁰ The Galatians needed to experience the fruit of their suffering by remaining under the guidance of the Spirit. Paul had similar fear among the Corinthians: "By this gospel you are saved, if you hold firmly to the word I preached to you. Otherwise, you have believed in vain" (1 Cor 15:2, NIV). The Galatians, like Corinthians, needed to hold firmly to the word that was first preached to them.

Did the Galatians ever suffer for their faith? Paul implies without specifying the nature of suffering by writing τοσαῦτα ἐπάθετε (you suffered so much). Bruce comments, "There is no reference to their being positively persecuted for the faith, like the Thessalonian Christians (1 Thess 2:14; 2 Thess 1:4f.). However, sufferings of any kind endured for the gospel's sake would indeed be pointless (εἰκῇ) if, after all, salvation could be attained by law-keeping)."⁶¹ As much as we may not pinpoint specific suffering(s) experienced by the Galatians, we generally know that Paul's calling and ministry to the Gentiles entailed suffering (Acts 9:16). Like other believers elsewhere, the Galatians must have experienced suffering from the hostile pagan surrounding (Acts 13:50; 16:22–24). In addition, Paul had labored hard in raising the Galatian congregation. Now, he expresses his genuine worry. In Galatians 4:11, with deep concern, he writes, "I fear for you, that somehow I have wasted my efforts on you." This fear is also explicitly expressed in Galatians 4:20; 5:4; and 6:8.

Summary of the Verse

With the understanding of the suffering the Galatians had gone through, Paul was worried that they stood to lose all that they had gained by their pain. If this happened, then Paul's reference to them as "foolish" stands unchallenged. They were drifting from what they once suffered for. So their drifting, according to Paul, in this verse, was potentially fruitless, and they stood to lose many things, including their suffering experience. Their pain would be wasted; because it would end up achieving nothing for them.

---

60. Ngewa, 98.
61. Bruce, *Epistle to Galatians*, 150.

Attributing the Receiving of the Spirit and the Work of the Spirit to Observance of the Law (v.5)

One last problem that Paul deals with in verse 5 is ascribing the reception of the Spirit and the working of the Spirit to the observance of the law. This must have been a deeply rooted belief in the teachings of Paul's opponents. Due to Judaizers' influence, observance of the law in Galatia had gained prominence to the extent that the reception of the Holy Spirit and the working of God in their midst had been credited to human effort.

> **Galatians 3:5 Greek Text:** ὁ οὖν ἐπιχορηγῶν ὑμῖν τὸ πνεῦμα καὶ ἐνεργῶν δυνάμεις ἐν ὑμῖν ἐξ ἔργων νόμου ἢ ἐξ ἀκοῆς πίστεως;
>
> **Translation:** Then does the one who gives you the Spirit and works miracles among you, (accomplish it) by the works of the law or by believing what you heard?

Paul begins verse 5 by the use of the conjunction οὖν, concluding the subsection. Is there a possibility that Paul was responding to his opponents in this verse? Judging by the way he maintains the dichotomy between the Spirit and the law, he was probably writing with the central tenets of Judaizers in mind.

The definite article ὁ agrees with the two substantival participles (ἐπιχορηγῶν and ἐνεργῶν) and refers to the unexpressed person – God the Father. The construction of the two participles, in the same case and connected by καὶ features the Granville theory, showing that the latter participle (in other cases a noun) refers to the same person expressed by the first.[62] In other words, the one who gives the Spirit and works miracles is the same person – God the Father.

Before looking at how the Galatians perceived what was happening to them, Paul, in this verse, points at two things that God the Father does (the one who called them – Gal 1:6). First, God the Father gives his Spirit to his people; he writes, ὁ οὖν ἐπιχορηγῶν ὑμῖν τὸ πνεῦμα (then does the one who gives you his Spirit). The use of the participle in the present tense ἐπιχορηγῶν as a durative/progressive present highlights the continuous aspect of God the Father supplying his Spirit. Second, God the Father is presented as a miracle worker, ἐνεργῶν δυνάμεις ἐν ὑμῖν (works miracles among you). In Galatia, God was active and "continually working" (taking ἐνεργῶν as a durative present)

---

62. Wallace, *Basics of New Testament*, 120.

miracles among his people. In 1 Corinthians 12:7–11, Paul listed some works of the Holy Spirit and the gifts the Spirit gives to each one, as the Spirit determines. The Spirit of God performed miracles in the ministry of Jesus (Matt 11:28). The verb ἐνεργέω, used to indicate God's performing mighty works among the Galatians, is also used in reference to God's work in the ministry of Peter (Gal 2:8), and is also used to depict God as a worker (1 Cor 12:6, 11).

In a rhetorical question, Paul challenges the Galatian believers on whether these workings of God the Father were accomplished either ἐξ ἔργων νόμου (by the works of the law) or ἐξ ἀκοῆς πίστεως (by believing what you heard or literally, "by the hearing of faith"). Syntactically, the use of ἐξ in these two instances focuses on means; both observance of the law and believing what is heard (gospel message) highlight the aspect of means. God did not perform miracles in their midst because of the observance of the law but because of believing what they heard. The preposition ἐν (among) has been taken as a dative of association, while the pronoun ὑμῖν as a dative of recipient.[63] Paul builds upon what he had addressed in verse 2, where he asked about their past lives. However, in verse 5, he asks them about their present life by using the present participles to refer to the continuous act of God giving his Spirit and performing miracles in their midst.

Summary of the Verse

In this verse, Paul talks about God the Father, whom the Galatians were deserting (1:6). He is the one who gives the Spirit and continues to work miracles among them. Interestingly, as a result of the Judaizers' teachings, the Galatians were now falsely ascribing these divine workings to the observance of the law. They were being persuaded to interpret the reception of the Spirit and the works of miracles among them as merited and based on their observance of the law. This proves that the Judaizers had taken captive the Galatian believers. Therefore, it was not just Christ that was no longer portrayed publicly as crucified, but also the roles of the Spirit and the Father were reinterpreted in light of the law. In order to return to the path of truth, life, and faith, the Galatians needed to rectify their understanding of God

---

63. Other uses for the rest of the verse are: The genitives ἔργων (subjective genitive), νόμου (objective genitive), and ἐξ (genitive of means), ἀκοῆς (subjective genitive), πίστεως (objective genitive).

(Father, Son, and Holy Spirit). The distortion of the theological concept of the person and work of God is a clear mark that they had drifted from the central tenets of the faith.

Conclusion of the Subsection (Verses 1–5)

In this section, Paul uses strong language to deal with serious faith matters concerning life and death. Indeed, there was a crisis in Galatia. They had landed into a theological error by accepting the teachings of the Judaizers. As explained above, the Galatians had foolishly turned from right to error, and neglected the one who called them. Also, their foolishness can be seen in the attempt to attain perfection based on the flesh as opposed to relying on the Spirit who began a good work in them. Furthermore, out of their foolishness and lack of spiritual discernment, the Galatians were tempted to ascribe the reception of the Spirit and the working of God in their midst to observance of the law.

The agitators infiltrated their midst and distorted the truth that Paul had preached. They attempted to destroy the very foundations that the apostles had laid. They sought to distort the apostolic message by emphasizing the law where Paul stressed the role of the Spirit; they emphasized works where Paul had emphasized faith. This was a great danger, and Paul feared for the worst – apostasy on the part of the Galatians. Judaizers, as Longenecker observes, had deceived the Galatians by claiming that they were only supplementing Paul's message by supplying what was lacking. He further adds,

> The strategy of the Judaizers was not to deny the importance of faith in Christ for salvation, but to affirm the necessity for Gentiles to accept at least minimal requirements of the Mosaic law for filling out their commitment to God and perfecting their Christian lives. It was not, therefore, an overt advocacy of legalism *per se*, but a call for Gentile believers to accept a lifestyle of Jewish nomism.[64]

Paul was not going to sit and watch things go down the drain; he would not allow the Judaizers to supplement or dilute the true gospel. Instead of addressing his opponents directly, Paul chose to address the Galatian believers

---

64. Longenecker, *Galatians*, 106.

and the false teachings which had corrupted his "brothers," whom he had preached to before.

Paul discusses the gospel message, salvation, and God (Father, Christ, and Spirit) in addressing these issues since the crisis in Galatia was both theological and practical. By accepting the message of the Judaizers, the Galatians were subjecting themselves (again) to slavery under the law. In these five verses, and in addressing the problem in Galatia, Paul successfully shows that the death of Christ, the crucified Christ, destroyed all forms of legal righteousness before God.

The following section details Paul's teachings with OT references. He invites the readers to consider the case of Abraham, the father of faith. The number of references to the Old Testament reveals Paul's high view of the OT Scriptures in light of Christ's redemptive work on the cross. In order to be restored to the path of truth, life, faith, and blessing, the Galatians needed to rectify their understanding of God (Father, Son, and Holy Spirit) and that of Scripture and salvation history.

Paul's Citation of the Old Testament (3:6–14)

In this section, we shall look at Paul's arguments and the use of Jewish Scriptures to this end. It will look at six quotations and the textual issues within their historical context. Where applicable, on cases with textual transformation, an explanation will be given in an attempt to account for the variations.

Faith Brings Blessing and Justification (3:6–9)

To be able to ground his argument, Paul appeals to the respectable OT patriarch, Abraham.[65] In a catena of OT quotations from verses 6–9, Abraham is mentioned several times. He illustrates that God's dealing in matters of righteousness has never changed! Salvation has all along been by faith and not by meritorious acts. In other words, Abraham's righteousness was not based on works but faith in God. Cole argues that Paul might have appealed

---

65. Hansen notes that Paul is citing Abraham for several reasons: To authenticate the validity and authority of the revelation to him, to show its consistency with the gospel, to show the place of the Gentiles in God's salvation agenda, to defend his mission to the Gentiles, and finally to refute the opponents' biblical basis for compelling the Gentiles to Judaize. Hansen, *Abraham in Galatians*, 171–74.

his case to Abraham and God's promise to him as a response to the Judaizers' reference to Moses and the law: "Judaizers might quote Moses; Paul will quote Abraham. Let them quote law; he will quote promise. If they appeal to centuries of tradition and the proud history of the law of Moses, he will appeal to the grander 'covenant with Abraham,' older by centuries still."[66] However, it should be noted that in Abraham, Paul sees a revelation of salvation that was solely based on faith. Thus, from the time of Abraham, Paul seeks to demonstrate that God's dealings with his people, in matters of salvation, remained unchanged.

Generally, exegetes agree that tracing Paul's argument in this section (Galatians chapters 3 and 4) is "extremely difficult to follow"[67] because Paul "goes far beyond the rules of historico-grammatical exegesis as followed by biblical scholars today."[68] This raises exegetical questions on the methodology used by the apostle, but this is something beyond the scope of this study. Paul conducts an elaborate exposition of Scripture to further his thesis. In verse 6, Paul quotes an OT Scripture, while in verse 7, he presents an exegesis of the quotation.

> **Galatians 3:6 Greek Text:** καθὼς Ἀβραὰμ ἐπίστευσεν τῷ θεῷ, καὶ ἐλογίσθη αὐτῷ εἰς δικαιοσύνην.
>
> **Translation:** (It is) just as Abraham "believed God and it was credited to him as righteousness."

In verse 6, Paul invites the readers into deliberation by quoting Genesis 15:6. This section is introduced and linked to the previous verse by the compound conjunction καθὼς. The author establishes a spiritual connection between those who have faith in Christ (those justified by believing the message of the gospel) and Abraham, the man of faith. He considers the case of Ἀβραὰμ, a respectable patriarch in the Old Testament. In a point that is summarized later in the next verse, Paul argues that Abraham was justified by faith apart from "works of the law" (3:10). The promise and crediting Abraham's faith as righteousness took place 430 years before the issuance of the law (Gal 3:17). Paul points out Abraham's case of justification by faith to

---

66. Cole, *Epistle of Paul*, 85.
67. Betz, *Galatians*, 137.
68. Longenecker, *Galatians*, 110.

confront and correct the misguided views and teachings of the Judaizers (also referred to as the circumcision party). He was pointing out that both Jews and Gentiles were justified by faith, just as Abraham, the father of the Jews (the father of all, including the Gentiles) who believe after him was justified by faith, not by observation of the law. The Galatian believers whom Paul was trying to bring back to the right-thinking were already justified by faith (had received the Spirit), as verse 2 states. The Judaizers were only misleading them; hence, Paul writes to straighten out their view of justification. Additionally, Paul's reference to Abraham in his arguments shows that his preaching was founded upon the OT teachings.

In Galatia, Paul and his opponents must have each used Abraham in their arguments concerning the faith and observance of the law, respectively. The Judaizers must have also used Abraham to argue that he obeyed God's command of circumcision (Gen 19:9–14). Longenecker comments, "Indeed, Abraham was the exemplar for Jews in all sorts of ways, and so might be expected to be appealed to in any arguments involving Jews. Seemingly, the Judaizers had instructed the Gentiles of Galatia that to be true children of Abraham, they had to be circumcised as Abraham himself was and as he was commanded in the covenant given him by God."[69] Therefore, Paul needed to set clear the biblical interpretation of Genesis 15:6 to rescue the Galatians from the confusion created by the circumcision party. Further, the example of Abraham must have resonated with the situation of the Gentiles. Betz projects the patriarch as a model of salvation among the Gentiles:

> For the Jewish mission to the Gentiles, however, Abraham was the very model of the one who converted from paganism to the true God and to the law. To this extent Abraham could have also been an attractive preaching theme for the Galatian opponents, an awe-inspiring figure from the distant past whom one could read about in the law and whose significance was that one should hold to his God.[70]

It was therefore important for Paul to come out clear on the salvation Abraham received, in relation to circumcision.

---

69. Longenecker, 109.
70. Betz, *Galatians*, 56.

Abraham was the father of the Jewish people (Gen 12:24; Isa 51:2; Matt 3:9); Israelites were naturally "the seed of Abraham" (Ps 105:6; Isa 41:8); and Jews considered their physical connection with Abraham a matter of pride (3 *Macc* 6:3). In the first-century Jewish literature, Abraham was a towering figure and was seen as the model of a devout Jew: "For Abraham was perfect in all his deeds with the Lord, and well pleasing in righteousness all the days of his life. . . ."[71] He was also depicted as a pagan who was determined to abandon idol worship in the quest for the true God.[72] Also, Abraham was portrayed as the first convert from paganism to the true God.[73] He was regarded as the father of many nations and that many nations would be blessed by his seed.[74]

In the Jewish tradition, Abraham was found to be faithful to God in times of testing.[75] It is unlikely that Paul and his opponents could have failed to refer to this towering figure in Jewish history. Under the name of Abraham, many themes in the Jewish Bible could be discussed. Some of the repeated motifs of Abraham's story in these writings are "father, people, covenant, circumcision, oath, posterity, blessing, and inheritance."[76] Therefore, when Paul discusses the issue of law, curses, blessings, and promise, we can be sure that his thought is primarily based on Abraham's story.

Further, it is noted that the Aramaic Targums, in Paul's day, speak of Genesis 15:6 in the context of Abraham's merit before God in rescuing Lot and his family from the four northern kings in Genesis 14.[77] In most of these references and interpretations, Abraham's deeds are emphasized over his faith in God. The Judaizers must have found plenty of evidence from these Jewish writings and pseudepigraphical materials to affirm their position on

---

71. *Jub* 23:10; Also see Charles, *Apocrypha and Pseudepigrapha*, 30. The book contains texts in English, and critical and explanatory notes to the several apocryphal and pseudepigraphal books featured. See also Perkins, *Abraham's Divided Children*, 65.

72. *Jub* 12; *Apoc Ab* 1–8; Philo, *Abr* 60–68; Josephus, *Ant* 1:55.

73. Josh 24:2–3; *Jub* 11:16–17; 12; *Apoc of Ab* 1–8; Philo, *Abr* 60–88; Josephus, *Ant* 1:154–57; Pseudo-Philo, *Lib ant* 23:5. See Garlington, *Exposition of Galatians*, 155.

74. *Sir* 44:19–21.

75. The following references for further study are listed by Garlington to show Abraham as a man of faith in times of testing: (*Sir* 44:19; 1 *Macc* 2:50–52; *T Levi* 9:1–14; *T Benj* 10:4; *T Abr* 17:2; *Jub* 23:10; 51:1–2; 16:20; 17:17–18; 23:10; CD 3:2–4; 16:1, 5–6; 2 *Apoc Bar* 57:1–3; Philo, *Abr* 275–6; m *Kidd* 4; 14). Garlington, *Exposition of Galatians*, 155. For more information and discussion, consult Longenecker, *Galatians*, 110–11, and; Betz, *Galatians*, 139–40.

76. Lührmann, *Galatians*, 57.

77. Longenecker, *Galatians*, 113.

the observance of the law. To the Judaizers, Paul must have unexpectedly interpreted Abraham's story to support his teaching on justification by faith. Against the Judaizers' central argument, Paul must have also argued that the covenant with Abraham predates the law that was issued several centuries later on Mount Sinai.

The call of Abraham in Genesis 12 and the subsequent covenant in Genesis 15 were key OT initiatives that were characterized by blessings. In the call to Abraham, the blessings to all families of the earth was announced (Gen 12:3). Although the majority of the Gentiles in Galatia were largely not conversant with the OT covenants and Scriptures, they certainly must have found an encouragement to know that their inclusion into the community of faith and blessing was long foretold.

In the Pauline corpus, Abraham is quoted or referred to by Paul several times to advance his teachings and arguments against false teachers. For example, in Romans 4, he appeals to the example of Abraham as a faithful patriarch. Abraham was not justified by works (Rom 4:2), but by faith (Rom 4:16), and Betz argues that "this faith is not the faith of who is righteous, but one who believes in God who justifies the unrighteous (Rom 4:5), who makes the dead alive, and who calls things that do not yet exist as if they do exist (Rom 4:17)."[78] This is the identity of the God that Abraham trusted.

In the Genesis 15:6 quotation, Abraham ἐπίστευσεν τῷ θεῷ (believed God); the verb ἐπίστευσεν is a constative aorist, looking at the action as a whole; and τῷ θεῷ is a dative of direct object. The verb πιστεύω means "having confidence in." Abraham had confidence in God to do what he promised (Rom 4:21). The promise of God and Abraham's faith features prominently in Abraham's encounter with God. Abraham believed God and his promises as trustworthy; therefore, he obeyed.

The conjunction καὶ introduces something special that happened as a result of Abraham's faith in God. Abraham believed and ἐλογίσθη αὐτῷ εἰς δικαιοσύνην (it was credited to him as righteousness). The verb ἐλογίσθη is a constative aorist, and the personal pronoun αὐτῷ is a dative of indirect object. The construction εἰς plus δικαιοσύνην is an adverbial accusative of termination with status as focus. The focus here is on the privileged status of righteousness that Abraham enjoyed before God. In line with Paul's argument, believers in

---

78. Betz, *Galatians*, 141.

Galatia were like Abraham because they came to God in faith; and the working of God's Spirit among them resulted from that faith response. Paul points out the ancient example of Abraham, a man who was justified by faith, before pointing at Jesus Christ. Succinctly, Abraham's portrayal of faith in God led to his declaration, by God, as righteousness.

Textual Issues

In this subsection, a comparison of quoted Bible texts[79] is carried out. For example, in this verse, Paul quotes from Genesis 15:6; but the way the quotation has been rendered raises some textual issues.

MT: וְהֶאֱמִן בַּיהוָה וַיַּחְשְׁבֶהָ לּוֹ צְדָקָה (Gen 15:6) (Then he believed in the Lord and he credited it to him as righteousness).

LXX: καὶ ἐπίστευσεν Αβραμ τῷ θεῷ καὶ ἐλογίσθη αὐτῷ εἰς δικαιοσύνην (Gen 15:6) (And Abram believed God and it was credited to him as righteousness).

UBS: καθὼς Ἀβραὰμ ἐπίστευσεν τῷ θεῷ, καὶ ἐλογίσθη αὐτῷ εἰς δικαιοσύνην (Even so, Abraham "believed God and it was credited to him as righteousness").

By comparing these texts, there are apparent textual issues that need to be pointed out. For instance, he name "Abram" is indicated in the LXX but missing in the MT. The same proper noun, though insignificant detail, is rendered as Ἀβραὰμ in the UBS text, but the LXX reads Αβραμ. In addition, the LXX rendered the verb ἐλογίσθη in passive voice (meaning, "it was credited to him") therefore avoiding reference to the name of God. The focus is put on the aspect of crediting righteousness, and the recipient (Abraham). Further, the Hebrew text renders the verb יַּחְשְׁבֶהָ as active (meaning, "he credited it"), making it possible to translate the verb with the third person singular pronoun. It is proper to conclude that these few textual issues do not changed the rendering of the Hebrew text in a way that raises questions. Betz notes that the way Paul uses Genesis 15:6 passage is different from the whole tradition of the interpretation of this text, although not erroneous.[80] Paul uses this text

---

79. Here and thereafter, the MT (based on BHS) translations are mine; LXX translations are based on NETS.

80. Betz, *Galatians*, 56–57.

to demonstrate that righteousness was reckoned to Abraham before his circumcision and giving of the law. The striking similarities in these three texts indicate that whichever the text the Galatians read (either MT or LXX), they would discover that Paul's base for his argument was correct and plausible.

Summary of the Verse

This verse expands the conversation in Galatia and seeks to find a biblical solution by looking at the history of salvation. It features the dichotomy between Paul, who preached justification by faith, and the Judaizers, who propagated justification through the works of the Torah. Paul's reference to Abraham demonstrates that faith is supreme over salvation by works. When Abraham heard the promise of God, he believed. Paul also indicates that "his" gospel was not a brand-new gospel but a gospel consistent with the OT. He finds an excellent example in Genesis, the example of Abraham, whose justification happened four centuries before the issuance of the law. Expectedly, Galatian believers would, therefore, be enlightened to realize that what Paul was preaching was indeed in accordance with the Scriptures; and that the false teachers were in error. Verse 6 establishes the basis for Paul's arguments that runs to verse 14. The next verse presents an exegetical conclusion of the Scriptural quotation in verse 6. Typically, one would expect an exegetical conclusion to precede a Scripture quotation; but these two verses render it differently.

> **Galatians 3:7 Greek Text:** Γινώσκετε ἄρα ὅτι οἱ ἐκ πίστεως, οὗτοι υἱοί εἰσιν Ἀβραάμ.
>
> **Translation:** Therefore, realize that those who have faith are sons of Abraham.

Through the conjunction ἄρα, Paul draws some implications of the OT quotation in the previous verse. Since Abraham believed God and it was credited to him as righteousness, Paul points his listeners to a certain realization, Γινώσκετε "understand"/"realize", which can be taken as a dramatic present. The verb Γινώσκετε can either be rendered as indicative (you understand/know) or imperative (understand/know). In this instance, Γινώσκετε has been rendered as an imperative and is consistent with the flow of verse 6, where he had issued a statement. Betz comments that what the Galatians were asked to recognize was not obvious.⁸¹ Paul keenly leads them to this important realization in verse 6. The realization concerns those who have faith οἱ ἐκ πίστεως (literally, "those out of faith"). The noun πίστεως has been taken as a genitive of possession, hence the phrase οἱ ἐκ πίστεως can be rendered as "those who *have* faith."

The verb εἰσιν has been taken here as a perfective present; thus the focus is not on the past action but a present reality. The Gentiles who exercise their faith become sons of Abraham. The noun Ἀβραάμ is a genitive of relationship, as such Paul wants his readers to understand that those who have faith in Jesus Christ are sons of Abraham. Garlington observes that the phrase οἱ ἐκ πίστεως is deliberately used against τοὺς ἐκ περιτομῆς (those of the circumcision) in Galatians 2:12, and ἐξ ἔργων νόμου (those of the works of the law) in Galatians 3:10 and Romans 4:14.⁸² Here, Paul points out a spiritual truth that those who have faith in Jesus Christ are spiritually connected to Abraham. True sonship to Abraham is not based on blood relations but faith. Although Abraham lived many centuries before the coming of Christ, he received the promise, revelation, and justification by faith. The promise that Abraham received later found fulfillment in Jesus Christ.

This verse makes an interesting association between the New Testament and Old Testament and between Christ and Abraham. Those who believe, (subjective view), even among the Galatians (whether Jews or Gentiles), are sons of Abraham (οὗτοι υἱοί εἰσιν Ἀβραάμ). Here, Paul redefines who the descendants of Abraham are, just as he redefines what it means to be a Jew in Romans 2:17–29. This redefinition at the spiritual level would disprove Judaizers, who based their identity on the physical connection with Abraham. In redefining what it means to be a descendant of Abraham, Paul finds his answer not in physical connection, but spiritual connection brought about by faith in Christ. The inclusion into this Abrahamic lineage is dependent on faith in Christ Jesus, the crucified one (and not on the observance of the law). Betz notes that the question of whether every Jew could claim the fatherhood of Abraham (Matt 3:9; Luke 3:8; 16:24; John 8:33) or whether all Israelites by

---

81. Betz, 141.
82. Garlington, *Exposition of Galatians*, 157.

birth are true Israelites (Rom 9:6; 2:28–3:3) was discussed both in Christianity and in Judaism.[83] Thus, presumably, it was a point of contention in each circle.

The issue of circumcision was central to the teachings of the Judaizers, and this stood in stark contrast to what Paul preached – justification by faith in Christ Jesus. Judaizers, on the one hand, wrongly defined the sonship to Abraham as comprising those who take after Abraham in the observance of the law, starting with circumcision. On the other hand, Paul redefined Abraham's children as "not the Law-people, but rather the faith-people."[84] The point raised by Judaizers was not a simple question to be easily dismissed. Judaizers knew that circumcision was instituted during Abraham's covenant with God, and the same sign of the covenant was reaffirmed later during the issuance of the law (Lev 12:3). Therefore, Paul must give a convincing interpretation of this aspect of the law touching on Abraham. Apart from providing a spiritual meaning to what it means to be a descendant of Abraham, Paul ties his instruction and response to the idea of υἱοθεσία (adoption as sons) in Galatians 4:5. So then, how did the Judaizers express the idea of Gentiles becoming descendants of Abraham? Bruce offers us a hint: "Galatians were being asked to become children of Abraham by adoption (since they were not his children by natural birth), and this, they were told, involved circumcision, just as it did for proselytes from paganism to Judaism."[85] Indeed, this was a deception that unsettled Paul and others who propagated the gospel of justification by faith.

Abraham's Covenant as a Response to the Human Problem in Genesis 3–11

God's covenant with Abraham and the promise to bless the nations should be looked at in the context of human history in Genesis 1–11. Christopher Wright and Jonathan Lunde, in *The Mission of God's People: A Biblical Theology for the Church's Mission*, observe that God's dealings with Abraham in Genesis 12 come as a cosmic solution to the curse and sin in Genesis 3. Concerning the promise to bless, Wright and Lunde observe, "Genesis 3–11 show how every dimension of life is tragically adrift from the original goodness of God's

---

83. Betz, *Galatians*, 142.
84. Martyn, *Galatians*, 299.
85. Bruce, *Epistle to Galatians*, 155.

purpose. The earth lies under the sentence of God's curse because of human sin. Human beings are adding to their catalog of evil as the generations roll past."[86] Thus, God's promise to Abraham seeks to reverse the curses of Genesis 3. In Genesis 12, God promises Abraham restoration of blessing pronounced before the fall (Gen 1–2) but lost during the fall (Gen 3). Concerning the promise to bless, "it is so emphatic that this promise is repeated five times in Genesis (12:3; 18:18; 22:18; 26:4; 28:14). There is a universal end in view. If humanity as a whole is subject to God's curse, then humanity as a whole must be reached by God's blessing."[87] In God's covenant with Abraham, God's promise to bless was good news to the entire humanity. It revealed God's heart for the nations.

Due to humanity's disobedience in Genesis 3, curses were pronounced by God. In these curses, the serpent was cursed (verse 14–15), the female-humanity (verse 16), the male-humanity, and the ground were cursed (verse 17–19). However, is the pronouncement in Genesis 3:14–19 a curse or mere punishment?[88] Notable in this curse pronouncement is the idea of death; that is, humanity returning to the dust, where they came from. Most commentators have associated the curse and death with the death-threat mentioned in Genesis 2:17 on those who would eat the forbidden fruit.[89] Since the fall of humankind consigned all humanity to death, the solution to the human puzzle needs to consider the extent of the fall. The call and the covenant God made with Abraham in Genesis 12 was God's initiative to once again bring blessings to all peoples of the earth. It reveals God's salvation plan of reversing the curses in Genesis 3:16–19 and bringing restoration of the blessings of God to humanity. Walton writes, "Before God resolved the Eden problem

---

86. Wright and Lunde, *Mission of God's People*, 60.
87. Wright and Lunde, 69.
88. There have been scholarly debates around this point. Those who believe that this Bible section deals with a curse pronounced by God argue that there is the mention of curses twice, and the fact that curses in this context emanate from man's transgression. I subscribe to this position because of the mention of curses which are pronounced as a punishment for human sinfulness. However, there are other interpreters like C. Westermann and J. Scullion who argue that it was only the serpent and the ground that were cursed, and that humanity was only punished with negative consequences resulting from their disobedience. See Westermann and Scullion, *Genesis 1–11*, 257. The same views are shared by Walton, *Genesis*, 236.
89. Wenham, *Genesis 1–15*, 83. He also lists scholars who dispute this position by arguing for lack of connection between Genesis 2:3 and 3:19. These scholars believe that death is part of the natural order of things.

(sin), he determined to resolve the Babel problem (deity falsely construed). Calvary resolves the Eden problem, but covenant resolves the Babel problem. It does so by revealing what God is truly like."[90] Walton is hesitant to admit that humanity was cursed in Genesis 3, but in the narrative of Genesis 12, he acknowledges that God is in the business of bringing people back into a relationship with him.

Summary of Verse 6–7

In verse 6, Paul uses Abraham and references salvation history to confront his opponents and set forth the biblical truth. God's call and covenant with Abraham represents a new project against the backdrop of the fall of humankind, with its resultant sin, curse, and separation from God (death). The mention of blessings in the story of Abraham is part of God's mission to bring something new (blessings and salvation) out of the gloomy narrative of curse and death. The antithesis of blessings and curses is also present in the promise God gave Abraham in Genesis 12:3, but the blessing is given prominence. Therefore, the covenant God made with Abraham in Genesis 12 answers the human enigma of sin and curses in Genesis 3. In Genesis 12:1–3, when God promised land, nation, and blessings, he was laying out a grand salvation project for humanity, which was fulfilled in the work of Christ on the cross.

Abraham represents a new era, an epoch where the inauguration of God's salvation plan was laid out not just for Abraham's physical descendants but the entire nations/families of the earth (Gen 12:3c). In Romans 5:17, Paul looks at the example of Adam and Christ. He writes, "For if, by the trespass of the one man [Adam], death reigned through that one man, how much more will those who receive God's abundant provision of grace and of the gift of righteousness reign in life through the one man, Jesus Christ." In application to the Galatian situation, those (Jews and Gentiles) who put their faith in Christ are no longer *in Adam* but *in Christ*. Paul in Galatians 3:26 emphatically writes, "you are all sons of God through faith in Christ Jesus." The redeemed people of God in Christ are now part of a community of faith and blessing. Again, in Genesis 12, God promised Abraham, וְנִבְרְכוּ בְךָ כֹּל מִשְׁפְּחֹת הָאֲדָמָה: (and in you, all families of the earth shall be blessed). On this, Paul did not look at the cross to see the inclusion of the Gentiles into the community of

---

90. Walton, *Genesis*, 402.

faith and blessing; instead, he retrospectively looked at the promise given to Abraham. The cross was a fulfillment of the salvation promise earlier given to Abraham.

In verse 7, the implication and interpretation of the quotation in verse 6 is highlighted. By redefining what it means to be a descendant of Abraham, Paul strongly indicates that Gentiles are treasured people in God's economy of salvation; because they were not an afterthought but part and parcel of God's original plan. In a nutshell, the two verses highlight God's redemption plan through Abraham. The verses describe Abraham's nature of righteousness before God – justification by faith.

The next verse reveals Scriptural testimony concerning the inclusion of Gentiles into the community of faith and blessing. God revealed his eternal plan of salvation to Abraham, and in that plan, God promises to bring blessings to all nations of the earth. Further, Paul proves that the gospel he proclaimed was not a new message, rather, it was a gospel that Scripture foresaw and foretold.

> **Galatians 3:8 Greek Text:** προϊδοῦσα δὲ ἡ γραφὴ ὅτι ἐκ πίστεως δικαιοῖ τὰ ἔθνη ὁ θεὸς προευηγγελίσατο τῷ Ἀβραὰμ ὅτι Ἐνευλογηθήσονται ἐν σοὶ πάντα τὰ ἔθνη.
>
> **Translation:** And the Scripture, foreseeing that God would justify the Gentiles by faith, preached the gospel in advance to Abraham that, "All the nations will be blessed in you."

In verse 8, Paul begins with an explanation which is then followed by an OT quotation to support his assertion. He makes an emphatic claim that the Scriptures foresaw that God would justify the Gentiles by faith, and thus the gospel was proclaimed in advance to Abraham. The verse is quoted from Genesis 12:3; 18:18; and 22:18.

The conjunction δὲ serves to continue the thought from the previous verse. That is why it is more appropriate to translate it as "and" instead of "but." The nominative subject ἡ γραφὴ presented with a definite article refers to the Scripture in its entirety, as one. The aspect of Scripture foreseeing is a personification figure of speech; Scripture is personified as seeing, as if with eyes. The action of the aorist participle, προϊδοῦσα, is antecedent to the action of the main verb (προευηγγελίσατο). The use of personification indicates two things. First, it reveals Paul's respect of Scriptures as the expression of God's will: "Paul saw the scriptures as alive, active, speaking, and even locking people up under sin (Gal 3:22)."[91] Second, the personification of Scripture speaks of something deeper than just being a text with God's oracles; it indicates that "Scripture is not a passive text to be quoted and interpreted by humans as they will. On the contrary, it is alive, having, as it were, eyes and intelligence and a mouth."[92] The Scripture communicates to us in a manner that is real (Heb 4:12). Thus, Paul asserts, that the Scripture foresaw that God would justify the Gentiles.

The phrase τὰ ἔθνη is translated as "the nations or Gentiles," with ἔθνη being accusative of direct object. The Gentiles will be justified ἐκ πίστεως (by faith – genitive of means). The idea of God reaching out to the Gentiles with salvation is taught in the Bible (Ps 22:27–28; 47:9; 67; 87; 117). Paul employs the phrase τὰ ἔθνη several times in Galatians to refer to his Gentile audience (Gal 1:16; 2:2, 8–9, 12, 14–15; 3:14).

Foreseeing the justification of the Gentiles by faith, the Scripture "preached the gospel in advance" to Abraham (τῷ Ἀβραάμ); the verb προευηγγελίσατο has been rendered as a constative aorist. The definite article (τῷ) is an article with the proper name; the noun Ἀβραάμ is a dative of indirect object. Abraham not only received a glimpse of God's salvation plan but personally experienced such salvation that involved justification by faith. He was a beneficiary of God's gracious gift of justification by faith. It is evident from this verse that Abraham received not only the gift of salvation but also the message about the place of the Gentiles in relation to the gift. The Gentiles who believe become sons of Abraham. The salvation and promise that Abraham received was a foretaste and first fruit of what God was going to accomplish in the fullness of time. In Abraham, God laid a paradigm of how he would save and bless his people – through justification by faith.

The OT quotation is introduced by the conjunction ὅτι, which is a standard way of introducing a direct or indirect quotation. The direct quotation from Genesis 12:3 (with echoes of Gen 18:18 or 22:18), gives part of the promise that Abraham received from God, Ἐνευλογηθήσονται ἐν σοὶ πάντα τὰ ἔθνη (all the nations will be blessed in you). The quotation has the phrase πάντα τὰ

---

91. Garlington, *Exposition of Galatians*, 158.

92. Martyn, *Galatians*, 300. Martyn also notes that in Philo and in the rabbinic traditions there are affirmations that Scripture sees and knows. Philo, *Leg Alleg* 3.118; Billerbeck, 3.538.

ἔθνη (all nations – nominative subject); the adjective πάντα adds emphasis. God's initial plan was universal; it went beyond the promised nation of Israel. Betz gives a helpful caveat that the phrase πάντα τὰ ἔθνη must be taken to mean those of the Gentiles who believe like Abraham.[93] The inclusion of the Gentile believers into the community of faith and blessing was not an alien concept in the Old Testament. In Romans 15:9–11, Paul quotes several OT texts with the theme of "nations" (Deut 32:43; 2 Sam 22:50; Ps 18:49; 117:1; Isa 11:10), thus demonstrating that the idea of reaching out to the nations runs through the Old Testament. Bruce writes, "the scripture embodies and perpetuates the promise, so that the good news which was 'preached beforehand' to Abraham is still preached by the scripture to those who read it or hear it or read, especially to those living in the age when the promise has been fulfilled."[94]

This verse emphasizes and expands the scope of application of God's sonship through Abraham. It demonstrates that Gentiles were in view when the gospel was first announced to Abraham. Paul points out that through the crucifixion of Christ, salvation had indeed come to Gentiles as per the promise earlier given to Abraham.

Textual Issues from the Quotation

In this verse, Paul supports his argument by quoting Genesis 12:3; 18:18; and 22:18. Below is an analysis of the texts. The quotation exhibits minimal modifications that are generally inconsequential to the meaning of the passage.

MT: וְנִבְרְכוּ בְךָ כֹּל מִשְׁפְּחֹת הָאֲדָמָה (Gen 12:3) (and in you all families on earth shall be blessed).

LXX: καὶ ἐνευλογηθήσονται ἐν σοὶ πᾶσαι αἱ φυλαὶ τῆς γῆς (Gen 12:3) (and in you all the tribes of the earth shall be blessed).

UBS: Ἐνευλογηθήσονται ἐν σοὶ πάντα τὰ ἔθνη (All the nations will be blessed in you).

The Hebrew כֹּל מִשְׁפְּחֹת הָאֲדָמָה (all families/clans on earth) is rendered in LXX using the phrase πᾶσαι αἱ φυλαὶ τῆς γῆς (all the tribes of the earth). The UBS text has πάντα τὰ ἔθνη (all the nations). Overall, these different

---

93. Betz, *Galatians*, 143.
94. Bruce, *Epistle to Galatians*, 156.

renderings in the three texts do not alter the meaning of what is communicated. However, it shows that either Paul was quoting from memory or translating directly from the MT. Still, any skeptic of Paul's gentile soteriology would, upon review of the MT and LXX, find Paul's case from the Old Testament and salvation history to be watertight.

Summary of the Verse

The announcement of the gospel to Abraham in Genesis 12 was good news to the entire humanity. It was a response to the problem of human sin and the curse pronounced in Genesis 3 on all humanity. God's promised blessings will remove the curse on humanity. Martyn relates this verse to the objections raised by Paul's opponents,[95] but this may not be entirely true in each of the verses. In this verse, it appears that Paul primarily reveals a biblical truth; and the issue of Judaizers occupies a secondary role in his thought.

The next verse gives a summary statement of the section that begins in verse 6. Paul seeks to demonstrate that those who are of faith (whether Jews or Gentiles) are blessed with Abraham, the man of faith. They become part of a community of faith, a community that is blessed with Abraham.

> **Galatians 3:9 Greek Text:** ὥστε οἱ ἐκ πίστεως εὐλογοῦνται σὺν τῷ πιστῷ Ἀβραάμ.
>
> **Translation:** So then, those who are of faith are blessed with the man of faith, Abraham.

Verse 9 makes a summary statement of the exposition of the OT quotations. The conjunction ὥστε ("so that" or "so then") is a result clause concluding Paul's thoughts from verse 6. Paul repeats the phrase οἱ ἐκ πίστεως in verse 7 to refer to the same group of those who believe. The definite article οἱ, also acts as a nominative subject, and reflects an anaphoric use of a definite article. As a plural in number, οἱ implies that those who believe are many, in other words, a community of faith. The genitive πίστεως is a qualitative genitive; providing a distinction between those who are of faith and those who are not. Those who are of faith, Paul writes εὐλογοῦνται σὺν τῷ πιστῷ Ἀβραάμ

---

95. Martyn wrongly presumes that in every verse, Paul makes a polemic response to his opponents. This is a far-fetched assertion, because the entire letter was not written against false teachers but to present the true gospel. Martyn, *Galatians*, 300.

(are blessed with Abraham). The verb εὐλογοῦνται is a durative present – the act of blessing began in the past and is still ongoing. The dative Ἀβραάμ has been taken as a dative of association. Those who believe enter into a community of blessings because of their faith. The idea of "blessing" is a promise made by God to Abraham and is extended to all descendants of Abraham who believe. Faith in God and his promises is the requirement for receiving this blessing and joining this community of blessing. Abraham was among the first person to enter into this community based on faith and not because of any meritorious act.

The ending τῷ πιστῷ means "the believing" or "the faithful." The adjective πιστῷ, in this case, has been used attributively. The definite article τῷ is used anaphorically; Abraham is portrayed as a "man of faith." In Hebrew 11, Abraham is also mentioned among the heroes of faith (Heb 11:8–19). Betz notes, "Abraham who in Judaism is the prototype of 'righteousness through obedience to the Torah' now has become the prototype of the 'men of faith.'"[96] Garlington observes that it is striking that Paul speaks of "faithful Abraham" (literally) rather than "Abraham who had faith" or believing Abraham (the majority rendering); Abraham was "faithful" in the broad sense because he believed against hope (Rom 4:18–22).[97] This is the reason for his justification.

It is possible that Paul implicitly refuted the Judaizers in this verse. Garlington observes,

> The polemic impact of the verse is that fidelity to God does not depend on law observance. This in turn implies that the Judaizers and their followers cannot be the sons of Abraham, because they refuse to walk "in his footsteps" (Rom 4:12). By the nature of the case, then, the Judaizers' program of converting the nations to the law in order to become the seed of Abraham is illegitimate and contradicts the very example of the patriarch himself, who was believing and faithful before circumcision and the advent of the Torah on to the stage of human history.[98]

---

96. Betz, *Galatians*, 143.
97. Garlington, *Exposition of Galatians*, 158.
98. Garlington, 159.

Therefore, the case of Abraham is consistent with Paul's proclamation and stands in contrast to the message of the Judaizers. In this verse, Paul succeeded in highlighting that blessings come to those who believe alongside Abraham.

Subsection Conclusion

In this subsection (Gal 3: 6–9), Paul presents his arguments using Genesis 12 as his primary text. He finds a historical example in Abraham to present his teaching on justification by faith. He demonstrates that his gospel was not a newly invented means of salvation but a divine anointed way of salvation from ancient times. Abraham's acceptance by God was not based on anything he did (or did not do) but solely on his faith in God and his promises. Paul then redefines the identity of Abraham's descendants – they are those who believe like Abraham. They are not those related to Abraham by blood but those spiritually connected to him by faith in God. In the context of Galatia, they comprised both Jews and Gentiles who have faith in Christ Jesus.

In addition, Paul argues that Scripture foresaw and foretold the gospel to Abraham; he received the promise that God would bless all the families of the earth. God's plan to bless is apparent in this section. Against the backdrop of Genesis 3, God's determination to bless all families of the earth is seen specifically in the call, covenant, and promise given to Abraham. The gospel from the beginning was based on faith and was inclusive of the Gentiles. Abraham's model of salvation highlights the way of salvation, and the scope of God's salvation, encompassing the entire world.

A quick follow-up question that comes to mind is: What about those not of faith or those not in the community of blessing? Paul deals with this category in the next section (Gal 3:10–12). He follows through the antithesis of blessing and curse that is taken from Genesis 12:3 and in the next verse, he looks at the issue of the curse within the context of the law. The answer he provides to the issue of curses is the same as what he had hinted in verse 1 – the crucified and cursed Christ.

The Law Brings Curse, Not Justification (3:10–12)

The following subsection (verses 10–12) introduces the concept of curse, but, just like the previous discussion of blessing, the arguments are drawn from the Old Testament. The subsection forms a continuation of Paul's thought that began in verse 1. The Galatians were trying to attain perfection through human effort, and seemingly, they were now being tempted to attribute the reception of the Holy Spirit and the working of God among them to the observance of the law. However, in this subsection, Paul refutes his opponents and demonstrates that the law brings curse, not blessings or justification. Those who do not belong to Abraham are not blessed; instead, they are cursed.

The subsection shifts from a discussion of blessing to curse. After dealing with blessings and justification, Paul points at the limitation and the problem with the law. Observance of the law does not bring any solution either. He shows the fate of those who rely on the observance of the law; theirs is not a promise but a judgment pronounced by the same law they sought to observe. Turning to verse 10, the first half contains a statement and the second half presents a quotation from the Old Testament.

> **Galatians 3:10 Greek Text:** ὅσοι γὰρ ἐξ ἔργων νόμου εἰσὶν ὑπὸ κατάραν εἰσίν· γέγραπται γὰρ ὅτι Ἐπικατάρατος πᾶς ὃς οὐκ ἐμμένει πᾶσιν τοῖς γεγραμμένοις ἐν τῷ βιβλίῳ τοῦ νόμου τοῦ ποιῆσαι αὐτά.
>
> **Translation:** For as many as are of the works of (the) law are under a curse; for it is written that, "Cursed is everyone who does not abide by all things written in the book of the law, to do them."

Paul uses the conjunction γὰρ to continue his thoughts from the previous verse. He uses the pronoun ὅσοι (as many as) to refer to all those (Jews and Gentiles) who were relying on the observance of the law for salvation. Those who were of the works of the law were the same group of people in Galatians 2:12 identified as the circumcision party. The phrase ἐξ ἔργων νόμου εἰσὶν (are of the works of the law), refers to those who were trying to attain perfection by the flesh (human effort), according to verse 3. In this case, the function of the noun ἔργων has been taken as subjective genitive while the noun νόμου as objective genitive. The verb εἰσίν has been rendered as a static present.

Those who are of the works of the law ὑπὸ κατάραν εἰσίν (are under a curse), but Paul does not specify the nature of the curse here, but he chooses to illustrate his point with an OT quotation. From verses 6–9, Paul argues that those who believe with Abraham are true descendants of Abraham. In verse 10, Paul looks at the contrary situation: those outside the community of faith and blessing. According to Paul, those who rely on the works of the law for justification are under a curse. The phrase ὑπὸ κατάραν features several times in the letter; as Longenecker notes,

> The preposition ὑπὸ is connected with the law, either directly or indirectly, a total of ten times in Galatians. In each occurrence it expresses a situation of being under the authority or power of that which it modifies: "under sin" (3:22), "under the law" (3:23; 4:4, 5, 21; 5:18), "under a pedagogue" (3:25), "under guardians and trustees" (4:2), and "under the basic principles of the world (4:3)." Here in verse 10 it is "under a curse," which Paul associates with the law.[99]

The application of the preposition ὑπὸ to κατάραν confirms that Paul is talking of a curse being like a sin; that is, having an enslaving power. Those under it are powerless and helpless and are certainly in need of liberation.

In the NT times, to be *under* a curse was a serious matter as discussed in the previous chapter. It meant that there was no prosperity, life, and posterity. The Judaizers would also not love to be under a curse or any binding spell. Majority of the people in the NT world feared curses or binding spells because they were thought to be an effective way of bringing misfortune. Gager quotes the renowned first-century Roman author, Pliny the Elder, who remarked on the widespread fear of curse and binding spells: "there is no one who is not afraid of curses and binding spells."[100] Paul in this verse highlights the distinction between what it means to be blessed and cursed. Betz infers, "not being blessed is the same as being cursed. Not belonging to the 'men of faith' is the same as belonging to the 'men of the Torah.'"[101] The curse that affected those that are of the law was the same curse uttered in Galatians 1:8–9 against those who preach a false gospel. Emphatically, Paul shows how serious it is to be outside the community of those who believe the true gospel.

Paul introduces a quotation from Deuteronomy 27:26 using the common introductory formula γέγραπται (it is written), an intensive perfect. The quotation comes from a context where Moses gave final remarks of the law as the Israelites prepared to enter the promised land. In this context, on Mt.

---

99. Longenecker, *Galatians*, 116.
100. Gager, *Curse Tablets*, 220.
101. Betz, *Galatians*, 144.

Ebal, the Levites pronounced twelve curses on those who would disobey the law of God. The Israelites' response with אָמֵן (Amen) affirmed the terms of the covenant which involved Israelites being God's people and Yahweh being their God. Their "Amen" response also confirmed that God would bless them when they obeyed but also curse them when they disobeyed his commands. Deuteronomy 27:26 pronounces a curse to a man who does not uphold the words of the law. This was a self-fulfilling curse upon the act of disobedience to the law; as Ryken et al. comment, "The curse seeks to deprive covenant violators of security, freedom, health, and blessings. Israel under curse will be partially or entirely constrained from enjoying certain blessings, resulting in a debasement of their God-given identity."[102] Likewise, in Deuteronomy 28, blessings were pronounced to whoever obeys the Lord and follows God's commands. In Israel, Yahweh was invoked to execute a curse on the violator,

> No specific penalty is prescribed for each offence mentioned, but Yahweh is called upon in effect to execute his curse on the wrongdoer. By their "Amen" the people as a whole dissociate themselves from such evil actions and those who practice them; the curse thus involves exclusion from the covenant-community.[103]

From the context, blessings follow those who keep the law, but curses pursue those who break the law. This is the context Paul quotes from in Galatians 3:10.

Paul writes, Ἐπικατάρατος πᾶς ὃς οὐκ ἐμμένει (cursed is everyone who does not abide). The truth is that everyone falls into this curse because no one can perfectly abide by God's laws. The nominative adjective Ἐπικατάρατος has been taken as an attributive adjective and the indicative present active verb ἐμμένει functions as a durative present. The adjective πᾶς (everyone) shows the scope of the curse. The curse has affected not just the Jews but also the Gentiles; literally, "everyone" has been affected by the curse. Martyn remarks, "The Law's curse falls both on those who are observant and on those who are not. By pronouncing a curse, the Law establishes a sphere of inimical power that is universal."[104] Therefore, the issue of curse was not a local issue to the

---

102. Ryken et al., *Dictionary of Biblical Imagery*, 187.
103. Bruce, *Epistle to Galatians*, 158.
104. Martyn, *Galatians*, 311.

Jews, rather, it was a universal problem that needed a solution for all. This assertion is consistent with the quotation of Genesis 12. The blessing of Genesis 12 was the solution to a universal problem of sin and curse in Genesis 3.

The curse was labelled on those who did not abide πᾶσιν τοῖς γεγραμμένοις ἐν τῷ βιβλίῳ τοῦ νόμου τοῦ ποιῆσαι αὐτά (by all things written in the book of the law, to do them). The phrase πᾶσιν τοῖς (all things), refers to the contents of what γεγραμμένοις (it is written), ἐν τῷ βιβλίῳ τοῦ νόμου (in the book of the law). The phrase τῷ βιβλίῳ τοῦ νόμου (the book of the law) refers to the Pentateuch as a whole, and not just the specific book of Deuteronomy.

Textual Issues

In Galatians 3:10, Paul quotes Deuteronomy 27:26, but with some textual variations. Also, the quotation seems to contradict the statement in the first part of the verse.

> **MT:** אָר֗וּר אֲשֶׁ֤ר לֹא־יָקִים֙ אֶת־דִּבְרֵ֣י הַתּוֹרָֽה־הַזֹּ֔את לַעֲשׂ֖וֹת אוֹתָ֑ם (Cursed is anyone who does not uphold the words of this law by doing them).

> **LXX:** ἐπικατάρατος πᾶς ἄνθρωπος ὃς οὐκ ἐμμενεῖ ἐν πᾶσιν τοῖς λόγοις τοῦ νόμου τούτου τοῦ ποιῆσαι αὐτούς (Cursed be any person who does not remain in all the words of this law, to do them).

> **UBS:** Ἐπικατάρατος πᾶς ὃς οὐκ ἐμμένει πᾶσιν τοῖς γεγραμμένοις ἐν τῷ βιβλίῳ τοῦ νόμου τοῦ ποιῆσαι αὐτά (Cursed is everyone who does not abide by all things written in the book of the law, to do them).

In this quotation, Paul does not complete the quotation of the verse in MT or LXX. The excerpt omits the last part of the verse: MT- וְאָמַ֥ר כָּל־הָעָ֖ם אָמֵֽן׃ (and all the people shall say, "Amen!"; LXX: καὶ ἐροῦσιν πᾶς ὁ λαός γένοιτο (and all the people shall say, "May it be!"). Several textual issues arise when the extant MT, LXX, and UBS texts are compared. We shall briefly look at the variations under the following subtitles.

MT and LXX

There are notable variations between the MT and LXX. The LXX translators added some emphasis to their text. For instance, the LXX inserts the adjective πᾶς after Ἐπικατάρατος; likewise, the adjective πᾶσιν is inserted after ὃς οὐκ ἐμμενεῖ ἐν. So, the LXX translator(s) must have modified the text; in the first instance, to emphasize that the curse applied to "all"; and in the second instance, to emphasize the totality of the law. The curse is applied to anyone who does not uphold or abide in "all" the words of the law. A safe but unsatisfactory reason for this variation is that the LXX translators may have used a different Vorlage. However, the issue deserves careful consideration. Essential to this study, the text seeks to convey what is evident in the Old Testament, that all people are under curse, because no one can fulfill the words of the law in its entirety.

LXX and UBS Text

The Septuagint and the UBS text also exhibit some variations. First, instead of using the LXX translation πᾶς ἄνθρωπος ὅς (any person who . . .), Paul, in this verse, drops the nominative masculine singular noun ἄνθρωπος (to read πᾶς ὅς – everyone who . . .). The Hebrew text uses the relative pronoun אֲשֶׁר (translated here as: anyone). Specifically, in this aspect, Paul is more inclined to the MT and seems to be translating directly from the MT. It remains interesting that the Septuagint translators introduced the noun ἄνθρωπος in their translation; although it does not alter, in any way, the meaning of the text.

Second, Paul's phrase ὃς οὐκ ἐμμένει πᾶσιν τοῖς γεγραμμένοις ἐν τῷ βιβλίῳ τοῦ νόμου τοῦ (who does not abide by all things written in the book of the law) also differs from the corresponding Septuagint text, ὃς οὐκ ἐμμενεῖ ἐν πᾶσιν τοῖς λόγοις τοῦ νόμου τούτου τοῦ (who does not remain in all the words of this law). Paul drops the preposition ἐν, which is situated before πᾶσιν in the LXX text. Also, instead of copying the LXX (ἐν πᾶσιν τοῖς λόγοις τοῦ νόμου τούτου – in all the words of this law), he writes πᾶσιν τοῖς γεγραμμένοις ἐν τῷ βιβλίῳ τοῦ νόμου τοῦ (by all things written in the book of the law). Unlike the NT text, the LXX phrase τοῖς λόγοις τοῦ νόμου τούτου (the words of this law), is a direct translation of the Hebrew text (אֶת־דִּבְרֵי הַתּוֹרָה־הַזֹּאת) – the words of this law). The apparent modifications demonstrate that Paul might have been quoting the LXX text from memory. These changes emphasize areas of interest to Paul, but the overall meaning of the text remains unchanged.

The Three Texts: MT, LXX, and UBS Text Compared

Further, the Hebrew הַתּוֹרָה־הַזֹּאת (this law), is rendered in LXX using the masculine singular demonstrative pronoun as τούτου; τοῖς λόγοις τοῦ νόμου τούτου (the words of this law). It emphasizes the law of Moses, but in the UBS text, the demonstrative pronouns are dropped. Bruce convincingly argues that Paul in his version generalizes this aspect; "it is not 'this law' (the decalogue) that he has in mind, but the written Torah (cf. Dt. 31:26; Jos. 1:8)."[105] In this case, it might be that Paul made deliberate changes so as to apply the issue of curse to the entire law. I concur with Betz that Paul's quotation is close to LXX; and concerning the textual variations in this verse, the changes identified do not substantially affect the message of the passage as found in the LXX.[106] Having mapped and accounted for the discrepancies of the texts, it remains puzzling how Paul interprets and applies the Deuteronomy text to a different unrelated situation.

How Paul Deals with the Deuteronomy Passage

There is contention among scholars on how Paul interprets Deuteronomy 27:26 and applies it to his situation. At first glance, it looks as if Paul is quoting a passage that does not support his claim. The first part of the verse argues that the curse affects those who rely on observing the law, while on the second part, the same curse is labeled on those who do not continue to do everything written in the book of the law. How should this be construed? Also, the context of the quote has raised many questions. One camp of scholars pointedly argue that Paul's interpretation goes against the original meaning of the passage.[107] The second camp comprises scholars who claim that Paul's interpretation of this OT passage is correct with the exception of genaralizing the curse and the change of the LXX text from the original.[108] The third group of scholars argue that Paul was interested in showing the unfulfillable nature of the Torah; that is, everybody is under the curse of the law because nobody

---

105. Bruce, *Epistle to Galatians*, 158.
106. Betz, *Galatians*, 145.
107. Lührmann, *Galatians*, 61.
108. Betz, *Galatians*, 145.

can keep the whole law. Here, Paul concurs with rabbinical teachers of his time who believed that one couldn't fulfill the entire Torah.[109]

The fourth group claims that Paul is arguing that those who do the Torah are under the curse; meaning, the emphasis is on doing rather than believing. The fifth camp's argument can be summarized as: "not the doing is under the curse, but not the doing of the Torah."[110] Das reconstructs Paul's argument (premise and conclusion) in this verse, "All who rely on the works of the law do not observe and obey all things written in the book of the law."[111] However, none of these solutions given is satisfactory. Biblically, on the one hand, no one is made righteous in the eyes of God by observing the law; on the other hand, by not doing the law, one comes under the curse pronounced by the same law. Hence, according to Paul, doing or not doing the law does not lead to salvation or blessing but a curse. In essence, the law was not intended to bring salvation or eternal life. Therefore, Judaizers should understand the limits of the law in terms of salvation. The law served its era, but the coming of Christ ushered in a new era whereby the law was fulfilled in Christ.

Summary of the Verse

In the previous section, Paul argued that those who are of faith are blessed along with Abraham. Further, he writes that all those who rely on the observance of the law and all those who do not continue to do everything written in it are under a curse. In the ancient world, just like in any other context, blessings were sought after, but curses were feared and shunned. Paul demonstrates that all those who rely on the observance of the law and those who follow it and end up not doing everything in it are all under curse. As much as this referred directly to the Jews, it also applied to the Gentiles who rely on anything other than God. They are also victims of this curse for the law cannot be fulfilled perfectly. Likewise, anyone who seeks to be perfected by it falls short of the expected end result (perfection). Paul's opponents also stood cursed by emphasizing the observance of the law over faith in Jesus. In this verse, Paul highlights the seriousness of the curse and prepares his audience to start thinking about deliverance from the curse's enslavement.

---

109. Betz, 145.
110. Betz, 146.
111. Das, *Paul, Law, and Covenant*, 146.

In God's salvation plan, the cursed state must be remedied for God's people to enjoy divine blessings.

Like in this verse, the next has two parts. The first part contains a statement, and the second part is a quotation from the prophetic section of OT. Again, Paul reiterates that justification only happens by faith and not by observance of the law.

Galatians 3:11 Greek Text: ὅτι δὲ ἐν νόμῳ οὐδεὶς δικαιοῦται παρὰ τῷ θεῷ δῆλον, ὅτι Ὁ δίκαιος ἐκ πίστεως ζήσεται·

Translation: And clearly no one is justified by the law before God; for, "The righteous will live by faith."

In this verse, Paul reiterates what he had earlier pointed out in Galatians 2:16. He begins this verse with the conjunction δὲ (translated as "and"), showing a progression of his thought. The adjective δῆλον translated as "clearly" shows that he is about to make a point clear, without a grain of doubt. He states that no one is justified, before God, by remaining in the law. Simply put, the law cannot justify anyone at all.

Categorically, he writes, ἐν νόμῳ οὐδεὶς δικαιοῦται παρὰ τῷ θεῷ (no one is justified by the law before God). Here he uses the negative οὐδεὶς (no one); in 2:16 he uses οὐ . . . ἄνθρωπος (no . . . man). He uses οὐδεὶς in showing that no one is "justified" (δικαιοῦται, customary present). The νόμῳ functions as a dative of means. Since the law justifies no one, Galatians needed to understand that justification by means of the law was impossible and unachievable. It is just like seeking perfection through human effort in what was Spirit-initiated. It does not work! Martyn notes, "By the power of its universal curse, the Law has established its own realm, and in that cursed realm, no one is being set right. Why not? Doubtless, because the Law has its business to pronounce a curse (v.10); but also because the source of rectification lies elsewhere."[112] This was a direct refutation to the lie that the Judaizers peddled. Paul proves the futility of such an effort. It only brings a curse upon oneself. He makes it clear that the justification he refers to is παρὰ τῷ θεῷ (before God). Justification by the observance of the law, though self-deceiving, can bring satisfaction in the eyes of men but cannot meet God's threshold.

---

112. Martyn, *Galatians*, 312.

The conjunction ὅτι (for) serves as an introductory formula to the quotation from Habakkuk 2:4, a quotation that talks about the righteous. The quotation Ὁ δίκαιος ἐκ πίστεως ζήσεται (The righteous will live by faith) is a Scripture he uses to support his argument. The function of the phrase Ὁ δίκαιος has been taken as an attributive adjective; and the phrase ἐκ πίστεως as a genitive of means. The verb ζήσεται (shall live) functions as a predictive future.

The quotation from Habakkuk 2:4 in its context is part of the Lord's answer to the questions prophet Habakkuk had raised. God's seeming inaction had confounded Habakkuk over rampant evil in Judah. In response, God promised to punish the wickedness of his people using the pagan Babylonians as his instrument of justice. This response sends Habakkuk into a deeper faith crisis; he wonders why God would punish his "righteous" people using a pagan nation. The Lord also promised to judge the iniquity of Babylon at the appointed time. In the meantime, as God executes justice by punishing wickedness, he promises to preserve the righteous (Hab 2:4). The just shall live by faith; "the Israelite who is rightly related to God will live through the trying times by being consistently faithful to God."[113] It is the faith of the righteous that will sustain them through difficult times. Garlington summarizes the response to Habakkuk: "And Yahweh's assurance to the prophet is just that the righteous person will live through the judgment and ultimately be vindicated ('justified') by his faith(fulness)."[114] The faith(fulness) of the righteous is what will ensure they are saved and finally vindicated.

Textual Issues

In Galatians 3:11, Paul quotes Habakkuk 2:4 to distinguish those who rely on the works of the law and those who have faith. When MT and LXX are compared, some changes are evident.

> **MT:** וְצַדִּיק בֶּאֱמוּנָתוֹ יִחְיֶה׃ (But the righteous man shall live by his faithfulness).
>
> **LXX:** ὁ δὲ δίκαιος ἐκ πίστεώς μου ζήσεται (Hab 2:4) (But the just shall live by my faith.)

---

113. Martyn, 312.
114. Garlington, *Exposition of Galatians*, 161.

UBS Text: Ὁ δίκαιος ἐκ πίστεως ζήσεται (The righteous will live by faith)

MT and LXX Variations

The second part of the verse features a quotation from Habakkuk 2:4. The adjective צַדִּיק which is translated as "righteous" can also be rendered as "just." The noun אֱמוּנָה that is translated faithfulness can also be translated as "steadfastness," or "fidelity." Instead of translating the Hebrew text to reflect בֶּאֱמוּנָתוֹ (by *his* faithfulness), the LXX reads ἐκ πίστεώς μου (by *my* faithfulness). The verb אֱמוּנָתוֹ has within it the pronominal suffix, 3rd person masculine singular, "his"; while the verb יִחְיֶה is Qal, imperfect, 3rd person masculine, singular. Although the change of personal pronouns (his/my faith) looks minor, it does make a difference. Paul omits the pronoun, something that some scholars think is an attempt to bring the quotation closer to the Hebrew or deliberately render the reference ambiguous.[115] The LXX text can be read in two ways: "the righteous shall live on the basis of my [God's] faithfulness," or "my righteous one shall live on the basis of faith/faithfulness."[116] Some of the other questions that this raises are: How should the prepositional phrase ἐκ πίστεως be rendered? Is it with the subject or with the verb? Silva persuasively argues that "it would be possible to construe the prepositional phrase (ἐκ πίστεως) with the subject rather than with the verb, which yields the translation 'he who through faith is righteous will live.'"[117] In an attempt to resolve the textual issues and hermeneutics of Paul, Silva makes a key observation:

> Paul was not careless when he quoted the Scriptures. True, the apostle's use of his Bible did not in every respect conform to methods that modern exegesis considers appropriate, but only a superficial reading of his letters could lead one to regard that use as invalid or irresponsible. On the contrary, it is clear that the very categories he used to present his understanding of Christ's work arose from a serious study of the OT that was both meticulous and comprehensive. Guided not only by the text's historical meaning but also by its divine authority, by the need to actualize

---

115. Silva, *Interpreting Galatians*, 165.
116. Longenecker, *Galatians*, 118–19.
117. Silva, *Interpreting Galatians*, 164.

the biblical message, by the power of literary associations, and by a Christological view of redemptive history, Paul succeeded both in setting forth the truth of the gospel and in teaching God's people how Scriptures should be read.[118]

Putting together the seemingly contradicting ideas within the same verse may look obscure and confusing to a modern reader who is armed with all the modern methods of exegesis and interpretation, but the original audience must have understood with clarity Paul messaage concerning the law. The righteous will live not only because of their faith but also because of God's faithfulness.

Summary of the Verse

In order to complement the quotation from the Law section, Paul quotes the prophetic section of the Old Testament (Hab 2:4). In the case of Habakkuk, God promised to deliver and vindicate his faithful people – those who are blessed. The verse looks at the insufficiency of the law to justify one before God. Abraham lived before the law and was justified on account of his faith in God. So, faith in God is all that is necessary for one to be justified. Habakkuk 2:4 is also similarly quoted in Romans 1:17 and Hebrew 10:37. The next verse highlights the dichotomy between law and faith.

> **Galatians 3:12 Greek Text:** ὁ δὲ νόμος οὐκ ἔστιν ἐκ πίστεως, ἀλλ' Ὁ ποιήσας αὐτὰ ζήσεται ἐν αὐτοῖς.
>
> **Translation:** And the law is not of faith, but "he who does these things will live by them."

The verse is introduced by the conjunction δὲ (translated "and"), highlighting continuation from the previous section. The definite article ὁ agrees with the noun νόμος, which functions as a nominative subject. Paul argues that ὁ δὲ νόμος οὐκ ἔστιν ἐκ πίστεως (and the law is not of faith). "The law" refers to the law of Moses or the book of the law (Pentateuch), in verse 11. The noun πίστεως can be taken as a genitive of relationship bringing out the idea that the law and faith are opposites in matters justification. The verb ἔστιν functions as a static present.

---

118. Silva, 167.

Garlington comments, "To say that the law is 'not of faith' is to affirm that the law and faith belong distinctly to different historical realms: the former does not occupy the same turf in the salvation-historical continuum as the latter."[119] Paul argues that the Torah has its own limitations. Longenecker quotes W. Gutbrod on the goal of the Torah, "The aim of the Torah is to show man what he should do and not do in order that, obedient to the Torah, he may have God's approval, righteousness, life, and a share in the future world of God."[120] According to Paul, the law and faith are distinct; "The gospel calls for faith, but the law requires works."[121] Galatians needed to understand this truth to avoid falling prey to the convincing arguments of the Judaizers.

In the second part of the verse, Paul quotes Leviticus 18:5 to further his argument. He introduces the OT quotation with an adversative conjunction ἀλλ' (but) and not with the common introductory formula (γέγραπται). He writes, Ὁ ποιήσας αὐτὰ ζήσεται ἐν αὐτοῖς (He who does these things will live by them). Hays comments, "Paul rejects the Law, not because of an empirical observation that no one can do what it requires but because its claim to give life, explicitly articulated in Lev 18:5 . . . is incompatible with the gospel story, which says that Christ had to die in order to give life to us (3:13–14; cf. 2:21)."[122] There are two aspects in Leviticus 18:5, they are: to "do" (that is, to be obedient or remain faithful) and "live." In this context, life was also brought about by obedience to the Torah. However, this way of salvation became temporary as the Scripture looked forward to the one who was to bring true life apart from the law.

Textual Issues

In Galatians 3:12, Paul quotes Leviticus 18:5 to show how the law mediated life: a man lived based on his obedience.

> **MT:** אֲשֶׁר יַעֲשֶׂה אֹתָם הָאָדָם וָחַי בָּהֶם (by which a man who does them will live).

---

119. Garlington, *Exposition of Galatians*, 162.
120. Longenecker, *Galatians*, 120.
121. Bruce, *Epistle to Galatians*, 162.
122. Hays, *Faith of Jesus Christ*, 179.

LXX: καὶ ποιήσετε αὐτά ἃ ποιήσας ἄνθρωπος ζήσεται ἐν αὐτοῖς (and you shall do them; as for the things a person does, he shall live by them.)

UBS: Ὁ ποιήσας αὐτὰ ζήσεται ἐν αὐτοῖς (he who does these things will live by them.)

The Hebrew text talks of הָאָדָם (the man) and LXX translated this with the noun ἄνθρωπος. Paul renders it using a combination of an article and a substantival participle (Ὁ ποιήσας – the one who does). The weight of the quotation is hinged on the verb, עשׂה and ποιέω, in Hebrew and Greek respectively. Obedience to the Torah was a precondition for life in the Old Testament. At least in this quotation, Paul positively portrays the law as "leading to life," when embraced with obedient attitude.[123] Obedience to the law provided a temporary means through which life was experienced before the fulfillment of the ultimate means in which life is received.

Paul's use of Leviticus 18:5 enhances his argument. The Judaizers failed to keep the law:

> As regards the Judaizers, this principle of life as a result of adherence to the Torah does not apply, because they have failed to observe the law in its overall salvific design, i.e. to lead Israel to Christ (3:23–25). In short, they live in the wrong age and will not relinquish the law in favor of a law-free gospel as procured by the death of the Messiah "on the tree." Herein resides their apostasy.[124]

The Judaizers failed to keep the law in totality, therefore they remained under the curse.

Ineffectiveness of the Law

In Galatians 3 and other portions of Pauline corpus, Paul not only argues positively about the law (Rom 7:12, 16; Gal 3:25; 1 Tim 1:8) but also presents ineffectiveness of the law in matters concerning righteousness (Gal 2:16, 19, 21; 3:2, 5). He esteemed the law and opposed the negative use of the law by the Judaizers. Some have argued that Paul's negative statements concerning the

---

123. Silva, *Interpreting Galatians*, 193.
124. Garlington, *Exposition of Galatians*, 165.

law's ineffectiveness arose out of conflict with Judaism.[125] However, as a former Pharisee, Paul's conversion to Christianity, and reflection of the work of Christ on the cross and its relationship with the law must have radically changed his perception of the law. In the past, some scholars have interpreted Paul's opposition to the law as simply due to its unfulfillable character.[126] Rudolf Bultman, as quoted by McLean, also added to the debate that Paul's rejection of the law was because "striving to observe the law often led to the sinful attitudes of self-reliance and boasting and not self-renunciation."[127] McLean gives a balanced appraisal of these earlier views: "These explanations for Paul's rejection of the law are anthropocentric, each focusing on a particular defect in the human person; either people are unable to keep the law, or they boast when they do keep it, or they have sinned and have thereby rendered the law impotent."[128] The problem with this approach is the fact that it is centered on humankind (human inability) rather than Christ. It also does not relate the law to the work or the era of Christ.

The central reason for Paul's rejection of the law was based on his belief that in Christ, God had inaugurated a new creation in which the law was no longer valid: "The law being designed for sinful humanity, was incompatible with the new age created for a redeemed humanity."[129] McLean notes that in Galatia Paul uses the term "law" in a broader sense to show that the Jews are under the "elemental cosmic powers" (τὰ στοιχεῖα τοῦ κόσμου) along with the Gentiles (Gal 3:19–25; 4:1–3, 8–10).[130] He concludes that "Paul does not argue that Christians *are not obliged* to follow the law, but rather that they *must not* follow the law. They must be freed from the old order in order to live exclusively in the new."[131] Christians belong to a new era that was marked by Christ's coming and fulfillment of the coming of the Spirit. Furthermore, Paul presents curse as something serious:

---

125. Silva, *Interpreting Galatians*, 193.
126. McLean, *Cursed Christ*, 113.
127. McLean, 113.
128. McLean, 114.
129. McLean, 116.
130. McLean, 118.
131. McLean, 119.

Paul's portrayal of this curse is very similar to his understanding of sin. Paul describes sin, not merely as the sum of wrong doings, but as a physical power which is both infectious and dangerous. Sin is an active, menacing, independent power which physically clings to the human flesh as a hostile power (Rom 7:17, 20) and enslaves people (Rom 5:12–14; 6:6–23; 7:14). Hence the phrase "under a curse" (ὑπὸ κατάραν) in Gal 3:10 is synonymous with the analogous phrase *"under* sin" (ὑπὸ ἁμαρτίαν) (Gal 3:22; Rom 3:9).[132]

The curse is a power that is dangerous and needs an effective remedy beyond what the law offers. The era of the law had a beginning and an end, as Schreiner comments:

> The era of law was enacted 430 years after the covenant with Abraham (Gal 3:17); hence, it was given at a certain point in history (Rom 5:13, 20; Gal 3:21). Paul describes the law as a child attendant that held sway over the people until the coming of Christ (Gal 3:24). But now that Christ has come, believers are not under the child attendant (Rom 6:14–15; Gal 3:25), which was designed for a period of infancy until Jesus Christ came and liberated those under the law (Gal 4:1–7).[133]

The coming of Christ thus ushered in a new dispensation.

Summary of the Verse

In this verse, Paul has argues that the law is not based on faith. Later in Galatians 3:19–20, Paul elaborates on the purpose of the law. The law was meant to serve as an interim arrangement until the coming of Jesus Christ. Now that Jesus has come, people should put their faith in him. He is the right remedy to the problem of curse; this is a prelude to what Paul discusses in the next verse.

Galatians 3:13 Greek Text: Χριστὸς ἡμᾶς ἐξηγόρασεν ἐκ τῆς κατάρας τοῦ νόμου γενόμενος ὑπὲρ ἡμῶν κατάρα, ὅτι γέγραπται, Ἐπικατάρατος πᾶς ὁ κρεμάμενος ἐπὶ ξύλου.

---

132. McLean, 123.
133. Schreiner, *Law and Its Fulfillment*, 39.

Translation: Christ redeemed us from the curse of the law by becoming a curse for us, for it is written, "Cursed is everyone who hangs on a tree."

In this verse, like in verse 1, where Paul highlights Christ crucified as the solution to the crisis in Galatia. Paul introduces a new idea of a cursed Christ. The author uses an OT excerpt and applies curses to Christ in a unique way. The noun Χριστὸς in the phrase Χριστὸς ἡμᾶς ἐξηγόρασεν (Christ redeemed us) functions as the nominative subject of the first part of the verse, while the personal pronoun ἡμᾶς functions as an accusative of direct object. It has been debated whether this personal pronoun ἡμᾶς refers to the Jews, Gentiles, or both (the entire human race). Martyn believes that there are good reasons to think that it refers to the whole human race.[134] In this pericope, Paul addresses both Jews and Gentiles as Galatians (3:1); and from verse 10, he establishes beyond doubt the universal nature of the curse by using the adjective πᾶς. However, it is in this verse he articulates the solution to the curse. In the previous verses, Paul established the cause, seriousness of the problem, and its universality. Humanity stands cursed, by God, because of its rebellion against God's way of salvation. The phrase ὑπὸ κατάραν depicts the seriousness, enslavement, and human helplessness in the cursed state.

Christ the Redeemer from the Curse (vv.13–14): Origin of the Verb ἐξαγοράζω

Paul argues that Christ ἡμᾶς ἐξηγόρασεν (redeemed us). The verb ἐξηγόρασεν, indicative is taken as a constative aorist; it shows the redemptive work of Christ as a historical event. The verb ἐξαγοράζω, also used in Galatians 4:5, has some association with the liberation of slaves. In the major periods of Bible history, liberation has been associated with the freedom from slavery in Egypt and Babylon.[135] In the Graeco-Roman world, the redemption of slaves was a common practice.

Is Paul strictly talking about redemption from slavery? Some scholars believe that Paul has a new form of bondage in mind, a bondage to the Torah. Besides, Paul likely has in mind redemption from the bondage of curse. Although this view has not received much scholarly attention, it remains a

---

134. Martyn, *Galatians*, 317.
135. Garlington, *Exposition of Galatians*, 165.

strong possibility. In the second part of the verse, Paul presents Christ as the right remedy to deliver humanity from the curse. Both the Jews and Gentiles were all enslaved under the malignant powers (Gal 2:4; 4:7; 4:24; 5:1; Phil 2:7), and Paul presents Christ as the hope for freedom to those under the curse.

The Curse of the Law

Emphatically, Paul writes, Christ redeemed us ἐκ τῆς κατάρας τοῦ νόμου (from the curse of the law). Here, the noun κατάρας functions as an objective genitive and νόμου as a subjective genitive. The phrase, τῆς κατάρας τοῦ νόμου is an *hapax legomenon* in the entire Bible. According to Garlington, τῆς κατάρας τοῦ νόμου is "the curse which the law brings and which, in this sense, the Law itself is."[136] In light of Galatians 4:8–10, Betz distinguishes that Gentiles who were not under Torah still stood cursed because they were under the "elements of the world."[137] The indisputable fact remains that both Jews and Gentiles were under a curse, and needed a deliverer. Those Galatians who had resorted to the observance of the law as a means of salvation stood cursed. The "curse of the law" that Paul refers to was the curse that was pronounced on the lawbreaker (Deut 27:26); in other words, it was the judgment that the lawbreaker faced. This cursed state meant death; and this was the context in which Paul introduced the idea of the cursed Christ.

Christ as the Means by Which the Curse is Removed

The next part of the verse shows how redemption was effected. Christ redeemed us by γενόμενος ὑπὲρ ἡμῶν κατάρα (becoming a curse for us). The verb γενόμενος ('by becoming') features an instrumental use of the participle. How did Christ become a curse? This question has received different answers among scholars. According to Garlington, "Paul consigns his Messiah to the curse that befell the apostate of Deut 21:23. The Messiah is treated by Israel as an outcast and thus brings the curses of Deuteronomy to a climax; but in the process, he liberates his new people from the 'bondage' which still curses the new Judaizers."[138] Naturally, curses bring death; but the crucified Messiah

---

136. Garlington, 167.
137. Betz, *Galatians*, 148.
138. Garlington, *Exposition of Galatians*, 166.

took upon himself the curse (death) so that in his death, those in him are released from the power of the curse and receive blessings and life.

A Curse for Us

The phrase ὑπὲρ ἡμῶν has been discussed widely by scholars. On this aspect, two issues are can be singled out: first, the pronoun ἡμῶν, and the second, the preposition ὑπὲρ. Paul writes that Christ became a curse ὑπὲρ ἡμῶν (for us). The identity of the personal pronoun ἡμῶν (objective genitive) has been understood to refer either to redeemed Jews alone or inclusive of the Gentiles. Garlington brings in the issue of priority; he believes ἡμῶν refers first to redeemed Israel, "believing Israel is first redeemed in order that this redemption might be extended to the Gentiles."[139] He quotes Donaldson, who similarly argues that Christ redeemed those under the law's curse so that Gentiles share in salvation on equal terms with Jews.[140] According to this view, Christ solved the curse at the level of the Jews so that the Gentiles might not struggle with the same problem. This view, in a way, localizes Christ's work on the cross by giving Jews the benefit of priority over the Gentiles, yet the only prerequisite to belonging to the community of blessing is faith in Christ.

The pronoun ἡμῶν should be interpreted within its context. Paul refers to Christ taking up the curse from those who have put their faith in him, those who have received the Spirit, and those who began in the Spirit and are committed to ending with the Spirit. The pronoun ἡμῶν thus refers to those who are spiritual descendants of Abraham, that is, those who have been redeemed into a community of blessing. This category encompasses redeemed Israel and believing Gentiles without ascribing priority or importance to either party. The central point is that Paul's opponents and anyone outside Christ stand accursed. Their curse remains because they have not trusted in the one who removes the curse. This is true to salvation from sin, Christ died for all, but only those who believe in him receive the benefits of his work on the cross.

The preposition ὑπὲρ (for/on behalf of) in verse 13 is used as a genitive of substitution, showing that Christ took upon himself the curse earmarked for humanity. The highlight here is the aspect of substitution or exchange. Alternatively, a choice of genitive of advantage will render the meaning of

---

139. Garlington, 173.
140. Garlington, 173.

ὑπὲρ as "for," thus bringing the idea of benefit. Similarly, Paul uses this language elsewhere to relate to Christ's work on the cross to the aspect of sin. In 2 Corinthians 5:21, with reference to the action of God the Father, Paul writes, ὑπὲρ ἡμῶν ἁμαρτίαν ἐποίησεν, (made him [Christ] to be sin for/on our behalf). Martyn examined this verse and pointed out two undeniable realities in the early Christian confession: (i) Sin can be transferred from one person to another, and (ii) God transferred our sin to Christ, thus bringing us freedom.[141] These points will be probed further in the subsequent chapters. However, there are other contexts in which Paul uses similar language. In 1 Corinthians 1:30, Χριστῷ Ἰησοῦ, ὃς ἐγενήθη σοφία ἡμῖν ἀπὸ θεοῦ, (Christ Jesus who became to us wisdom from God). Longenecker describes the act as "an exchange curse."[142] In light of these observations, a curse was transferable from one person to another,[143] and so it is logical that Christ took upon himself the curse of humanity.

On the second part of the verse, Paul uses the introductory marker ὅτι γέγραπται (for it is written– the verb γέγραπται functions as an intensive perfect) to introduce a quote from Deuteronomy 21:23. Paul cites Deuteronomy 21:23, a chapter where a series of judgments were pronounced on those who sin by committing abhorrent offenses. It is written that if a man was put to death and his body was hung on a tree because of a capital offense committed, the body should not be left to stay overnight. Instead, it should be buried the same day because anyone hung on a tree was under God's curse.

In this citation, even before hanging, those who sin were already subject to the curse that the law pronounced. The criminal death (hanging on a tree) was in itself a punishment for an offense committed. The practice of hanging criminals was a common ancient practice to deter rebels and serve as a public warning (Num 25:4; Josh 10:26–27; 2 Sam 21:6–9). It was applied to a few selected violations, and underscores the serious nature of a curse. Bruce notes that exposure of a criminal's corpse on a tree or pole was not to be prolonged beyond sunset because it was an affront not only to human decency but to God himself.[144] In the Bible, there were several instances where corpses were

---

141. Martyn, *Galatians*, 319.

142. Longenecker, *Galatians*, 121.

143. Instances of transference of a curse in the Bible and in antiquity are looked at in chapter 4.

144. Bruce, *Epistle to Galatians*, 164.

hanged upon a pole but removed before nightfall. In the case of the five kings of the Amorites, Joshua killed and hung them on trees, and in the evening, their bodies were lowered down (Josh 10:26–27). In the case of Jesus hanging on the cross, Jews were cautious not to leave a corpse hanging on a tree during Sabbath eve (Mark 15:42; John 19:31). Looking at the sociorhetorical intertexture of this verse, Paul reconfigures a criminal hanged on a tree to a crucified Messiah who becomes accursed so that he can be an end to the curse suffered by humanity. Incidentally, Paul finds a parallel verse in the law and reconfigures it on the crucified Lord. Although exceptionally, Jesus was not a criminal, the two thieves crucified with Christ on the cross were facing the consequences of their wrongdoing; but on the cross, Christ was embracing a divine punishment upon himself, so as to liberate those ὑπὸ κατάραν (under a curse).

Textual Issues

In Galatian 3:13, Paul uses an excerpt from Deuteronomy 21:23 to expound his idea of curse and the connection with the hanging on a tree. In its original context, the entire verse refers to a corpse of an offender that should not be allowed to remain hanging on a tree after sunset because it was thought to attract a curse and defilement of the land.

> **MT:** כִּי־קִלְלַת אֱלֹהִים תָּלוּי (for he who is hanged is accursed of God).
>
> **LXX:** ὅτι κεκατηραμένος ὑπὸ θεοῦ πᾶς κρεμάμενος ἐπὶ ξύλου (for anyone hanging on a tree is cursed by God.)
>
> **UBS:** Ἐπικατάρατος πᾶς ὁ κρεμάμενος ἐπὶ ξύλου (Cursed is everyone who hangs on a tree).

MT, LXX, and UBS Variations

Paul in his text omits the phrase ὑπὸ θεοῦ, which is present in LXX, thus emphasizing the idea of cursedness without focusing on the origin of the curse. Although in Rabbinic theology, the "curse of God" was interpreted as blasphemy against God,[145] Paul was not afraid to admit that God the Father cursed Christ. His interest, at this point, was to highlight the absolute nature of the curse. He was not unsure whether the curse came from God: he

---

145. Betz, *Galatians*, 152.

certainly knew it was from God, the Lawgiver. Betz holds a contrary opinion in arguing that "the curse associated with the law came to an end, in that the law itself cursed Christ (cf. 2:19)."[146] In my opinion, God the Father cursed Christ; the law did not curse Christ because Christ never broke the law (Heb 4:15c); he willingly and purposefully took up the curse of humanity in a manner of exchange. Christ did not break the law, nor was he under the "elements of the world"; therefore, he did not need a curse-bearer for himself. He was sinless, thus qualifying as the ultimate curse-bearer for humanity. Also, Martyn wrongly presumes that the law and not God pronounced a curse on the crucified one.[147] Evidently, God gave the law; so, he should not be absolved from being the one who cursed humanity. The law as a means provided the basis for understanding wrongdoing and its repercussions. However, humanity failed to observe all the things written in it and so stood cursed. Christ's role becomes that of a liberator who redeems those under the oppressive power of a curse.

LXX and UBS texts clearly use a different word for curse; LXX reads κεκατηραμένος (participle perfect passive nominative masculine singular) while the UBS reads Ἐπικατάρατος (cursed; nominative masculine singular), but basically, the same idea is communicated. NETS translated the Hebrew name for God אֱלֹהִים as θεοῦ but with no definite article, perhaps hinting that the translator(s) were unsure whether to ascribe the origin of a curse to God or not. Concerning the variations on this verse, Paul may not have been using a different *Vorlage*. Paul likely modified the MT and LXX in a way that advanced his arguments as he sought to formulate a Christology on curse that flowed from the Old Testament to the New Testament.

The idea of a crucified and cursed Christ must have made the Judaizers stumble (1 Cor 1:23; Gal 5:11), as Bruce observes that "the identification of the crucified Jesus with the Messiah was a blasphemous contradiction of terms."[148] Longenecker acknowledges that the Jewish Christians must have been confused on how to understand Christ as both Messiah and cursed, as he says, "The process as to how early Christians came to understand Jesus as both Messiah and accursed may be obscure, but their conclusion is clear:

---

146. Betz, 61.
147. Martyn, *Galatians*, 321.
148. Bruce, *Epistle to Galatians*, 166.

the curse of the cross was 'an exchange curse' wherein Christ became a curse for us."[149] Further, in the depiction of Christ as cursed, Longenecker argues that Paul refers to Jewish pre-Pauline confessional statement.[150] However, in my opinion, the idea of cursed Christ was a Pauline formulation. First, as seen above, the idea of the "curse of God" in Jewish circles was blasphemous; therefore, a Christology around it would have been impossible. Second, it is unlikely that this was a pre-Pauline statement because assuming the south Galatia hypothesis is true, the dating of this letter would be about AD 49, making this letter one of the earliest writings of the New Testament. Arguably, the statement originated from Paul's reflection on Christ's redemptive event on the cross. The crucified and cursed Christ became a solution to the human enigma of sin and curse. Also, a proper Christology would solve deep issues like those faced by the church in Galatia.

Christ's Redemption from the Curse

On the cross, Christ secured human redemption from the curse. Naturally, even in the Bible, curses bring death; but the death of Christ is significant because it terminates the curse on humanity. It liberates those ὑπὸ κατάραν (under a curse). Simply, it is *the* death that reverses the curse upon humanity. The death of Christ is the death that stops human deaths, caused by curses, from running through human generations. It is the death that reverses the curse of Genesis 3. It is the death that stops curses and ushers in blessings, life, and freedom. This atoning death on the cross brings freedom to all those under the law, that is, both Jews and Gentiles (Rom 2:14; Gal 4:5). The singular adjective πᾶς is significantly used to highlight the extent of the curse; the curse has affected every person. Christ's redemption benefits all who put their faith in Christ. As a progression of thought, Paul in verses 10–12 portrayed the law as ineffective in granting righteousness from God, but in verse 13, he offers the right antidote – Jesus Christ. As Martyn remarks, "The greater power arrived then in the person of Christ, who embodied the faith Paul had just contrasted with the Law (v.12)."[151] Jesus Christ brings hope for humanity because of his work on the cross – those who seek to be perfected

---

149. Longenecker, *Galatians*, 122.
150. Longenecker, 123.
151. Martyn, *Galatians*, 217.

by the same Spirit that began the good work of salvation. Bruce quotes M. D. Hooker who raises a good point on how exactly Jesus took the curse for believers to receive blessings:

> Paul does not explain how one who is made a curse becomes a source of blessing; but since it is "in Christ" that the blessing comes, and since it is by being identified with the one true descendant of Abraham that the Jews and Gentiles receive the promise, it is clear that the curse has been annulled – transformed into blessing. This can only be through the resurrection: the judgment of the Law – that Christ was under a curse – has been withdrawn; God himself has vindicated his Son as righteous, and those who have faith in him are reckoned righteous and live.[152]

Christ's resurrection from the dead is a clear mark that the sting of the curse (death) has been defeated. In addition, the resurrection of Christ proved that Christ was indeed the suitable curse-bearer for humanity.

Summary of the Verse

In verses 10 and 12, Paul depicted humanity as under curse, but in verse 13, he conveyed the idea of deliverance through Christ. Thus, Jesus became the solution to the human enigma of the curse. This was achieved by Christ "becoming a curse for us." On the cross, Christ took a substitutionary role to satisfy divine justice, on behalf of humanity that is ὑπὸ κατάραν. Thus, the death of Christ became the death that reversed the curse that enslaved humanity.

Biblically, the curse on humanity was first pronounced in Genesis 3 upon humankind. However, Abraham's covenant with God in Genesis 12 was a foundational divine step in removing the curse and bringing blessings to all nations. From the beginning, even before Abraham (Heb 11:4, 5, 7), God's dealings with humanity in matters concerning salvation were based on faith. Abraham's salvation experience is an example of justification by faith before the issuance of the law on Mount Sinai. The law of Moses was limited in its purpose; it served in the meantime as it awaited the manifestation of the promised "Seed," Jesus Christ (Gal 3:19). Paul uses the book of Genesis as

---

152. Bruce, *Epistle to Galatians*, 168.

his primary text to highlight the antithesis of curse and blessing and demonstrate the scope of God's plan of blessings to the nations. Abraham heard and experienced the gospel of justification by faith and understood that God's redemptive plan encompasses all nations.

Importantly, verse 13 applies Christ's death on the cross for the universal problem of curse affecting humanity. Both Jews and Gentiles were under the curse: The Jews were under the Torah, while the Gentiles were under the same curse because in their pagan ways, they acted in disobedience to God's revelation. According to Romans 2, the Jews were under curse, not because the law itself was a curse but because they had broken the law (Rom 2:27). Gentiles were under curse because they had not acted according to the revelation (the witness) that God had given to them about his will (about what is good to do and what is evil to avoid). The Gentiles had the law written in their hearts and were guided by the Spirit of God through their consciences (Rom 2:14–15). When they acted against their conscience, that was a sin. In Romans 1:18, Paul establishes that the wrath of God is revealed against all the godlessness and wickedness of men who suppress the truth by their wickedness. Therefore, the godlessness of both Jews (despite having the law) and Gentiles equally earns them a curse.

The last verse of this pericope shows the purpose of redemption through Christ. Paul gives twofold reasons why redemption was accomplished: It was so that the blessing of Abraham might come to the Gentiles, and so that we might receive the promise of the Spirit.

> **Galatians 3:14 Greek Text:** ἵνα εἰς τὰ ἔθνη ἡ εὐλογία τοῦ Ἀβραὰμ γένηται ἐν Χριστῷ Ἰησοῦ, ἵνα τὴν ἐπαγγελίαν τοῦ πνεύματος λάβωμεν διὰ τῆς πίστεως.
>
> **Translation:** (He redeemed us) in order that in Jesus Christ, the blessings of Abraham might come to the Gentiles, so that we might receive the promise of the Spirit through faith.

Paul now reverts to his prime text (Gen 12) and the main point introduced in verse 6 by considering Abraham, the man of faith. Having redeemed us, Paul uses two purpose clauses (ἵνα) to present the purpose of the redemption. In verse 12, Paul wrote, Χριστὸς ἡμᾶς ἐξηγόρασεν, the personal pronoun ἡμᾶς as established above refers to those who have faith in Christ. Likewise, in verse 14, the benefit of Christ's redemptive work and deliverance from the enslavement of curse applies to those in ἐν Χριστῷ Ἰησοῦ (in Christ Jesus), taking Christ Jesus as a dative of sphere. The idea of being "in Christ Jesus" is the same spiritual connection that Paul establishes between Abraham and believing Jews and Gentiles.[153] The next phrase that deserves attention is ἡ εὐλογία τοῦ Ἀβραάμ (the blessing of Abraham). The noun ἡ εὐλογία functions as a nominative subject while Ἀβραάμ functions as a genitive of reference. The phrase, "blessing of Abraham" is an expression drawn from Genesis 28:3–4, where Isaac, Abraham's son, blesses his son, Jacob. This could also refer to the blessings of land and descendants given by God to Abraham in Genesis 12:1–3. To further his argument, Paul is primarily interested in the promise of blessing and spiritual descendants of Abraham, the man of faith.

The focus on the Gentiles is reiterated in verse 14. Paul writes, ἵνα εἰς τὰ ἔθνη ἡ εὐλογία τοῦ Ἀβραὰμ γένηται ἐν Χριστῷ (in order that in Christ, the blessings of Abraham might come to the Gentiles). The subjunctive aorist middle verb γένηται (rendered "might come") with the use of ἵνα at the beginning of the verse is a construction that shows purpose. The phrase εἰς τὰ ἔθνη functions as an adverbial accusative of termination with focus on the beneficiary (the Gentiles). The emphasis of Gentile inclusion into the community of blessing under Christ, was a promise that was foretold to Abraham. According to Galatians 3:8, Abraham received this promise of justification of Gentiles by faith. Originally, Abraham was a Gentile; he was a pagan before God called him and made a covenant. What made the difference was that Abraham believed in God, and it was credited to him as righteousness. The same promise of inclusion of Gentiles into the community of faith and blessing was mentioned several times in the New Testament (Luke 24:49; Acts 1:4–5; 2:33; Eph 1:13). The fulfillment of this promise is seen in Jesus; *in* Christ, all nations are liberated from the curse and are ushered into a community of blessing. Now, Gentiles and Jews have become one *in* Christ. Therefore, the first purpose clause ἵνα shows that one of the functions of Christ's redemption was for the blessing of Abraham to come to the Gentiles.

In the second part of verse 14, the second purpose of Christ's redemption is introduced by the purpose clause ἵνα. Paul writes, "Christ redeemed us,"

---

153. Campbell, *Paul*, 82. He argues that the phrase ἐν Χριστῷ is instrumental – that is, "the blessing of Abraham upon the Gentiles is ultimately the work of God's initiative, which has been wrought through the work of Christ."

ἵνα τὴν ἐπαγγελίαν τοῦ πνεύματος λάβωμεν διὰ τῆς πίστεως (so that we might receive the promise of the Spirit through faith). "The promise of the Spirit" (τὴν ἐπαγγελίαν τοῦ πνεύματος) is received διὰ τῆς πίστεως (through faith).

The phrase τὴν ἐπαγγελίαν τοῦ πνεύματος is somehow problematic because it is not explicit in the promises to Abraham in Genesis 12:1–3. In acknowledging that in the Old Testament "the blessing of Abraham" is not associated with "the promise of the Spirit," Calvin sought to bring a solution by suggesting that Paul did not mean to refer to the gift of the Holy Spirit, as in the Acts parallels, but that the phrase should be translated as "the spiritual promise."[154] This suggestion is solution-oriented and does not appreciate the tension that is common in Scripture. In this verse, Paul strongly alludes that the pre-announced gospel to Abraham implicitly contained the promise. Was Abraham aware of the promise of the Spirit?

According to Paul, Abraham received this promise, just as he received the good news beforehand. This is a new revelation that Paul seems to convey. According to Galatians 3:3, Paul reminded believers in Galatia, by using the rhetorical question, that they received the Spirit not by observance of the law but by believing what they heard. Paul seems to assume that Abraham received the promise of the Spirit the moment he believed in God. The gift of the Spirit is ordinarily received when one believes. On the Galatians' situation, Betz comments, "when the Galatians received the Spirit, this could not have been an illegitimate, premature, or deficient event; they must have experienced nothing less than the fulfillment of the solemn promise God had made to Abraham."[155] They received what was long promised to the patriarch. There are numerous references to the promise of the Spirit, though not directly referring to Abraham (Isa 4:2–6; 11:1–2; 32:15; 42:1; 44:3; 61:1; 63:11; Ezek 36:26–27; 37:14; 39:29; Joel 2:28–29). Also, the promise of the Holy Spirit is explicit in the New Testament (Acts 1:4; 2:14–21, 33, 38; Rom 5:5; Eph 1:13). The promise is prominently featured in the letter to the Galatians (3:16–18, 21, 22, 29; 4:23).[156] Therefore, Paul is not making an unsubstantiated statement in the Bible; rather, he intertwines a revealed biblical truth to the idea of Christ's redemption. However, it is worth noting that this verse only

---

154. Torrance, Torrance, and Parker, *Epistles of Paul*, 56.
155. Betz, *Galatians*, 153.
156. Garlington, *Exposition of Galatians*, 170.

introduces the idea of promise that is discussed at length in the subsequent verses and chapters.

During the Pentecost, the coming of the Spirit was then the fulfillment of a promise given by God during the Old Testament, first to Abraham then later to the prophets. The coming of the Spirit, just like the inclusion of the Gentiles into the community of faith and blessing, was not an afterthought but part and parcel of God's plans from the beginning. Consequently, the Gentiles now receive the long-given promise of the Holy Spirit. In Acts 2, the Spirit of God, according to the prophecy of prophet Joel (2:28–29), was poured onto all people, Jews and Gentiles alike, in Christ.

Summary of the Verse

This verse highlights the benefits that believers experience through Christ's redemption and deliverance from the curse. Through Christ's redemption, believers receive the promise of the Spirit; and the blessings of God also flow to the nations. Therefore, the concept of the crucified and cursed Christ obliterates all kinds of enslavement to the law and curse. As a result, believers are ushered into a community of faith and blessing because of Christ's death.

Conclusion of the Exegetical Section

In Galatians 3:1–14, Paul refutes the Judaizers who had infiltrated into the congregations he had established and caused a theological confusion that consequently affected the behavior of the Galatians. The false teachers emphasized the observance of the law of Moses (justification by works) over justification by faith. This message was in stark contrast to what Paul had formerly taught the Galatians. Galatians had begun well by upholding the apostolic message, but sadly, they were now quickly being dragged away by false teachers who put undue emphasis on the law. Apostle Paul, a well-trained Pharisee, understood the law quite well and what it can achieve, "Paul questions whether the law can achieve at all what it promises: to give righteousness, life, Spirit, and blessing. He demonstrates that faith in Christ can bring all of this, whereas on the path of the law one always remains in the world of sin, death, flesh, and curse."[157] Therefore, Galatians needed to reconsider their stand and refocus on the crucified and cursed Christ.

These challenges that the Galatians faced led Paul to put forward a Christology (of the crucified and cursed Christ) that elevated the redemptive work of Christ on the cross. Paul quotes from six OT Scriptures to demonstrate that being justified based on works was a futile process that only leads to curse and death; but being justified by faith leads to blessing and life in Christ. In Galatians 3, Paul responds to the Judaizers and finds an opportunity to set forth the truth about the cursed and crucified Christ. Galatians needed to have faith in the Lord's anointed one, the one ordained by God, to remove sin and curses and provide redemption. In his reference to the patriarch Abraham, Paul sought to show that his gospel (justification by faith) is not a new gospel but a gospel announced to Abraham. This very gospel guaranteed Abraham's justification. Paul also, in his arguments, established from the Scriptures that God's salvation plan has always included the Gentiles from the beginning.

Significantly, Paul establishes the universal problem of curse, and presents the crucified and cursed Christ as the universal remedy of the curse. The solution to the challenges raised by the Judaizers in Galatia can only be remedied by presenting Christ as crucified and cursed. The Gentile believers who were formerly enslaved should not succumb to the Judaizer's message that seeks to bring them again under curse. The Jewish believers who have put their faith in Christ should no longer revert to the law which they had been saved from. A new era has dawned! The coming of Christ has ushered in a new era of salvation, and both the Gentile and Jewish believers should live in this new era. The right message of the crucified and cursed Christ is the message that can redeem and deliver humanity from any form of enslavement. Those who believe in Christ are redeemed, freed, blessed, and receive the promise of the Spirit. In the rest of Galatians 3, Paul continues his discussion on the promise given to Abraham and law given to Moses. He explains the purpose and the era of the law in relation to the coming of Christ.

Up to this point, we have looked at the understanding of curses in the Bible world, and the exegesis of Galatians 3:1–14. The next chapter looks at the comparison and analysis of the findings from chapters 1–3. It achieves

---

157. Lührmann, *Galatians*, 53.

this by looking at the connection between the world of the Bible and the key features of the biblical text. It investigates the removal of curses in the ANE and Graeco-Roman world to establish the background behind Paul's statement of redemption and the cursed Christ. It highlights the contextual information necessary to interpret and appreciate Christ's role as a curse-bearer. A modern hermeneut should seek to understand the original setting of Paul's audience to apply the message appropriately.

CHAPTER 4

Comparison and Analysis

Introduction

Having looked at the understanding curses in the ancient world, and exegetical issues in Galatians 3:1–14, we now turn to the comparison and analysis section. In this chapter, the exegetical findings and gleanings from the ancient world are compared and analyzed in order to rightly appropriate Paul's message in its original context. It has already been ascertained, in chapter two, that Paul used ideas and language drawn from the Jewish and Hellenistic cultures. Also, it has been identified that Paul's discussion of curses matches with the judicial (pleas for justice and revenge) use of curses in the ancient world. Further, it has been noted that the judicial function of curses was the most common application of curses in the ancient world.

The present chapter looks at how ANE and Graeco-Roman contexts enable us to better understand Paul's statement of the crucified and cursed Christ within the context of Galatians 3:13. Part of the questions explored are: How did the Galatians, within their cultural context, understand Christ as the substitutionary victim of divine justice? What was the most probable understanding of Paul's original audience that the crucified Christ became a curse "for us"? It is worth repeating that Paul's idea of the cursed Christ was a concept that was rooted in the understanding, use, practice, and functioning of judicial curses both in the ANE and Graeco-Roman world.

This chapter focuses on the critical examination and comparative analysis of similar concepts and themes both in the Bible and the world of antiquity. Key features and correlations for hermeneutical consideration are identified.

The study demonstrates that Paul based his understanding of the rich cursing and blessing practice in the ancient world, a context where Paul's substitutionary ideas of curses emanated from. Again, the present chapter looks at the satisfaction of God's wrath and divine justice in the death of Christ, something that the law of Moses could not achieve. From these comparative analyses, it will be explicit that removing curses and satisfaction of justice could only be done through the death of an agent (Christ) and not through the law. The crucified Christ was that agent. To arrive at this conclusion, this chapter looks at ways in which curses were removed; but significantly, it highlights Christ's unique role in removing the curse and making the blessing flow to all nations. It underscores how the death of Christ puts believers (both Jews and Gentiles) in the pathway of blessings that God initially intended in Genesis 1–2 and in Genesis 12 through the promise to Abraham. Believers *in Christ* are spiritually connected to the promise given to Abraham.

Moreover, the study demonstrates that the cross of Christ was not a miscarriage of justice but a satisfaction of divine justice. The "sting" of the curse pronounced against humanity in Genesis 3 and the curse of the law, was once and for all removed by the death of Christ on the cross. In addition, by being united with Christ, believers participate in the death and life of Christ and thus live a new life under the guidance of the Holy Spirit. Christ becomes the one through whom many people live and become blessed.

Removal of Curses in the Ancient World

Generally, people in the ancient world, whether Jews or Gentiles, were familiar with ways in which curses and binding spells were removed. The ancients were not just familiar with the widespread nature of curses but were also well versed with ways in which curses could either be prevented or canceled. They believed that one could beforehand prevent being accursed, but they also believed that pronounced curses could be removed or reversed.

In Galatians 3:1–14, especially in verse 10, Paul establishes that all humanity stands accursed. Before prescribing a remedy for the curse, an average person living in the first-century Graeco-Roman society was readily aware of this crisis and options in which *defixiones* and binding spells were negated. In the ancient world, it was first necessary to determine the actual cause of a misfortune experienced by the individual or community to see if it was a result of a curse. Hence, in a situation or occurrence deemed to be a consequence of a curse (like depression, certain diseases, deaths, and so forth), a professional was consulted to diagnose and prescribe the best remedy or countermeasure. The goal of the expert was not just to determine the cause of the misfortune but also "the reestablishment of a harmonious balance; his purpose, the disengagement of malicious powers from their target, the victim; his means, ritual."[1] Unsurprisingly, the services of these curse professionals had a great demand among the ancient people. In verse 10-14, Paul identifies the human problem of the curse, the solution at the cross, and the restoration of blessings through Christ.

In the subsection below, we generally look at possible ways in which curses were reversed in the ancient world (in both Jewish and Graeco-Roman contexts). The background understanding of how curses were negated in the ancient world enables a modern reader of Galatians 3:1–14 to appropriate the message in its initial context before applying it to the modern context. Also, a deeper understanding of how victims of *defixiones* and imprecations were released from the power of curses will hopefully lead a modern reader to a greater appreciation of Paul's Christology regarding the issue of curses. Below is a survey of how curses were undone in the ancient world to help us put into perspective Paul's Christology that presents Christ as the ultimate curse-bearer. The subsection also looks at parallels in the Bible.

Scapegoat Rituals

Hudson B. McLean in his dissertation titled, *The Cursed Christ: Mediterranean Expulsion Rituals and Pauline Soteriology* (1996), extensively explored the scapegoat (apotropaeic) paradigm and rituals in Judaism and Graeco-Roman religion. In Judaism, the idea of the scapegoat in Leviticus 16:20–22 was part of the practices during יוֹם הַכִּפֻּרִים (the day of atonement). On this day, two goats were offered; the first goat was sacrificed for the sins of the people, while the second goat (scapegoat) was sent away to the desert, supposedly carrying away people's iniquities and transgressions. Philo's translation of Leviticus 16:21 equates the "crooked deeds," "rebellions," and "sins" with "curses." "The one on whom the lot fell [that is, the purification goat] was sacrificed to God, the other was sent out into a trackless and desolate wilderness bearing on

---

1. Lührmann, *Galatians*, 275.

its back the curse which had been laid upon the transgressors." (*Spec. Leg.* 1.188[Text 1]). Philo's synonymous understanding of sin and curse is startling but not surprising; because a curse, like a sin, is disastrous and brings condemnation and death. In the same wavelength, McLean remarks on the essence of the ritual, "the scapegoat ritual embodies that once sin had blighted the people, it would work itself out upon them unless a substitute could be provided upon whom it might be discharged."[2] This establishes one of the means by which both sins and curses (sometimes looked at synonymously) were removed in the Jewish religious background.

Likewise, in the Graeco-Roman religion, apotropaeic rituals were widespread. Apotropaeic rituals were conducted as a result of the disruption of social harmony. McLean writes,

> Life in the ancient world was governed by taboos and sacred laws, many of which were connected with issues of purity and defilement, to duties owing to the gods (εὐσέβεια) and to the consequences of neglecting these duties.... In other cases, defilement resulted from willful transgression of a taboo or sacred law. These defilements could manifest themselves in the form of curses.[3]

Thus, the scapegoat became the substitute victim upon which a curse was discharged for the restoration of societal order. People in antiquity, and especially in the first-century Mediterranean world, believed in the possibility of transferring a curse to an innocent victim (scapegoat). McLean further argues, "Apotropaeic rituals take advantage of this very feature of transferability by selecting a victim upon whom this physical infection could be transferred, and by expelling the victim, the curse is also expelled."[4] Thus, it was not a strange idea to Paul's first hearers that a curse could be transferred to an innocent victim. It must have been a mind-boggling idea to Paul's first hearers to read about Christ as a cursed victim. Nevertheless, the concept of transferring a curse to an innocent victim (in this case, Jesus Christ) was an existing cultural resource and foundation upon which Paul built his Christology. If

---

2. McLean, *Cursed Christ*, 77.

3. McLean, 71.

4. McLean, 72. For detailed discussion, consult McLean, pages 72–73, especially on examples of apotropaeic myths/stories in the Graeco-Roman world.

the Galatians were fully persuaded that they were ὑπὸ κατάραν, under a curse, (according to Paul's arguments in Galatians 3:10), then they would deeply grasp the need for an effective substitutionary victim upon whom their curse might be transferred to.

In the Graeco-Roman religion, the substitutionary victims included both animals and human beings (slaves, criminals, the poor).[5] The evil or curse was transferred to the victim with the sole expectation that the accursed party became liberated, at the expense of the victim. Once the "reversal rituals" were performed, the victim was expelled from the community to remove the curse; in some cases, as McLean points out, this was followed by the victim's execution.[6] In this case, the execution (or the death of the substitutionary victim) was critical because it signified the removal of curses from the individual or community. When this idea is related to the death or the idea of a crucified Christ, it strikingly becomes a real possibility that Paul's audience must have understood the death of Christ on the cross in relation to the innocent human apotropaeic victim executed as a substitute. Also, Paul in Galatians 3:1–14 refers to the removal of curses from a community of faith, those *in Abraham* (and by extension, those *in Christ*).

Apotropaic Rituals in the Bible

Apart from the prominent scapegoat reference in Leviticus 16, there are other instances where this phenomenon is attested in the Bible. In 2 Samuel 21:1–10, when there was a famine[7] for three successive years in Israel, King David inquired from the Lord, and it was revealed to him that the famine was due to the murder of the Gibeonites who lived in Israel. In other words, a covenant (בְּרִית) made between the Israelites and Gibeonites (Josh 9:16) had been broken. In order to end the national suffering and to make peace, the Gibeonites demanded that David hands them over seven male descendants from the house of Saul to be killed. David agreed to these terms, and behold, the three-year famine ended! Again, in the story of Jonah's disobedience to God's call to go to Nineveh (Jonah 1:1–10), the sailors interpreted the sea

---

5. McLean, 73.

6. McLean, 75.

7. In the Bible, famine was mostly seen as a curse from the Lord for disobedience to his commands (Deut 28:15–19).

disturbances as a punishment from the gods because of wrongdoing. In order to silence the raging sea, they cast lots to find out the guilty person, and the lot fell on Jonah. Interestingly, Jonah agrees to be cast into the raging storm not just for the sea to calm but also for the safety of the rest of the sailors. In this case, Jonah became a human apotropaeic sacrifice. The idea of one dying for many is also remotely expressed in the New Testament. In response to the Sanhedrin who were plotting against Jesus, the high priest named Caiaphas said, "You do not realize that it is better for you that one man die for the people than that the whole nation perish" (John 11:50 NIV). In the subsequent verses (John 11:51–53), it is clear that the high priest gave this response after a revelation that Jesus would die not only for the Jewish nation but also for the scattered children of God and to make them one. From these few biblical examples, the apotropaeic practice was a cultural feature in the classical, Hellenistic, and Roman periods. McLean observes a similar pattern between the suffering of Christ and ancient scapegoat rituals:

> There are notable parallels between the passion of Christ and the apotropaeic paradigm. Like many expulsion victims, Christ was given a special meal in preparation for his death (the Last Supper), was flagellated and invested with special garments (Mark 15:17; Luke 23:11; Matt 27:28–29). Finally, Jesus was expelled from society by being condemned as a criminal.[8]

Therefore, the apotropaeic ritual was one of the ways in which curses were removed in antiquity. It is possible that Paul's audience understood the crucified and cursed Christ in terms of apotropaeic practices. The scapegoat paradigm also had some historical support from early Christian writers.

Historical Association of the Crucified and Cursed Christ to the Scapegoat Concept

Historically, key figures in the history of the church have associated the cursed Christ with the scapegoat. The *Epistle of Barnabas* (written in either the late first or early second century) draws a direct connection between Christ and scapegoat (Ep. Barn. 7.7–9). The scapegoat bears the curse of humanity. Also, in both the epistles of Barnabas and Tertullian (Adv. Marc. 7.7) the corporate

---

8. McLean, *Cursed Christ*, 105.

sin of the people is described as a curse. In addition, Justin Martyr states that Christ was "sent off as a scapegoat." (*Dial.* 40.4).

Further, Origen of Alexandria explicitly compares Jesus to both human apotropaeic victims and the Levitical scapegoat. He wrote, "The apostles not only dared to show to the Jews from the words of the prophets that Jesus was the prophesied one, but also to the other people that Jesus, who had been recently crucified, voluntarily died for humanity, like those who died for their fatherland, to avert plague, epidemics, famines and shipwreck." (*c. Cels* 1.31.) This is also an interpretation taken by the fifth century Gregory of Nazianzus I.[9] The early writers carefully detailed how the scapegoat foretells the death of Christ. When this understanding of a scapegoat is applied to Christ, it becomes clear from the background information that Christ was the innocent (a cultural/religious prerequisite) substitutionary victim through whom the curse of humanity was removed. The historical support adds weight to the interpretation of the concept of the crucified and cursed Christ, but there were several other ways in which curses were removed.

Sacrifice Rituals

Another way in which curses and binding spells were destroyed in the ancient world was through sacrifice. Some scholarly studies have established that Paul's concept of atonement was based on the idea of sacrifice. It is common knowledge that many of the ancient religions had sacrifice as a common characteristic.

Traditionally, scholarship has argued for the Jewish sacrificial concept as a basis for Paul's portrayal of Christ as cursed.[10] This view is widely supported by many OT references that prominently feature the theme of offering sacrifices. There was a wide range of sacrifices offered in the Old Testament: whole burnt-offering, the sin offering, burnt offering, and thank-offering, among others (Lev 1–5. The number of sacrifices affirms the prevalence of this theme and practice in Judaism.

A careful look at passages in the Old Testament reveals some vital aspects concerning the practice of sacrifice. First, sacrifice in the Jewish religion distinctively involved animals like bulls and lambs, and, in some cases, birds

---

9. McLean, 106.
10. McLean, 22.

like pigeons and turtles. Recognizably, from the Bible (Lev 18:21), human sacrifice was not allowed in the Jewish religion. Second, the animals offered for sacrifice were to be without blemish (Lev 1:3). Third, the one offering the sacrifice presented the animal by laying a single hand upon its head (Lev 1:4). It has been widely construed that the practice of laying hands on the sacrificial victim symbolized the transference of sin. However, McLean thinks otherwise:

> The imposition of a single hand did not imply that the offerer's sins were transferred to the victim but only that a particular animal was offered by a particular person (or group), and that it was being sacrificed for his benefit. Thus, the victim was not a substitutionary victim. No confession of sin was made over a purification victim because the intention was not to transfer sin.[11]

This argument still does not make much difference because the idea of beneficiary still retains the idea of transference; that is, by laying of hand upon the sacrificial victim, the worshipper/beneficiary pointed to the victim that died on the victim's behalf. Therefore, the practice identified the person presenting the sacrifice as the beneficiary. Fourth, the animal was sacrificed (2 Chr 29:22–24). In other words, the sacrificial victim died. This relates closely to the idea of the crucified Christ. The perfect sacrifice died in order to benefit the guilty person. Indisputably, the death of the sacrifice was the essence of the sacrifice; the victim's death became the reason the offerer lived. In short, the sacrificial victim was the lifeline substitution to the offerer. Fifth, the sacrifice was followed by a ritual in which the animal's blood was sprinkled against the sides of the altar (Lev 1:5, 15).

Having looked at the practice of sacrifice in the Old Testament, what was the general purpose of the sacrifices?[12] First, these sacrifices were made as an act of worship to God; some sacrifices appeased God's wrath,[13] some were offered as an honor to God,[14] and so forth. In other words, the sacrifices were offered based on will. Second, the sacrifice benefited the offerer; it could be by cleansing or removing sin, disfavor, a show of gratitude, or even for the

---

11. McLean, 28.
12. The scope and focus of the paper do not warrant a detailed look at each of the sacrifices.
13. *Ant* 7.333; Cf. 2 Sam 24:8–25.
14. Philo, *De Spec Leg* 1.195–97.

well-being of the people.¹⁵ In summary, this religious observance to God was for the good of the offerer and the entire community.

Some scholars argue that Paul had a developed theology of sacrifice with a foundation and overtones from Jewish sacrificial theology in the New Testament.¹⁶ McLean presents a contrary opinion that needs to be recognized at this point. He raises several objections in an attempt to disqualify the sacrificial paradigm as a basis for Paul's atonement theology. He argues:

> First, a sacrificial victim did not "represent" the offerer as his substitute, nor did it bear human sin. Hence, by killing the victim, "human sins" were not "destroyed." Second as we have seen, it was not the animal's death but the application of the blood which accomplished the purification. Finally, the purpose of Jewish sacrifice was not to atone for "human sins," but to purify the temple.¹⁷

This quotation raises several points of discussion which, because of the scope of the study, we have not delved into; overall, McLean's conclusion is agreeable – that Paul might have used the Jewish understanding of sacrifice and transformed or adapted it into something different. The adaptation of OT themes was not a new phenomenon. Many NT passages interpret Christ's death in sacrificial terms. For example, in John 1:29, when John the Baptist saw Jesus, he exclaimed, "Look, the Lamb of God, who takes away the sin of the world" (NIV). Again, the book of Hebrews, drawing from the Jewish sacrificial analogies, presents Jesus not only as a superior high priest but also as a sacrifice (Heb 7:23–8:6; 9:11–14).

The practice of sacrifice was also prevalent in Graeco-Roman religions.¹⁸ In the Greek religion, approved types of domestic animals were offered to Olympian or chthonic (earth) deities; part of the sacrifice was burned at the altar, and part of it was consumed by the worshipper(s).¹⁹ Plato defined piety as "knowledge of sacrificing and praying."²⁰ The Greek offerer of the

---

15. *Ant* 11.137; cf. 11:110; 15.419.
16. McLean, *Cursed Christ*, 41. McLean is referring to James Dunn, *Romans 1–9*, 181.
17. McLean, 42.
18. McLean extensively discusses Greek sacrifices in pages 52–64 in *Cursed Christ*.
19. Aune, *Dictionary of New Testament*, 920.
20. Plato, *Euthyphro*, 14c.

sacrifice entertained some expectations that good things would flow from their pious acts, although with no guarantee.[21] In his study, McLean examined the Olympian sacrifice (a parallel of thank-offering in the Jewish religion) and concludes that it lacks significant comparison with Paul's concept of the cursed Christ. In his finding, he argues that there is no evidence that the victim of the sacrifice became defiled or accursed in the course of the ritual.[22] As a result, McLean disqualifies the sacrificial option as Paul's foremost reference in Galatians 3:1–14:

> The fact that the purification-offering was not cursed or used as a substitutionary victim strongly suggests that Paul is not employing sacrificial concepts in this text. Indeed, there is no text in the Jewish tradition which contains a teaching that a righteous man can vicariously atone for the sin of others by becoming accursed and sinful.[23]

For sure, the idea of a cursed Christ was exclusively Pauline. As noted earlier, in formulating his Christology, Paul must have radically modified some aspects of the Jewish sacrificial theology. McLean has pointed out a major difference between sacrificial ritual and apotropaeic ritual that is of relevance to the current discussion. On the one hand,

> a sacrificial victim of the Jewish or Greek Olympian type was not offered as a substitute for the community, nor did it bear their defilement, curses or sin. Rather, this sacrifice was pure, undefiled offering, and as such, it represents human goodness and purity. It is on account of this fact that it was an appropriate gift for the deity.[24]

On the other hand,

> apotropaeic rituals are the reverse of this. The victim stood as a substitute for an endangered group. By the imposition of society's evil, it became desecrated and therefore unsuitable to be offered to the deity. Such victims did not represent human

---

21. Burkert, *Greek Religion*, 55.
22. McLean, *Cursed Christ*, 64–65.
23. McLean, 51.
24. McLean, 75.

goodness and purity, but human defilement and cursedness. The victim, polluted by the imposition of this impurity, must either be banished or destroyed in order to prevent its return.[25]

These first two options represent a possible understanding of Paul's concept of the crucified and the cursed Christ among his audience.

Herbal Antidotes

In the ancient world, the context where *defixiones* was a predominant reality, people used spells to break other spells. Some *magoi* would prescribe some herbal formula to counter *defixiones*.[26] The procedure to remove a curse or a binding spell using herbal antidote contained some strict instructions and rituals as prescribed by a *magoi*. Gager translates one of the tablets that shows how the effects of binding spells and curses were undone using herbal antidotes:

> If someone should be charmed and cursed, this is how you can release him: cook seven *pedeleonis* plants, without roots, when the moon is decreasing and without using water; cleanse it as well as yourself, as you do this before the threshold outside the house on the first night; burn and fumigate the birthwort plant; then return to the house without looking behind you and you will release him (from it).[27]

The specified plant was thought to have the power of removing the effects of curses and binding spells. However, this remedy covered other categories of curses apart from the judicial and revenge pleas. As such, it is unlikely that Paul equated this antitode with Christ. Paul developed the solution of curses around a person and not on herbal prescription.

Wearing Amulets, and the Stone of Hermes

To counter binding spells, ancient people used counterspells in the form of amulets to wade off spells. This was a preventive measure against any potential curses. The Greek word for amulets, "*periapta*" and "*periammata*," means

---

25. McLean, 75.
26. Gager, *Curse Tablets*, 237.
27. Gager, 237, 239.

"things tied around." Amulets were wrapped on some parts of the body, usually the neck, an arm, or a leg. "These objects might be simple pieces of string; colorful embroidered bands; engraved stones and rings; or strips of metal, papyrus, and other materials inscribed with special formulas, then rolled up or folded and carried about on a string, in a pouch or in tubular containers."[28] It was believed to guarantee protection to the wearer from any potential threat, whether known or unknown enemies. The use of plant amulets is attested in one of the prayers probably from the first millennium, addressed to god Marduk in Akkadian which Kitz has translated as follows, "[67]May the plant-amulet set around my neck not let any evil approach me. [68]May it drive away any evil curse, any utterance portending unfavorable things."[29] The use of a countermeasure like amulets mainly applied to *defixiones* and binding spells that served self-interests (like protection against a personal rival) and not judicial curses. In the ANE, the most familiar category of these amulets was the Lamaštu amulets used to ward off malicious activities of the demoness Lamaštu.[30] Due to the fear of curses or being cursed, some ancient people resorted to putting on amulets for protective purposes.

The purpose of wearing amulets was "to shield the bearer from all forms of harm and danger. By extension, that is by virtue of their ability to ward off unforeseen disasters, some also guaranteed success and prosperity."[31] In a world where *defixiones* and magic were used in every sphere of life, people took countermeasures to guarantee their safety from real or imagined foes.

Apart from wearing amulets, *defixiones* were also countered by wearing some special stones. It was believed that putting on the stone of Hermes would ward off life-threatening spells and release the victim or client from all forms of curses.[32] As much as Paul's audience may not have comprehended the work of Christ through this ancient means, nevertheless, they were for sure aware of this means. Paul knew that the problem of curses was something serious and internal and therefore needed a divine solution.

---

28. Gager, 219. Amulets were also written to protect mothers and their unborn children from malignant and abortifacient demons. These were used to wade off, banish, contain, drive off, and chase away demons. Kotansky, *Dictionary of New Testament*, 271–73.

29. Kitz, *Cursed Are You!*, 330.

30. Kitz, 286.

31. Gager, *Curse Tablets*, 220.

32. Gager, 239.

Cursing Curses and Exorcism

In the ancient Near Eastern societies, especially among the Akkadian, the curse specialist known as *āšipu* helped remove the effects of curses from those who were cursed. He used curses to counter curses. As a specialist, "he loosened, removed, dismissed and unbound imprecations. He cursed curses with curses. He also dealt with the surrounding of the victim. He traveled to private residences and directed the performance of rites for and by the sufferer."[33] He was thought to be effective in arresting effects of curses that got manifested in the form of illnesses, disease, and other misfortunes. Based on their examination, the specialist might prescribe the use of protective plaques that were hung on the doorways and gateways.[34] Apart from cursing former curses, some other curses were returned to the sender or source as attested in the Akkadian tablet as follows, "May he (Enki) return the conditional curse to its former place (of origin)! May he abolish the conditional curse from that man!"[35] It was believed that when the previous curse was cursed, the victim regained blessings.

Removing curses by exorcism was also a common ancient practice. In the Mesopotamia, exorcism was done to remove the harm caused by a witch. As Graf shows, "the rite will lead to the healing of illness, but will also repair the social failures and lack of success caused by the intervention of a demon, triggered by a sorcerer or witch."[36] This assumption of witches and sorcerers behind every misfortune informed the ancient thinking, as Graf continues to say, ". . . explanations attributing odd behavior to a binding spell implied that other people, sorcerers and demons, were responsible, and an exorcism could reestablish the former social position."[37] As can be observed, this means of removing curses or misfortunes sought to cancel the harmful work of witches and sorcerers. Paul did not develop his Christology based on verbal pronouncements or magical use of the name of Jesus to remove curses but based on the person and the death of Jesus Christ.

---

33. Kitz, *Cursed Are You!*, 3.
34. Kitz, 3.
35. Kitz, 333.
36. Graf, *Magic in Ancient World*, 172.
37. Graf, 166–67.

It has been proved from a lead tablet dated in the sixth century AD that Christians invoked the name of Jesus to exorcise and release people from the oppressive powers of curses.[38] It is unclear if this practice was influenced by Galatians 3:13 or surrounding cultural-religious practices. We may conclude that people at this time must have interpreted Christ's work on the cross as having power over *defixiones* and any other form of magic.

Confession

As acknowledged before, wrongdoing was a basis of one becoming guilty and thus incurring a judicial curse. Many judicial curse tablets inscribed on tombs warned plunderers of a curse on the occasion that the grave was disturbed. Judicial curses inscribed on the grave were activated the moment one destroyed or plundered the tomb. However, some inscriptions like the Nerab I tablet promises cessation of a curse and beginning of blessings should the plunderer experience "a change of heart" and take care of the tomb and inscription.[39] It was believed that the effects of curses would stop should the offender acknowledge his wrongdoing.[40] Therefore, confession offered ancient people some hope of release from maledictions.

From this survey of ways in which curses were removed in the ancient world, as modern readers of Paul's letter, we can make a few informed conclusions concerning the background framework of Paul's audience. First, the ancient people in the classical, Jewish, Hellenistic, and Roman world believed that curses can be prevented beforehand or could be removed once uttered. They were cognizant of the devastating effects of curses, so they would promptly seek an effective solution to prevent or remove them. Where necessary, they would consult curse experts to diagnose and prescribe the best remedy and/or rituals. When this was done accordingly and the curse annulled, they expected that blessings and social harmony would be restored.

Second, the several ways in which curses were removed attests to the fact that there were analogies that could be compared to the example of Christ. Within the ancient cultures, there were some aspects of transferability of curse and sin, sacrifice and scapegoat concepts, the innocence of the substitutionary

---

38. Gager, *Curse Tablets*, 224–25.
39. Crawford, *Blessing and Curse*, 115.
40. Kitz, *Cursed Are You!*, 340–41.

victim (whether human or animal), the death of the cursed victim, and the eventual flow of life and blessings to the beneficiary. These similar concepts in the Bible and the ancient world context form the bedrock on which Paul based his Christology. Of course, he did not borrow everything from the ancient background, but he transformed the ancient understanding of removing curses by putting Christ at the center and as the ultimate solution for the curse. One lingering question that still begs for an answer is: If the ancient people had a variety of ways of undoing maledictions, why were they still fearful of curses?

The Persistent Enigma of Curses in the Ancient World

Despite having several possible ways of dealing with curses, people in the ancient world still lived in fear of curses. Both in private and public life, every happening and occurrence continued to be interpreted through the lenses of curse and blessing. Is it that the prevalence of fear of curse among the ancient people was a confirmation that the counter-measures for *defixiones* were ineffective? One fact is explicit, the fear of curse in the ancient world proves that the curse problem remained unsolved despite having a variety of ways of dealing with curses. The perpetual fear of imprecations also prominently highlights the helplessness of people to effectively deal with the problem of curses once and for all.

Shortcomings and ineffectiveness characterized the options that the ancient cultures offered in remedying a curse. The curse countermeasures only managed the problem and did not offer an ultimate solution. For example, the Akkadian *māmīt pašāru* (curse-releasing) ritual had a limited dual role: "It principally bans active, extant evils. These malevolences are enticed to go elsewhere, down into the river, up in the sky like smoke, down into the earth, or they are destroyed outright and burned."[41] Notably, the maledictions were not removed and obliterated, instead they were only "enticed to go elsewhere," and could perhaps inevitably return. In one way, the solutions offered by the ancient cultures toward curses (like banning or using herbal solutions and

---

41. Kitz, 331.

amulets) indicate that the ancients failed and were limited in their ability to provide an effective solution to the enigma of curses.

Again, through the countermeasures against curses, it can be deduced that the ancients looked at curse as something external that only requires external measures. In another way, speculatively, the fact that the powers of curses were "enticed to go elsewhere" might be a hint that the ancient people profoundly realized their limitation as human beings to deal with the problem of curse decisively. Simply, curses were beyond their powers; they must have understood that powers behind curses were beyond the human sphere, and so, it would only take a "higher power" to remove them. It was in such a context that Paul wrote to the church in Galatia addressing emerging concerns from the Judaizers. He develops a Christology that highlights the real panacea to the human enigma of curse. He presents Christ as *the* solution to the problem of curses. The answer Paul gave concerning curses was not that of amulets and herbs but of a divine Person. Christ became a curse so that in his death, he could remove death and its powers.

The Uniqueness and Sufficiency of Christ's Death as a Remover of All Curses

In Galatians 3:1–14, Paul developed a Christology as the panacea for the phenomenon of curse. He presented the crucified Christ not only as a curse-bearer but also as the ultimate curse-breaker. Paul's solution is a person, Jesus Christ. The use of amulets, animal sacrifices, and rituals to break curses in the ancient world fell short of God's ordained way in which curses were broken. The provision of God's ordained means was necessary because God understood the human inability to deal with sin and curses: "Sinners cannot put themselves right with God, yet justice requires the 'satisfaction' of God's demands. The death of Jesus, freely offered as a gift to God the Father, outweighs in value and therefore compensates for all the sins of humanity."[42] As seen earlier, the ancient world had plenty of ways in which curses were annulled, but Christ's death on the cross became the effective solution to the human enigma of curses. Curses cannot be broken by rituals or animal sacrifices but by a person, Jesus Christ. Paul presents Christ's death as effective

---

42. Travis, *Christ and Judgement*, 181–82.

in dealing with the human curse because he represented all sinners, and by his death, he destroyed the power of the curse.

Essentially, (judicial) curses in the Bible emanate from willful disobedience of or rebellion against God's law; obedience brings blessings while disobedience brings ruin (Lev 26; Deut 26–30). When God's people sinned, God judged them, whether as individuals or as nations (Gen 18:25; Exod 20:5–6; Ps 96:13). In the case of the Old Testament, no one stood before God to rescue humanity. The animal sacrificed functioned as a temporary means as it waited for the ultimate sacrifice: Jesus Christ. In some instances, patriarchs and prophets would stand before God and the people to plead for mercy (Gen 18:27–33; Deut 9:25–29).

The same truth is vivid in the New Testament; wickedness and suppressing of truth brings God's wrath (Rom 1:18; 12:19; Eph 5:6; Col 3:6). God provided a way through Jesus Christ, a way in which people can live and be blessed. In 1 Thessalonians 1:9–10, Jesus is referred to as the one who rescues believers from the eschatological wrath of God. In the next section, we look at the concept of the crucified and cursed Christ, the one specially ordained by God to take away the human curse.

The Concept of Crucified Christ

In Galatians 3:1, Paul discusses the death of Christ in addressing the problem in Galatia. Intentionally, he highlights the centrality of the death of Christ in his kerygma and theology; that is, before introducing the issue of curse and the cursed Christ. Initially, Paul had preached to the Galatians a gospel that exalted the person and the work of Jesus Christ on the cross; but all that suddenly changed! The Galatians were now quickly deserting the one who called them and were drifting from the truth to a different gospel that was no gospel at all (Gal 1:6–7). They were being lured into a different gospel that was "cross-less"; a belief that was contrary to the apostolic tradition. To put it simply, the genesis of the problem in Galatia stemmed from preaching a false gospel that did not exalt the crucified Christ, hence led to a cursed state.

The death of Christ carries much significance in Paul's thought. Picking the discussion from the incarnation of Jesus, Christ took a human form and became "like us"; He identified himself with humanity, and so he was able to represent humanity in every way, yet retaining his deity (Phil 2:.6–7). When Jesus Christ was crucified, the Bible is clear that believers were equally crucified with him, in a spiritual sense. This aspect of believers' union with Christ is evident in texts like Galatians 2:20, "I have been crucified with Christ and I no longer live, but Christ lives in me. The life I now live in the body, I live by faith in the Son of God, who loved me and gave himself for me" (NIV). Further in Galatians 3:26–28, Paul writes, "So in Christ Jesus you are all children of God through faith, for all of you who were baptized into Christ have clothed yourselves with Christ. There is neither Jew nor Gentile, slave nor free, male nor female, for you are all one in Christ Jesus." From these verses, believers are closely identified with the experience of Christ. For instance, when Christ died and rose, believers equally died and were resurrected *in Christ*. The underlying principle that guarantees this union is being *in Christ*. Having believed in Jesus Christ for salvation, believers are ushered into a deep spiritual union with their Master. Therefore, when Paul argues that Christ became a curse "for us," he anchors his argument on the principle of believers' union with Christ, so that believers, through this identification, have a share in the life of Jesus Christ. The death of Christ is unique because it benefits all those who believe or are spiritually united with him. It is a substitutionary death with a universal application, potentially benefiting all those under the curse.[43]

In Galatians 3:10, Paul categorically argues that all humanity is under a curse. The judicial curse has affected all because, in one way or another, all have broken God's laws and covenant. The accursed state of humanity is hopeless unless external and divine help is provided. An effective solution to this enigma needs more than a mechanical or ritualistic solution. Rather, it needs a solution that considers the seriousness of curses and human inadequacy to offer an effective solution.

As demonstrated, Paul's audience was much aware of the belief and practice of blessing and cursing. They lived in a society where curses were feared and understood that the ultimate penalty and goal of a curse was death. In short, blessings bring life, but curses take away life. Therefore, when Paul taught that the crucified Christ became a curse for us, his audience must have initially found his Christology surprisingly deep. Then upon reflecting on Paul's arguments, they must have, within their cultural background, deeply related the death of the cursed Christ with the prevailing apotropaeic rituals,

---

43. For reference of the theme of union with Christ in Paul's letters, see Campbell, *Paul*.

substitutionary death, the transference of the curse concept, the innocence of a sacrificial victim, and removal of curses, among other analogous concepts in their world.

The death of Christ on the cross is the death that terminates other deaths caused by the curse. The death of Christ took away the "sting" that was due to lawbreakers or covenant breakers. Therefore, those who have been united with Christ in his death are delivered from the curse on the basis that the death of Christ satisfied God's justice. Bruce comments, "The curse of Dt. 27:26 was pronounced at the end of a covenant-renewal ceremony and had special reference therefore to the covenant-breaker. Christ accordingly underwent the penalty prescribed for the covenant-breaker."[44] He bore upon himself the curse of all lawbreakers so that through his death, the cursed can be delivered and the blessings of God flow to all nations. Thus, the solution of curses that God offers through Christ is unique in the sense that it not only solves the problem of curses but also ensures that God's blessings (promised to Abraham) flow to the Gentiles. Jesus, and not Abraham, becomes the new linkage to the community of blessings, that is, a community of those who are in Christ, a community that upholds the true gospel of justification by faith.

The scope of Christ's redemptive work and solution to curses also reaches wide to the cursed state of the earth. Christ is the solution to the curse in reference to the law and the cosmic curse of Genesis 3. In Genesis 3:17–18, the ground was cursed due to man's transgression. Kitz raises a crucial point while discussing "difficult life" as one of the harms against a curse victim.[45] She writes, "The lightest hoped-for injury in a malediction is a strenuous, disappointing existence. Impoverishment as indicated by insufficiency of food and/or difficulty in maintaining life on even the most fundamental level."[46] Other catastrophic events that make life difficult and bring painful deaths include floods, droughts, and plagues, among others. In an interesting observation, she notes that "these types of curses do not directly target a person. They target rather the environment around the person, principally the arable soil on which human beings depend for basic sustenance."[47] Kitz

---

44. Bruce, *Epistle to Galatians*, 164.
45. Kitz, *Cursed Are You!*, 201.
46. Kitz, 201–2.
47. Kitz, 202.

illustrates this curse-injury with Yahweh's curse in Genesis 3:17, where the ground is cursed, and life is made difficult for humanity.

In Genesis 3:17–18, a curse was pronounced on the land, אֲרוּרָה הָאֲדָמָה (cursed is the ground). Due to Adam's sin, the ground was cursed to produce thorns and thistles; and work on the ground would be toilsome. Biblically, on the one hand, the land that God blesses is productive and well-watered (Gen 2:8–14; Deut 33:13–16); on the other hand, the land that is cursed is unproductive and desolate (Gen 3:18). Thus, the curse on the ground made it difficult for humankind to work and live on it.

The death of Christ on the cross provided a solution to the curse that was pronounced in Genesis 3 due to Adam's disobedience. It provided a solution to the "sting of difficulty." In Romans 8:18–23, Paul points out that ματαιότητι ἡ κτίσις ὑπετάγη (creation was subjected to frustration/emptiness). In this context, he discusses the subjection of the whole creation to frustration, the present fallen state of creation, and the eschatological liberation of creation from decay and frustrations it was subjected to. Paul alludes to and gives a commentary of Genesis 3:17–19 and 5:29 without quoting them directly. He notes that Adam's transgression brought about death and "bondage to decay" (Rom 5:12–14), and affected not only humanity but also all material creation until the present time.[48] As a judgment to man's sin, God the righteous judge cursed his creation (Gen 3:17), hence the present frustration.

Clearly, according to Paul, both Christians and creation presently experience suffering that emanated from the fall of man in Genesis 3. Paul writes in Romans 8:22 that πᾶσα ἡ κτίσις (the whole creation) has been groaning from the fall of man, as in the pains of childbirth right up to the present time. The adjective πᾶσα stresses the scope of the creation, and many scholars have interpreted the phrase πᾶσα ἡ κτίσις as encompassing the entire universe – including human beings, animals, and plants.[49] However, the subjection was not without hope. Moo rightly argues that the hope mentioned in Romans 8:20 refers to the *protoevangelium* (literally, "a first gospel") promise in Genesis 3:15.[50] He comments: "The creation, then, though subjected to frustration

---

48. Fitzmyer, *Romans*, 505.

49. Moo, *Epistle to Romans*, 513.

50. Walton, *Genesis*, 235–36. Walton is of the contrary opinion, arguing that there is no sufficient basis to support the messianic interpretation of Genesis 3:15. Although, he also

as a result of human sin, has never been without hope; for the very decree of subjection was given in the context of hope."[51] The Scripture looked forward to the promise of God of the one who will deal with the consequences of the fall of man, including curses.

To Paul, this was not the whole story; the whole creation longs for an eschatological transformation that is yet to be revealed. According to Romans 8:19, the creation awaits with ἀποκαραδοκία (eager expectation) for the children of God to be revealed; a time when creation will also be liberated. In Romans 8:23, Paul introduces the idea of redemption (ἀπολύτρωσις) within the context of creation, showing that (Christ's) redemption goes beyond God's salvific plan for human beings. Redemption is also discussed in the context of curses in Galatians 3:13. Fitzmyer discusses the extent of this redemption although, in this context, the name of Jesus Christ is not mentioned:

> It [redemption] is no longer considered from an anthropological point of view; it is now recast in cosmic terms. Human bodies that are said to await such redemption (8:23) are merely part of the entire material creation, which is itself groaning in travail until such redemption occurs. For the Christ-event is expected to affect not only human beings, but all material or physical creation as well. And yet, it is strange that in all of these verses (18–23) there is no mention of Christ Jesus.[52]

In summary, Jesus Christ is presented as the hope of liberation of humanity and the rest of creation.

The Concept of the Cursed Christ

The idea of the cursed Christ is a unique feature of Pauline Christology. Christ, the blameless Lamb of God, took upon himself the curse labeled against humanity because of disobedience to God. He took upon himself the penalty for the curse. He suffered a death that was supposed to be suffered by wrong-doers. His death was, therefore, substitutionary so that those who trust in him share in his life. On the cross, while paying the penalty of

---

acknowledges that such a stand does not deny Christ's victory over Satan or water down the messianic interpretation of the OT theology.

51. Moo, *Epistle to Romans*, 516.
52. Fitzmyer, *Romans*, 505–6.

humanity's curse, Christ was a representative figure.[53] Calvin wrote: "This is our acquittal: the guilt which we were liable for punishment was transferred to the head of the son of God."[54] The punishment to which we were liable was inflicted on Jesus Christ, the just and innocent one. He took away the curse, which was God's judgment upon man. Also, Travis boldly highlights Christ's substitutionary role on the cross:

> ... he entered into and bore on our behalf the destructive consequences of sin. Standing where we stand, he bore the consequences of our alienation from God. In so doing, he absorbed and exhausted them, so that they should not fall on us. It is both true and important to say that he "was judged in our place" – that he experienced divine judgment on sin in the sense that he endured the God-ordained consequences of human sinfulness.[55]

He accomplished all this for the benefit of humanity.

As a result, those who put their faith in Christ are rescued from the jaws of death. A corresponding verse to Paul's thought pattern is highlighted in 2 Corinthians 5:21: "God made him who had no sin to be sin for us, so that in him we might become the righteousness of God". McLean quotes J. F. Collange, who rightly argues that "Christ was made sin in the sense that he personified all the sins of man, he is the curse incarnate."[56] Paul argues that the sinless Christ was made to be sin, for the purpose that through this identification, believers might gain his righteousness. It is true that gaining this righteousness only comes through the believer's union with Christ; by being united with Christ, believers do not "infect" Christ with the sinful nature, but instead, Christ confers on them his righteousness. Christ identified himself with the accursed humanity through his incarnation, although he was without sin and curse. He became like the kinsman redeemer to be able to redeem his own from the curse. He took upon himself the penalty of the lawbreaker and became the sacrificial victim that dies to stop other subsequent deaths. He brought the power of the curse to an end and brought blessings to God's entire creation.

---

53. See Hays, *Faith of Jesus Christ*, 176.
54. Calvin, Lane, and Osborne, *Institutes of Christian Religion*, 2.16.5.
55. Travis, *Christ and Judgement*, 199.
56. McLean, *Cursed Christ*, 110.

Significant Themes on Curse and Blessing in Galatians 3:1–14

In this subsection, we look at some apparent themes in Galatians 3:1–14 that can be better understood in light of the ancient world's social, religious, and cultural practices. Some themes must have stood out prominently to Paul's audience in the discussion of blessing and curse in Galatians 3:1–14.

"Who Has Bewitched You?" (Gal 3:1)

In Galatians 1:8–9, with the use of a strong language, Paul issues anathema (a curse) to those preaching a gospel contrary to the apostolic tradition. To be accursed or being an object of anathema means "to be delivered up to the judicial wrath of God."[57] The curse he pronounces, and the strong language he uses demonstrates the seriousness of the issue at hand; for matters concerning salvation are matters of life and death. Also, in a context where there was the great fear of curses, Paul's statement in 3:1 ("Who has bewitched you?") cannot be taken without a second thought. Just as it has been pointed out in chapter 3 of this study, Paul did not strictly mean to say that the Galatians were under some sort of power of a sorcerer or magician. In fact, the Judaizers were not known to be sorcerers or magicians. Paul, while talking to an audience that understood curses and witchcraft, used chastising language against the Galatians to point out that they were indeed behaving oddly as those under the powers of a spell. Paul's audience certainly knew what that meant. A person under the power of a spell was certainly confused, behaved strangely, and was out of mind. The Galatians began their journey of faith on a right footing with the life-giving gospel but had now resorted to a futile quest.

The Phrase ὑπὸ κατάραν (Gal 3:10)

Paul's depiction of humanity as "under a curse" in Galatians 3:10 must have deeply provoked his audience. To be under a curse in the ancient world was not a simple matter since it brought a crisis both at personal and communal levels. Moreover, a person under a curse was equally under divine judgment. The most outstanding aspect of curses is that they brought death and not life. Therefore, Paul's audience must have read this verse with intensity and

---

57. Hawthorne and Martin, *Dictionary of Paul*, 200.

seriousness that may escape many modern readers. If indeed they were under a curse, then they urgently needed help.

Blessing (Gal 3:14)

In a world where the concept and practice of blessing were prevalent, Paul's audience must have attached a greater value to the idea of blessing. In the ancient world, a blessing was thought to bring life, health, wealth, and harmony to individual and communal spheres. The content of blessing was all-encompassing prosperity, including success in crop farming and animal keeping, begetting of children to sustain a lineage, health, and generally, good life.[58] More so, ancient people understood blessings in the context of curses; they understood life in the context of deaths occasioned by curses. Therefore, Christ's promise of bringing blessings to the nations echoed loudly against such a backdrop.

Redemption (Gal 3:13)

In discussing the work of Christ on the cross, Paul mentions the idea of ἀπολύτρωσις (redemption). In antiquity, the term was loaded with meaning because, in the Greek *agora* (marketplace), redemption applied to the manumission of slaves. The term "applied to the process whereby something or someone is rescued from forfeiture by the payment of a price."[59] The ancient people understood that a ransom had to be paid for redemption to take place. For instance, in the Old Testament, when a dangerous bull killed a man or a woman, the owner was to be stoned to death as per the law. However, he could redeem his life by paying whatever penalty was demanded (Exod 21:28–32; the same applied to the redemption of firstborn males – Num 18:15–16). According to Paul's writings, the blood of Christ was the ultimate price for redemption (Rom 3:24–25; Eph 1:7). Therefore, through Christ, believers are redeemed (Col 1:14), from wickedness (1 Tim 2:6; Titus 2:14), and the curse of the law (Gal 3:13).

When the idea of redemption is looked at in the context of curses, it becomes clear that those accursed by God need redemption. They need to be unbound and released from the malicious powers of curses. Notably,

---

58. Grüneberg, *Abraham*, 100.
59. Williams, *Paul's Metaphors*, 122.

the purpose of the Akkadian *māmīt pašāru* (curse-releasing) ritual was "to 'loosen' the threatened harm in conditional imprecations. It was proactive and preventative. It 'untied' annoying 'bonds.' Banning was also a feature. For once the provisional malediction is 'loosened,' its extant but latent injury must be sent on its way – far away, never to return."[60] Christ's redemption and freedom are thus necessary to unbind and set free those that are ὑπὸ κατάραν.

These few identified themes in Galatians 1:1–14 must have resonated well and evoked deeper reflection among Paul's audience who lived in the first-century context, where magic, cursing, and blessing practices were widespread. Therefore, it is prudent for a modern reader to pay close attention to the meanings of these terms within their original setting to appreciate the impact they had on the first hearers before providing a modern application.

Redemption required a ransom to be paid. On the cross, Christ paid what was due for human redemption. The primary point is that the price for humanity's release has been paid; as to who received the payment remains a non-issue because it overstretches Paul's image. In referring to Christ's redemption, Martyn comments, "If one says that the deliverance involves the paying of a price, then to ask for the identity of the person or power to whom the price is paid is, as regards to Paul's intentions, to press the image too far."[61] The main point in Paul's analogy is that Christ's sacrifice settled God's anger and justice against humanity. Christ's work on the cross decisively dealt with sin and its consequences (curse) and restored God's blessings among his people. The sacrifice of Christ once and for all paid the price for the willful disobedience of humanity; precisely benefiting those in Christ.

Conclusion

Up to this point, we have established that there were many ways through which the ancient people reversed or removed curses, and the Bible audience had knowledge of these prevailing means of removing curses. The undying fear of curses in the ancient world serves as a strong hint that the issue of curses remained despite having several avenues of removing it. The chapter presented the crucified and cursed Christ as the ultimate solution to the

---

60. Kitz, *Cursed Are You!*, 313.
61. Martyn, *Galatians*, 317.

human problem of curses. Christ became the innocent substitutionary victim that was sacrificed to end curses. He became the scapegoat that was sent away bearing curses of the people. Through his death on the cross, he removes curses and brings blessings to the human race. Paul reformulated these ideas and presented an elevated Christology that addressed the issue of curses.

Christ satisfied God's justice by paying the penalty due for sin. He took upon himself the judgment of God that was supposed to be carried by the disobedient. He bore upon himself the divine judgment so that through his death, the sting of the curse (death) is terminated for all who believe and receive him. Also, in this chapter, we have looked at themes that can be better understood by interrogating Paul's background. Presumably, Galatians 3:1–14 was interpreted by Paul's first readers with attention to the sociocultural themes within their surrounding environment.

CHAPTER 5

Application to the African Context and Contribution from the African Context

Introduction

Just as the context of the original readers helped them understand the meaning of Paul's statement on curses, the African context makes an important contribution in illuminating the relevance of this passage for us today. The focus is, but is not limited to, the Marakwet worldview on the issue of curses. Using the four-legged stool metaphor, this application section looks at the parallels to the African context.[1] The preceding chapters already covered the theological context, the literary context, and the historical context.

This chapter states the Marakwet cultural experience, function, and understanding of curses as a means of justice for application purposes.[2] It looks at correlation, similarity, and difference with the Jewish, Hellenistic, and Roman

---

1. This leg in the stool analogy enables the reader to understand the biblical text from a familiar point, by looking at "shared mutual interests." This is where the reader's context and the Bible's context interact and the points of contact with the biblical text are identified. Mburu, *African Hermeneutics*, 67–70.

2. The researcher comes from the Marakwet community and speaks Marakwet language, and has in the past served as a pastor within the same community. Therefore, he is familiar with the community's cursing practices, experiences, and has faced ministry situations interpreted as emanating from curses. However, in coming up with this work, there was need to clarify some issues related to cursing from older people in the community. This was important not only to mitigate the age limitation of the researcher, but also to ensure that the Marakwet cultural beliefs on curses are faithfully represented. In this regard, the following resourceful persons were consulted for the purpose of this study: Mr. John Kisitei, Mr. Philemon Chemweno, Rev. Joseph Kitur, Rev. Laban Kittony, Rev. Richard Cherop, and Rev. Robert Biwott.

understanding of curses. The chapter examines practices and motifs within the African cultural setting and ancient setting, and how these aspects influence the application of Galatians 3:1–14. It explores some insights that can be drawn into biblical scholarship and perspectives necessary for faithful and healthy biblical interpretation of the biblical text. This is a necessary step in the process of application of the biblical text in the contemporary setting. The main research question for this chapter is: What are some of the cultural curse elements and practices in Marakwet and other African cultures that can help apply Christ's substitutionary role as a curse-bearer in Galatians 3:13? Although the chapter deals with the Marakwet cursing practice, relevant studies in other African cultures are also consulted. In the discussion, several other subquestions are explored. These questions include: What are some of the curse categories in African cultures with cursing practices? What is the relationship between curses and justice? What is the ultimate goal of a curse? What are some of the offenses that necessitate cursing? How are curses administered? Who administers curses? What are the effects of curses on family and generations? How are curses averted? Who reverses curses? What is involved in the removal of curses? Are there substitute concepts for curses in African cultures?

This chapter proposes some cultural parallels when the antiquity context is considered alongside the contemporary African understanding and function of curses. It establishes with similarities the fact that Paul's concept of the cursed Christ is analogous to the concept of curse in Marakwet culture; they have a shared paradigm, but not without differences. Therefore, an African cultural understanding of curses can expand our understanding of cursing practices beyond the extant information on ancient contexts. The exploration of the Marakwet worldview in this chapter is only necessary for applying the biblical text.

In this application chapter, the three worlds of the author, the text, and the reader are merged. Tate rightly notes, "Meaning resides in the conversation between the text and reader with the world behind the text informing that conversation. Interpretation is impaired when any world is given preeminence at the expense of neglecting the other two."[3] Therefore, having looked at the text, ancient context, and the analysis section in the preceding chapters, the

---

3. Tate, *Biblical Interpretation*, 6.

present chapter highlights common motifs and stylistic features in the world of the author and the reader. It discusses the theme of justice and the significance of Christ's role in solving the human problem of curse.

The Presence, Fear, and Power of Curses in Marakwet Culture

Tokuboh defines a curse as:

> An invocation (a calling down) of harm or injury upon a person or people, either immediately or contingent upon particular circumstances. It is an utterance of a deity or a person invoking a deity consigning person(s) or thing(s) to destruction or divine vengeance. It is a malediction – the opposite of a benediction – or imprecation: an evil inflicted on another.[4]

It is pointed out in this definition that invocation of a curse is directed to the deity, but also that a person or a deity can utter a curse. The purpose of a curse is also stated as causing misfortune or harm to the target object.

Cursing and blessing practice is[5] a common phenomenon in the Marakwet culture, the root words for a curse are *ban* and *chub (keban or kechub means to curse)*. The terms refer to the act of pronouncing a curse on someone. Cursing is commonly practiced both at the personal and at the communal level, as is explored below. The prevalence of cursing practice is seen in the experiences and identifiable stories locals give concerning the reality and effects of curses. For example, stories of families reduced due to a series of deaths occasioned by curses are common. Also, narratives of selected mad people, odd behaviors, and unexplained realities are used to prove the existence of curses.

Curses are feared not only because of their dreadful consequences but also because of people's lived experiences concerning those accursed. Besides, the reality of the spiritual world, which is invoked in cursing, is more real in the African cosmology.[6] Primarily, curses bring death; and naturally, people fear death. Traditionally, it is believed that a curse has a negative effect, first, on the

---

4. Adeyemo, *Is Africa Cursed?*, 11.

5. The use of present tense highlights that the age-long practice is still prevalent in Marakwet society today.

6. Mburu, *African Hermeneutics*, 33.

offender(s) and second, on the offender's family. If not reversed, it is believed that curses can obliterate a whole family lineage. In the Marakwet culture, a curse is thought to be an effective means of executing justice; a curse "is a powerful instrument of justice and is most unlikely to be used except against offenders."[7] Mostly, it is used when an offender (such as a thief, land grabber, bandit, or murderer) is unknown, and no one claims to know the violator. It is believed that the curse effectively tracks down the unknown offender. It is therefore feared because of the potential destruction it brings. The fearful attitude toward curses is also attested in other in other communities like the Kikuyu community in Kenya, as noted by Wachege:

> In many African communities, the fear of curses and cursing is real. A curse is a disturbing anguish in life and living. It does not matter whether one is a leader; educated or uneducated; restless youth or an elder; medicine man or a soothsayer; sorcerer or witch; polygamist or monogamist; celibate churchmen and women, or laity; man endowed with virility and fecundity; or woman blessed with femininity cum fruitfulness; pauper or billionaire; a peace maker or a peace breaker. The underlying factor is that of curse and cursing phobia.[8]

In Marakwet culture, the fear of curses is explicit because several meetings are held before resorting to a curse. The Marakwet culture allows up to three gatherings by the adult community members before a communal curse is finally pronounced. In the meetings, a thorough investigation is carried out to locate the offender. During this period, which is spaced several days apart, individuals and families are offered a chance to interrogate their family members concerning the matter before the curse is finally uttered in the fourth gathering. No one wishes that a judicial case goes to the fourth stage/meeting. A final resort to a judicial curse highlights humanity's ultimate inability to know all things; thus, the communal curse invites the higher being(s) to take charge due to human inadequacies. The supreme deity (Asis) is believed to be the supreme, all-powerful, omniscient, arbiter of all things,

---

7. Kipkorir and Welbourn, *Marakwet of Kenya*, 9.
8. Wachege, *Curses and Cursing*, 1.

and a guarantor of what is right.[9] In a case where a thief or murderer is not located even after lengthy investigations, the community invites the supreme deity to take up the case. Interestingly, judicial curses were also used in the ancient world as a final option in seeking justice and revenge. Crawford notes that in the ancient world:

> Curses appear to be the last resort in situations when conventional means fail to provide needed security: where hidden tombs cannot defeat the cleverness of grave robbers, where respect for the dead does not prevent the living from jealously effacing a predecessor's name from a record of his or her accomplishments, or where sickness can only be prevented by incantations.[10]

In the ancient world where justice was elusive, the use of imprecations became the best antidote to the injustices inflicted upon innocent persons; judicial imprecations promised to offer redress to the afflicted party. In Marakwet culture, people fear curses uttered by the community; and in other African cultures, people greatly fear curses uttered by a parent because they are thought to be powerful, serious, and effective.[11] For example, among the *Agĩkũyũ* people (the largest ethnic group in Kenya), curses uttered by the Smith clan are feared, but a curse uttered by a mother is feared the most because of its serious repercussions.[12] Parents are thought to have the power to curse or bless.

The practice of cursing and blessing also offers lenses through which people interpret reality around them. In the Marakwet culture, people interpret a series of deaths and misfortunes in a family as emanating from a curse. When consecutive deaths happen in a family, the first assumption is to scan through history to see whether there was a curse directed to the family or a family member due to a wrongdoing. In some cases, where the cause of the deaths was ambiguous and beyond human understanding, people consulted

---

9. Kipkorir and Welbourn, *Marakwet of Kenya*, 8.
10. Crawford, *Blessing and Curse*, 97.
11. Evans-Pritchard, *Nuer Religion*, 166.
12. Wachege, *Curses and Cursing*, 3–4.

professional magicians (*kipses*)[13] to help detect the cause of the deaths. When the cause is established, it is then referred to Ōsis,[14] who are believed to be able to remove curses.

According to the Marakwet culture, a curse affects those who heard about the plot and those who saw the offender committing the offense but adamantly maintain silence on the matter. Thus when the offender(s) is cursed, they also curse the 'eye' that saw and the 'ear' that heard about the crime but choose not to reveal what they saw or heard about the offense. The effect of curses on accomplices is also attested in other cultural groups in Africa. For example, in Nuer's traditional culture, "a man who has witnessed a killing, though he has no part in it, yet if he keeps silence, will suffer misfortune because 'it is like as though he had hidden the [dead] man.'"[15] Equally, in the biblical world, judicial curses affected the wrongdoer and the associates of the offender. A two-sided lead curse tablet discovered on the island of Delos (dated between the first century BC and the first century AD) also shows that those who participated in the crime also suffered the harm of the curse. Versnel translated side A of the tablet: "Lords gods Sykonaioi . . . , Lady goddess Syria . . . Sykona, punish, and give expression to your wondrous power and direct your anger to the one who took away my necklace, who stole it, those who knew of it and those who were accomplices, whether man or woman."[16] From these cultures, offenders and their sympathizers are deemed guilty of the offense and are not excluded from the penalty of the curse.

In the biblical world context and contemporary African contexts, a curse could be removed by a substitutionary victim. In the Graeco-Roman religions, the pronouncement of a curse was feared, and Mclean notes that

---

13. Kipkorir and Welbourn, *Marakwet of Kenya*, 15; Kipkorir notes that *kipses* (reed-blowers) are on a high demand because they are believed to have powers not only to locate the cause of a misfortune, but can also help remove the bad omens.

14. Ōsis are a group of respectable people invited to determine a case between warring parties. These are not traditional specialists but are highly respectable individuals in society, who are known to be wise, fair, and calm, because of these attributes, they are seem as worthy to mediate community matters to the spiritual world. When there is a dispute in a community, the people agree to invite these mediators and arbitrators (the precondition being that they come from communities unrelated to the community in question). Their work is to hear, probe, and impartially determine the case at hand. Traditionally, their assessment and verdict is taken as authoritative and final.

15. Evans-Pritchard, *Nuer Religion*, 174.

16. Versnel, "Beyond Cursing," 67.

"once unleashed in a society, there was the genuine possibility of physical contagion and social disruption. This contagion or curse will work itself out on society unless a substitutionary victim is provided upon whom it might be discharged."[17] McLean acknowledges that this is a foreign concept to the modern mind. However, this view is untrue in some modern African contexts where cursing and blessing practices are still an ongoing reality.

Categories of Curses in Marakwet Culture

In Marakwet culture, curses can be placed into two categories. The first category deals with curses that are uttered at a personal level and are based on personal interests, while the second category deals with judicial curses that are pronounced mainly by the community. These two categories are briefly discussed in the following subsection.

Curses Motivated by Self-Interest

One of the common usages of curses in the Marakwet culture is for personal interests. Curses in this category are predominantly used against a competitor, a rival, or an enemy. A curse is used to seek control, manipulate, and influence events and occurrences against others (an individual or a group). Like the Greek *magoi*, the Marakwet *kipses*[18] dispenses curses for personal interests. Often, people contact these professionals, who are thought to possess innate powers, to enable them to defeat a competitor or torture or kill an enemy. Curses under this category affect whoever is the target. The traditional dispenser of curses can order a curse beyond one's social and cultural boundaries. In some cases, *kipses* can order the client to bring an item belonging to the target person, which may involve collecting the soil from the footprint of the target person. In addition, the client has the option of naming the type of harm to be inflicted on the target person. It is believed that the effects of the curse may be manifested in the form of infertility or insanity, among others.

---

17. McLean, *Cursed Christ*, 71.

18. Again, in the Marakwet culture, *kipses* are traditional specialists believed to have innate powers to diagnose the cause or reason for a misfortune. They could also prescribe or dispense solutions to the problems identified. These people were greatly feared because they could maliciously use their powers to manipulate and seek control over others through magic, witchcraft, and sorcery.

Comparatively, this category bears a resemblance to the ancient curses that were used against competitors in the arenas, such as business, sports, courts, love, and marriage.

Judicial and Revenge Prayers

In the Marakwet culture, curses are not only used in personal matters but also in concerns that threaten communal life. In a matter that affects communal life, curses are uttered against the offender(s). Unlike the former category that deals with personal and subjective matters, judicial curses are impartial and are uttered on extreme cases concerning the community.[19] This curse category is the final resort when a known offender persists in negative behavior that disrupts life in the community. Further, it is a final resort when an injustice is done against a member of the community by an unknown offender. Traditionally, the goal of judicial curses was to ensure that justice was delivered, the threat was eliminated, and vengeance applied. This category does not involve minor offenses but major offenses that threaten community life. For instance, robbers and murderers are potential victims of this nature of curse. Judicial curses were (and still are) deemed as effective in dealing with both known or unknown offenders.

In contentious matters that pertain to community life, neutral and respectable individuals (*Ōsis*), are invited to provide impartial and objective judgment on the matter. These individuals who are invited to mediate and arbitrate the matter, are drawn from a different community unrelated to the concerned parties. They impartially listen to all parties and serve as mediators and judges, and their final verdict is considered authoritative and final. Expectedly, each party upholds the final verdict. However, in cases of appeal, which are very rare, the dissatisfied party may still ask for a constitution of another team of *Ōsis* to deliberate on the matter. In cases where no offenders confess or are identified, during the fourth meeting, the *Ōsis*, in the presence

---

19. Recently, in the year 2017 and 2019, the Kenyan national media houses documented cursing ceremonies in the Marakwet community targeting cattle rustlers. One of the cursing function against cross-border bandits was done by Marakwets jointly with the neighboring community (Pokot). The video links are provided in the bibliography. Rutto, "Elders Turn to Curses."

of the community, utters a curse to locate and kill the offenders.[20] The cursing event is participatory; the *Ōsis* utters the curse words while the community participates in the process by responding in agreement or affirmation to the curse words.

The *Ōsis* party, involved in cursing or removing curses in the Marakwet culture, has some characteristics that can be highlighted; because this can be related to the person of Christ as a remover of curses. *Ōsis* is a respectable person(s), known to be fair and at peace with other people and the spiritual world. Hence, this stresses the fact that a curse can only be removed by a person of high moral standing. In the Bible, Jesus Christ is the blameless Lamb of God, who was tempted in every way yet was without sin (Heb 4:15). The final verdict given by the *Ōsis* was upheld by everyone in the community. Similarly, the removal of curses by Jesus Christ is final and benefits those in the community of faith.

In the Marakwet culture, curses are also deemed to automatically take effect in judicial cases, even without the curses being pronounced. For example, when an injustice is done to a person (especially to the most vulnerable persons like widows, the poor, strangers, elderly, persons living with disability, and orphans), the judicial and revenge prayers of these helpless and vulnerable persons are thought to be taken up by the deity who revenges and administers justice on their behalf. Evans-Pritchard notes the same belief among the Nuer concerning the "curse of the heart." He notes that the unspoken curse was by itself fully-pledged if the grievance was genuine.[21] He also highlights that Nuer people feared when an aggrieved party died with a legitimate concern that was not righted because the person could still seek settlement after he was gone.[22] This demonstrates that some African people believed that God hears cries expressed in the form of curses and listened to the unexpressed groans of the oppressed, by responding accordingly.

Culturally among the Marakwet, it is known that the only penalty for a judicial and revenge curse is death. The death punishment is thought to be an effective way of eliminating the offender(s) who has/have become a threat to

---

20. Culturally, apart from *Ōsis*, those people identified with two specific totems, namely, Kobilo and Shokwei, also qualify to pronounce communal curses.

21. Evans-Pritchard, *Nuer Religion*, 170.

22. Evans-Pritchard, 173.

community life and relations. The penalty is also believed to be apt revenge for the wrong(s) committed. Recognizably, a curse under this category is uttered as a result of persistent wrongdoing that damages communal life; and therefore, the curse functions to ensure that justice is executed and revenge settled. The power behind judicial and revenge curses or prayers lies not only in the invocation of the deity[23] but also in the communal unanimity on the prayers made.

The Object of Judicial and Revenge Prayers

The judicial and revenge prayers are directed to the traditional deity. The imprecations invoke the deity to take up the matter and ensure that justice is fully served and vengeance unleashed. In the Marakwet culture, the supreme being, known as *Asis* (literally, "sun"), is entreated to take up the judicial prayers of the community to an unspecified deity. That is the reason why cursing, like burials, is usually conducted before sunset. Judicial prayers are to be conducted during daytime in the presence of *Asis* because it is believed that the deity should be able to see, hear, and relay the judicial grievances of the people to the supreme deity. Thus, the *Asis* deity serves as a messenger to the unspecified deity who resides beyond the sun.

Additionally, some prayers are directed to the Marakwet deity of justice called *Illat* (the god of thunder and lightning). In Marakwet cosmology, *Illat* is thought to be the deity involved in the implementation of justice and revenge.[24] For instance, in controversial cases that concern the moving of a land boundary, *Illat* is invited to provide a just ruling of the case. It is expected that the deity impartially demarcates the piece of land in question. According to some lived experiences, when the judicial prayers are made, the god of lightning strikes and rightly demarcates the land during a thunderstorm, with some clear signs using items like stones, leaves, and gullies, among other visible signs. In cases of oath-taking and treaties, the individuals involved may invoke a self-curse by asking *Illat* to strike them in case they disown or deviate from the stipulated agreement. In Marakwet, an oath (*muma*) is equally seen as

---

23. It is also observed in the Nuer culture that cursing and blessing practice were effective because of the invocation of the deity. See Evans-Pritchard, 172.

24. Kipkorir and Welbourn, *Marakwet of Kenya*, 10.

a serious matter because it involves a self-curse.[25] Also, during oath-taking, rituals are conducted by the parties involved to determine a guilty person.

Execution of a Judicial Curse

In ancient societies, as discussed earlier, curses uttered by human beings were directed to a deity who was supposed to examine the authenticity of the case and enact justice or revenge. The supreme deities could at their disposal delegate the enforcement to subordinate deities. Concerning the ANE culture, Kitz comments,

> The deities always govern curses. They listen to the petition, they judge the circumstances, and they act if deemed appropriate. When they do act, the gods and goddesses can execute the curse's injury in many ways. This divine backdrop forges a strong link between the governing deity and the power behind the execution of the punishment. It is a divine power that can directly inflict the punishment or delegate it to agents.[26]

In any case, justice or revenge was served whether by the higher deity or by the subordinate divine being(s). In the ANE, some of these deities that were charged with the execution of the penalty of the curse were associated with animals.[27] In other cases, one's enemies (human beings) were expected to enforce the harm, especially in curses that began with the words "may your enemies. . . ." It was thought that the supreme deity could consign implementation of the curse penalty to one's enemy.[28] In this case, the enemies became agents used to inflict harm on the curse target. It suffices to provide an Akkadian example. In this instance, the highest deity Šamaš delivered his judgment, but Girra implemented the harm of the curse, thus, "⁶Šamaš, let Girra the Burner burn them. ⁷Let Girra deceive them. Let Girra scorch them.

---

25. Kipkorir and Welbourn.
26. Kitz, *Cursed Are You!*, 194. For extensive discussion of executionary deities in the ancient world, see pages 170–96 of Kitz's work.
27. Kitz, 182.
28. Some biblical examples that can illustrate this phenomenon of human agents include: Leviticus 26:17; Deuteronomy 28:25a.

⁸ᵇLet Girra obliterate them. Let Girra incinerate them."[29] This ancient feature of supreme deities relegating the execution of a curse is also well attested in the African culture.

As expressed before, in the Marakwet culture, curses are directed to the supreme deity *Asis* (the sun deity). However, similar to the ancient cultures, at the disposal of *Asis,* the execution of harm against curse victims could alternatively be delegated to *Illat* (the thunder and lightning deity).[30] The *Illat* is known to be a subordinate executioner deity of curses; and is believed to strike a victim to death through lightning and thunder. In the Marakwet cosmology, the supreme deity seems to be distant, and so people expected Illat to deliver justice: "regular prayers are not said to him [*Asis*]; as he appears so remote as to have no immediate effect on day-to-day activities."[31] In cases where the land boundary is a matter of dispute, *Illat* is expected to deliver justice on the matter by visibly marking the right boundary lines.

Removal and Reversal of Judicial and Revenge Curses

As it has been pointed out, it is believed that judicial and revenge curses bring physical death. A curse brings death to the family of the offender(s) and potentially the entire community, if not removed. It is believed that the effect of a curse starts with the offender(s), followed by a series of deaths among the immediate family members (young and old), then later, it follows the family lineage. However, in a surprising turn, after the family of the offender(s) has been eradicated, the curse, sort of loses control and, pursues those who were present during the cursing event. It is thought that the curse may even pursue those who cursed the offender (the arbiters – *Ōsis*) present[32] because, in a way, they committed murder indirectly by issuing a death

---

29. Kitz, *Cursed Are You!*, 181.

30. Elizabeth Mburu in her work looks at the African worldview and argues that the supreme deity in African cosmology was distant and unknown. As a result, he delegated duties and responsibilities to lesser spirit beings, gods, and divinities who interact with humanity directly: Mburu, *African Hermeneutics*, 27.

31. Kipkorir and Welbourn, *Marakwet of Kenya*, 8.

32. In Nuer culture, it is believed that one needed to be sure that the judicial curse has a basis on a certain injustice, otherwise the curse can become ineffective or pursue those who pronounced the curse. See Evans-Pritchard, *Nuer Religion*, 165.

verdict. This partly explains why people dread curses and fear being present on the occasion when the community pronounces a curse. Effectively, the curse moves step by step and steadily with an insatiable appetite killing many people before it can be reversed. Therefore when a curse has ravaged a family, *Ōsis* are called to cancel it.

In reversing curses, two situations need to be first noted. First, in cases where the unrepentant offender is known, it is necessary to remove the curse once the known offender died, to avoid spreading to the family of the offender. Thus, once the offender dies, *Ōsis* are recalled to annul the curse. Second, in cases where the offender was unknown, the curse affected not only the offender(s) but also the crime associates (those who saw or heard but chose to conceal the offender(s). The collaborator who heard about the crime but chose not to reveal the offender is cursed to be dumb, and the person who witnessed the crime by seeing but remained silent is cursed to be blind. In the long run, the effects of the curse could only be halted when and after some of the remnants of the affected family acknowledged the wrong and requested the community to meet and summon the *Ōsis* so that the curse could be removed. In this case, the offender's family took the place of the deceased to ask for forgiveness with the anticipation that the curse might be removed. This is a bit different from the idea of the cursed Christ because, in Christ's case, the one who died was both innocent and a solution to the curse. Although the differences are evident, some observations can be made. Sin is the root cause of curse in Galatians 3, as perceived in the light of Genesis 3, and a curse results in death unless it is reversed. Providentially, Christ is the God-given means for the reversal of curses for all those in Christ.

Ways of Preventing and Removing Curses in the Marakwet Culture

Again, curses are shunned by all individuals and communities. A curse is avoided or prevented when a guilty party confesses or admits having committed injustice or a wrong. In such cases, a penalty is administered. Culturally, in Marakwet, the payback is usually eight times what was stolen. Further, curses are prevented by ensuring that one does not inflict any form of injustice on another person. Also, as previously noted in Nuer culture, curses could be avoided by ensuring that an injustice committed against a person was righted before the person died. At all costs, people in the Bible and traditional African societies avoided situations that could bring curses, especially judicial and retribution prayers. However, in cases where a curse is not prevented, the pronouncement and consequences of a malediction become inevitable. Even so, there were (and still are) ways in which the harm of a curse could be reversed. At least in many African cultures, curses are not irreversible.

In Marakwet culture, there are ways in which curses are removed. First, a curse is canceled through a ritual ceremony known as *kelyop* (to cleanse). In this ritual, the community gathers to cleanse, reverse, and "sweeten" the curse words they had previously uttered. The impartial team of *Osis,* with the affirmative verbal response of the gathering, pronounces life where it had (previously) pronounced death; and pronounces blessing where it had pronounced a curse. During the ceremony, a black goat[33] is sacrificed and wholly consumed by the gathering. It is worth noting that nothing is eaten during the initial cursing event, but when removing a curse, the people present share a meal. Culturally, the cleansing ceremony is repeated annually for four years for the curse to be pronounced fully reversed and removed. Curses are understood to be serious when they are pronounced and also when they are being canceled. In Nuer culture, the effects of a curse were stopped either through a confession of the wrongdoing or by a sacrifice to the traditional deity.[34]

Substitutionary Concept on Curses

In the Marakwet culture, the substitutionary concept was remotely evident in the judicial curses. For instance, when a community gathered to curse a known violator, the people conducted the practice on the basis that it was better for one offender to die than for the rest of the immediate family or community to suffer. In cases where an offender was known to be a murderer or a perennial thief, a family would give up one of their own to be cursed, especially when the violator perpetually subjects the family to paying fines

---

33. Culturally, the unblemished goat is used for this purpose; but an unblemished sheep is used for *tisyo* (atonement). This illustrates that the remover of curses should be spotless. In the Bible, Christ is the perfect sacrifice from God (Heb 10:10).

34. Evans-Pritchard, *Nuer Religion*, 175.

for stolen goods or (domestic) animals. The resultant social disharmony, societal disequilibrium created by the offender, and relationship breakdown was once and for all solved by eliminating the disrupter. In this case, a family gave up one of their own to be cursed instead of the whole family bearing a curse. The substitutionary victim then died for the rest of the community to live in peace, although in this case, the substitutionary victim was a nuisance to the community.

Likewise, in the biblical world, people believed that a curse could be transferred from one person to another. Therefore, when Paul talks of Christ taking upon himself the curse of humanity, he was not exclusively proposing a peculiar concept but a practice that was present in the first-century Mediterranean world.

In the Old Testament, the idea of whether a curse could be transferred to a person is explicit in Genesis 27:12–13, in the case when Rebecca offered herself to bear the curse which her son, Jacob, could have incurred by impersonating to be Esau. In other words, she was willing to bear the curse that was supposed to affect Jacob.

Proclaiming Jesus Christ in a Cultural Context with Belief in Curses

The idea of a crucified and cursed Christ presents some implications that can be categorized as theological and pastoral for the church in Marakwet and in other African contexts with cursing practices.

Theological Implications

African Christology should relevantly address the issue of curses in African cosmology. The issue deserves attention, just as Paul addressed the issue in the early church. The question of John V. Taylor, is worthy of consideration:

> Christ has been presented as the answer to the questions a white man would ask, the solution to the needs that Western man would feel, the Savior of the world of the European world-view, the object of adoration and prayer of historic Christendom. But

if Christ were to appear as the answer to the questions that Africans are asking, what would he look like?[35]

The present study is not intended to comprehensively answer this critical question; but it seeks to consider what it would mean to Africans from cultural contexts where cursing practice is a reality that Jesus became a curse for us. Several implications can be mentioned to this effect. First, the study on judicial curses enriches the doctrine of Christology. The application of the death of Christ on the cross on issues of curses provides a solution to the cultural problem of curse and cursing. In a context where cursing is practiced, Christ can be seen as a deliverer and restorer of humanity from the fear and bondage of curses. Christ delivers his own from the oppressive powers of death and darkness into marvelous freedom.

Second, the study on curses enriches the doctrine of soteriology and ecclesiology. Christ's redemption and atonement deal with the problem of sin and the human enigma of curses. Deliverance from curses remains an area that has not received much scholarly attention, partly because curses have been categorized with magic, sorcery, and divination; and as a result, branded primitive and retrogressive practices. Discussion around the issue of curses has the potential to expand our idea of what Christ's salvation encompasses. Apostle Paul mentioned that Christ became a curse for us so that the blessing of God might flow to the nations. This bears some ecclesiological implications; the universal church is a community of blessings, a community where the life of God flows. In a context marred with myriads of challenges and hopelessness, the church in Africa should embrace the identity and calling to be a community of blessing and hope. The church, under the lordship of Christ, is a life-giving community.

Third, the articulation of Christian faith and kerygma in the African context should address issues of relevance in Africa, like curses. As seen in this study, the worldview of the Marakwet (and by extension, other African cultures) on curses can serve well in shedding light on an African understanding of Galatians 3:13. The death of Christ is significant because, through this single death, humanity receives freedom and redemption from sin and curses. He died our death so that believers can live and inherit blessings.

---

35. Taylor, *The Primal Vision, Christian amid African Religion*, 16 cited in Bediako, *Jesus in Africa*, vii.

Pastoral Implications

The concept of the crucified and cursed Christ brings true liberation from the power and fear of curses. Since Christ took away our curse upon himself, believers, even for those from contexts where cursing practices are not prominently practiced, should enjoy this marvelous freedom. Although talking about the law, Paul exhorts the Galatians not to subject themselves to the yoke of slavery (Gal 5:1); but to use their newfound freedom not to indulge in sinful nature but to serve one another in love (Gal 5:13). Christ's freedom from curse should lead believers not into sin but to righteous living. Therefore, Christians in contexts where curses are practiced should be delivered from the fear of curses because of Christ's liberation and redemption. They should not visit traditional specialists for curse removal but should trust in the work of Christ on the cross as the final and authoritative victory over human and divine curses. Believers in Christ have been united with Christ, and through Christ's death, God annulled the curse.

To be able to proclaim Christ's deliverance in cultures where the fear of curses is a reality, the church and theologians (especially from cultures where curses are not believed in) need not underrate contextual experiences of those who believe in the reality of curses. At the same time, the issue of curses should not be superficially wished away with a short prayer. Because of the lack of a clear articulation of Scriptural teachings in addressing the matter, many African Christians resort to traditional means of removing curses. It suffices to give an example of what this approach looks like. In this study, we established that wrongdoing is the basis of judicial curses. The judicial curse seeks to bring judgment or vengeance where the injury had been caused. At the same time, we noted that confession was one of the common ways in which curses were removed in the ancient world. If an offender experienced a "change of heart" and acknowledged the wrongdoing, the curse was nullified. Similarly, we observed that in the Marakwet culture, the curse was prevented or annulled if the violator admitted their offense. When people in African societies (including Christians) resort to traditional means of removing curses, they are always taken through a process of identifying the root cause of the curse before it is removed. The aim is always to diagnose the cause and prescribe traditional rituals involving the shedding of animal blood. This presents an ample opportunity for pastors, evangelists, theologians, and missiologists to relevantly articulate the doctrine of repentance and confession of sins, and the efficacy and finality of the blood of Christ that was shed on the cross in dealing with curses. First John 1:9 promises that "if we confess our sins, he is faithful and just and will forgive us our sins and purify us from all unrighteousness" (NIV). The sting of the curse upon humanity can be removed by coming to Christ in confession and belief; he promises to bless and to give his Spirit to those who come to him in faith.

Conclusion

In this chapter, we have looked at the understanding, belief, practice, and function of curses in the Marakwet culture, and by extension, other African cultures. Judicial curses were also a prominent category of curses in African societies, antiquity, and the present. Curses were widely feared because of the negative consequences they were (and still are) believed to bring on individuals, families, and communities. Furthermore, the study established points of similarities and differences between ancient cultures and contemporary African cultures. Again, it may be stated that the ancient Bible context and contemporary African contexts share parallel themes on cursing practice. From these two contexts, there are striking similarities in cursing practices. Although the modern African context is far removed from the Bible context, both in time and space, there are apparent analogous concepts in both cultures. Studying African cultures with cursing practices positively helps to understand the nature and seriousness of curses as we seek to build a Christology around it and apply Paul's message. Therefore, understanding Paul's message to the Galatians within its Graeco-Roman context and African context can bring a meaningful application in a way that the Western Christian community has not. In this study, African cultures where cursing is practiced can help provide categories of application of the Bible message in a profound way that Western scholarship has been unable to do.

CHAPTER 6

Conclusions and Recommendations

Introduction

The present chapter summarizes this work by looking at some key findings. This is done by looking at the key conclusions arrived at in each of the chapters. The second section deals with recommendations for further study. The recommendation section presents some suggestions for possible areas of further research.

The first chapter introduced the thesis, scope of the work, the problem, methodology, literature review, and procedure for the study. The scholarly literature surveyed in the introduction shows that there has been much scholarly activity done on Galatians 3:1–14. These studies include Paul's view of the law, Abraham, curse, and the use of the Old Testament in the New Testament. Some of the biblical criticism methods used in this text include intertextuality, rhetorical criticism, and speech act theory. However, the present study used a socio-rhetorical approach to investigate the connection between curses and justice to be able to understand the concept of the crucified and cursed Christ within its historical and cultural context. The motivation behind this study was stated as understanding the application of the death of Christ on the issue of curses.

In chapter two of this study, it was demonstrated that the curse of Galatians 3 needs to be seen within the ANE and the Graeco-Roman contexts. It was argued that the cursing practice was real in the classical, Hellenistic, and Roman worlds. Curses and binding spells were used in areas of sports, the business world, courts, love, sex, and marriage. We noted that these types of curses were primarily employed against personal rivals in the areas mentioned. We also established a distinctive category of judicial curses or prayers that were uttered against wrongdoing. The purpose of this category was solely to deliver justice and administer vengeance. The ancient people also used this type of curse to protect graves from plunderers and to protect one's name and writings even after one had died. The widespread belief and fear of curses can be attributed to the fact that the curses worked. In addition, we also saw that curses had a wide range of ramifications (including cessation of posterity or lack of advancement), but the judicial prayers had death as the ultimate end. A judicial curse sought to terminate the life of the victim. It was believed that a curse was equally effective when the targets were either known or unknown. In addition, the ancient people interpreted reality using curses. They looked at happenings around them using the lenses of curses and blessings. We noted that Paul employed the cultural understanding of ANE and the Graeco-Roman world in coming up with a Christology that addresses curses. He based his understanding of curses on the judicial use of curses in the ancient world.

The third chapter dealt with the exegesis of Galatians 3:1–14 and OT quotations. The chapter demonstrated that the curse of Galatians 3:13 has a relationship to the curse as stated in Genesis 3. The curse of the law in Galatians 3:13 has a relationship with the curse on humanity and the ground in Genesis 3:16–19.

In the exegetical section, Paul addresses the problem that led the Galatians to abandon the true gospel and the apostolic heritage to follow the misleading teachings of the Judaizers. The Galatians had abandoned the gospel of justification by faith and were now resorting to a different gospel that was not a gospel at all. They had begun well in the power of the Spirit but were now trying to complete what God started by means of human effort. To Paul, this was utter foolishness. To be able to correct this doctrinal anomaly, Paul developed a robust theological foundation that centered around the person and the work of Christ on the cross. He looked at the example of Abraham, the one who received God's promise that all nations would be blessed through him. Paul established that the gospel he preached was an agelong gospel that Abraham received from God through this patriarch. Paul reveals that, in God's plan, Gentiles have a share in God's salvation.

Paul observes that the era of the law preceded the coming of Christ, the law ruled. The law temporarily pointed out to people what was right and wrong, but it also stood as a reminder of man's inability to fulfill its demands in totality. That same law that was supposed to bring life to those who observed it also cursed humankind. Humans' disobedience of God's laws brought the curse that the same law stipulated. Because of this, Paul argues that all humanity stands accursed. The crux of the problem is that humanity is helpless and unable to free itself from this oppressive power of curse. Paul demonstrates that the work of Christ on the cross brought a solution to the problem of curses. Christ died on the cross, becoming a curse on our behalf. This is a blessing to all that are connected to Christ. The purpose of Christ's work enables Gentiles to receive God's blessings promised to Abraham and to receive the promise of the Holy Spirit. Paul taught that although humanity was under a curse, God had provided a solution to the curse through his Son, Jesus Christ.

The fourth chapter of this study analyzed the preceding exegetical section and the antiquity context. It looked at the social and cultural concepts in the ancient biblical world that aid an interpreter of Galatians 3:1–14. It concluded that Paul's writing can be better understood in light of the socio-cultural background of the Bible text. It also concluded that Paul's language and ideas were rooted in the Jewish and Graeco-Roman contexts. The chapter looked at the cross of Christ and the curse on Christ as the satisfaction of divine justice.

A major section of the chapter looked at ways in which curses were removed in the ancient world. In the ancient world curses and binding spells were removed through scapegoat rituals, sacrifices, herbal antidotes, wearing of amulets, and the stones of Hermes, cursing of curses and exorcism, and finally through confession. This understanding is important for a modern reader in order to appropriate and understand the meaning that the immediate audience derived from Paul's letter. Although there were variety of ways in which curses were removed, the ancient people still feared curses; an indication that the available avenues remained limited and ineffective. In a world with a variety of ways of dealing with curses, how was Christ the effective solution to the problem of curse? In answer to this question, the chapter looked at the uniqueness of Christ as the ultimate curse-bearer and curse-remover. He is the God-ordained means of removing the human curse.

On the one hand, his deity guaranteed his connection with God. On the other hand, his incarnation affirmed him as a representative of humankind.

Further, in this section, in considerable detail, we have separately explored the concept of the crucified and cursed Christ; and examined some terms that have meaningful background information for a modern reader of Galatians 3. These themes and phrases include: "Who has bewitched you?"; the phrase ὑπὸ κατάραν; blessing; and redemption. We established that these terms could be better understood by investigating the social context of the ancient world. This interrogation is possible through the socio-rhetorical approach. Finally, in this chapter, we established that Christ is the ultimate bearer and remover of all curses. He is the one who solved curses once and for all. He took away the penalty of man's disobedience (death) and satisfied God's justice. Through this, believers in Christ from all nations receive blessings and the promise of the Holy Spirit.

Chapter five of this study sought to highlight two key points. First, the Graeco-Roman context portrays a worldview that bears a resemblance to the Marakwet cursing practice. Second, interpreting Galatians 3:13 in view of the Marakwet worldview on curses and blessings does not amount to eisegesis but, in fact, sheds light on the understanding of Galatians 3:13 in a way that no other commentator has done before.

The section explored the Marakwet cultural understanding and functions of curses. Additionally, the study established some parallels with the ancient world context and noted some areas of difference. In the Marakwet culture, the theme of curses and blessings is widely prevalent. Curses are pronounced on different occasions, but this study's interest is the judicial use of curses. When one transgressed or committed a life-threatening offense and/or failed to assume responsibility, a curse would be invoked in the presence of adult members of the community. Traditionally, this was a way the wronged party sought justice. It is believed that after an unspecified period, the curse would find the unknown offender, and its effects would be public. It is believed by the Marakwet people that curses have a destructive power on individuals, families, and communities. In addition, it is believed that curses first affect the individual offender and then the family of the offender. A cursed individual brought a cessation of life and blessings; and ushered in a period and series of deaths in a family line, extending to generations. As noted, it is believed that curses can totally obliterate a family line unless revoked. A revocation of curses only happens when the affected party (the family that has suffered generational consequences of the curse) recognizes their wrongdoing committed in the past and willingly confesses. This process can take several generations or deaths; so that those who ultimately and willingly confess may end up being the children or grandchildren or great-grandchildren of the offender. As noted earlier, in the Marakwet culture, removing curses is not an event but a process; it is not an individual affair but a communal matter. It involves the healing of broken relationships, revocation of a curse, and restoration of blessings.

In Galatians 3:10, Paul established that all humanity stands cursed. However, in Galatians 3:13 the death of Christ on the cross became the ultimate price for redemption; and through this death the penalty that was upon humanity was paid in full, once and for all. Therefore, believers from all nations need to come to God in confession to receive blessings and the promise of the Holy Spirit. It has been established from the ancient contexts and in select modern African cultures that curses were (and still are) used distinctively to deal with judicial matters. Hence, the present study has filled a scholarly gap by looking at the connection between justice and curse in both the ancient and modern African contexts and highlighting Christ as the center of redemption from the oppressive power of curse.

Recommendations

The present study has not explored all that needs to be explored in regard to the crucified and cursed Christ. It, therefore, recommends some areas of further study. The first recommendation deals with studying the African socioreligious practices in comparison with practices in the biblical world. This study has established that there are striking similarities between traditional African practices and Bible antiquity contexts. These similarities, and differences, should be studied more critically to be able to have a meaningful application of the Bible text. There is a need for studies on how African culture can be a tool in engaging the Bible text.

Second, there still remains the theological task of further formulating a Christology that deals with sin and curses, and by extension, Christ's power over practices such as sorcery, magic, and witchcraft. These are areas in which a biblical application of the death of Christ can make much difference both on theological and pastoral levels. This involves looking at deliverance and redemption from a broader perspective.

Third, there is a need to explore further the doctrine of confession as a biblical resource in dealing with curses and bringing healing and restoration to families and communities.

Bibliography

Adeyemo, Tokunboh. *Is Africa Cursed?* Nairobi: Christian Learning and Materials Centre, 1997.
Adeyemo, Tokunboh (General Editor), *Africa Bible Commentary*. Nairobi: WordAlive Publishers, 2006.
Aland, Barbara, Kurt Aland, Johannes Karavidopoulos, Carlo Maria Martini, Bruce M. Metzger (eds.). *The Greek New Testament: A Reader's Edition*, Stuttgart: Deutsch Bibelgesellschaft, 2014.
Alt, Albrecht, Rudolf Kittel, Hans Bardtke, Hans Peter Rüger, Joseph Ziegler, Karl Elliger, Wilhelm Rudolph, Gérard E. Weil, Adrian Schenker, and Deutsche Bibelgesellschaft, (eds.). *Torah, Nevi'im u-Khetuvim: Biblia Hebraica Stuttgartensia*. 5th ed. Stuttgart: Deutsche Bibelgesellschaft, 1997.
Anderson, Jeffrey Scott. *The Blessing and the Curse*. Eugene: Wipf and Stock Publishers, 2014.
———. "The Nature and Function of Curses in the Narrative Literature of the Hebrew Bible." PhD Thesis. Ann Arbor: UMI, 1992.
Aune, D. E. *The New Testament in Its Literary Environment*. Library of Early Christianity, vol. 8. Philadelphia: Westminster, 1987.
Austin, J. L. *How to Do Things with Words*. 2nd ed. The William James Lectures 1955. Oxford: Clarendon Press, 1990.
Bediako, Kwame. *Jesus in Africa: The Christian Gospel in African History and Experience*. Theological Reflections from the South. Yaoundé, Cameroun: Editions Clé and Regnum Africa, in association with Paternoster, 2000.
Betz, Hans Dieter. *Galatians: A Commentary on Paul's Letter to the Churches in Galatia*. Hermeneia Commentaries. Philadelphia: Fortress Press, 1979.
Burkert, Walter. *Greek Religion: Archaic and Classical*. Malden: Blackwell, 2012.
Calvin, Jean, A. N. S. Lane, and Hilary Osborne. *The Institutes of Christian Religion*. Grand Rapids: Baker Book House, 1987.
Campbell, Constantine R. *Paul and Union with Christ: An Exegetical and Theological Study*. Grand Rapids: Zondervan, 2012.

Carson, D. A., and Douglas J. Moo. *An Introduction to the New Testament*. 2nd ed. Grand Rapids: Zondervan, 2005.

Charles, R. H., (ed.). *The Apocrypha and Pseudepigrapha of the Old Testament in English*. Vol. 2: *Pseudepigrapha*. Oxford: Clarendon, 1977.

Chilton, Bruce. *Rabbi Paul: An Intellectual Biography*. New York: Doubleday, 2004.

Classen, C. J. *Rhetorical Criticism of the New Testament*. Boston: Brill Academic, 2002.

Cole, R. Alan. *The Epistle of Paul to the Galatians*. Tyndale New Testament Commentaries 9. Grand Rapids: W. B. Eerdmans, 1989.

Cousar, C. B. *Galatians*. Interpretation, A Bible Commentary for Teaching and Preaching, Atlanta: John Knox, 1982.

Crawford, Timothy G. *Blessing and Curse in Syro-Palestinian Inscriptions of the Iron Age*. American University Studies, vol. 120. New York: Peter Lang, 1992.

Das, A. Andrew. *Paul, the Law, and the Covenant*. Peabody: Hendrickson, 2001.

Dunn, James D. G. *The Epistle to the Galatians*. Black's New Testament Commentaries. Peabody: Hendrickson, 1993.

Erickson, Millard J. *Christian Theology*. 3rd ed. Grand Rapids: Baker Academic, 2013.

Evans, Craig A., and Stanley E. Porter, eds. *Dictionary of New Testament Background*. Downers Grove: InterVarsity Press, 2000.

Evans-Pritchard, E. E. *Nuer Religion*. New York: Oxford University Press, 1956.

F. F. Bruce. *The Epistle to the Galatians: A Commentary on the Greek Text*. New International Greek Testament Commentary. Grand Rapids: W. B. Eerdmans, 2002.

Faraone, Christopher A., and Dirk Obbink. *Magika Hiera: Ancient Greek Magic and Religion*. New York: Oxford University Press, 1997.

Fitzmyer, Joseph A. *Romans: A New Translation with Introduction and Commentary*. The Anchor Bible, 33. New York: Doubleday, 1993.

Friberg, Timothy, Barbara Friberg, and Neva F. Miller. *Analytical Lexicon of the Greek New Testament*. Victoria: Trafford, 2005.

Gager, John G., ed. *Curse Tablets and Binding Spells from the Ancient World*. New York: Oxford University Press, 1992.

Garlington, Don B. *An Exposition of Galatians: A New Perspective/Reformational Reading*. 2nd ed. Eugene: Wipf and Stock, 2004.

George, Timothy. *Galatians: An Exegetical and Theologica*. The New American Commentary, vol. 30. USA: Broadman and Holman, 1994.

Graf, Fritz. *Magic in the Ancient World*. Revealing Antiquity 10. Cambridge: Harvard University Press, 1997.

Grüneberg, Keith Nigel. *Abraham, Blessing and the Nations: A Philological and Exegetical Study of Genesis 12:3 in Its Narrative Context*. Beihefte Zur

Zeitschrift Für Die Alttestamentliche Wissenschaft, 332. New York: Walter de Gruyter, 2003.

Hansen, G. Walter. *Abraham in Galatians: Epistolary and Rhetorical Contexts*. Journal for the Study of the New Testament 29. Sheffield: JSOT press, 1989.

Harvey, J. D. *Listening to the Text: Oral Patterning in Paul's Letters*. Grand Rapids: Baker, 1998.

Hawthorne, Gerald F., and Ralph P. Martin, eds. *Dictionary of Paul and His Letters*. Downers Grove: InterVarsity Press, 1993.

Hays, Richard B. *The Faith of Jesus Christ: The Narrative Substructure of Galatians 3:1–4:11*. 2nd ed. The Biblical Resource Series. Grand Rapids: W. B. Eerdmans, 2002.

Hock, R. F. "Paul and Greco-Roman Education." In *Paul in the Greco-Roman World: A Handbook*, edited by J. P. Sampley, 198–227. Harrisburg: Trinity Press International, 2003.

Hurd, John C. "Reflections Concerning 'Paul's Opponents' in Galatia." In *Paul and His Opponents*, edited by Stanley E. Porter, 129–148. Pauline Studies, vol. 2. Leiden: Brill, 2005.

Jeffers, Ann. *Magic and Divination in Ancient Palestine and Syria*. Studies in the History and Culture of the Ancient Near East, vol. 8. Leiden: E. J. Brill, 1996.

Joshua, Nathan Nzyoka. "A Christian Response to Curses in Africa." In *Christianity and Suffering: African Perspectives*, edited by Rodney L. Reed, 145–166. Carlisle: Langham Global Library, 2018.

Keener, Craig S. *Galatians*. New Cambridge Bible Commentary. Cambridge: Cambridge University Press, 2018.

———. *Galatians: A Commentary*. Grand Rapids: Baker Academic, 2019.

Kennedy, G. A. *New Testament Interpretation through Rhetorical Criticism*. Chapel Hill: University of North Carolina Press, 1984.

Kipkorir, B. E., and Frederick Burkewood Welbourn. *The Marakwet of Kenya: A Preliminary Study*. Nairobi: East African Educational Publishers, 2008. First Published 1973 by East African Literature Bureau.

Kitz, Anne Marie. *Cursed Are You! The Phenomenology of Cursing in Cuneiform and Hebrew Texts*. Winona Lake: Eisenbrauns, 2014.

Kotansky, R. D. "Demonology." In *Dictionary of New Testament Background*, edited by Craig A. Evans and Stanley E. Porter, 269–73. Downers Grove: InterVarsity Press, 2000.

Lightfoot, J. B. *Saint Paul's Epistle to the Galatians: A Revised Text with Introduction, Notes, and Dissertations*. New York: Macmillan, 1896.

Little, Lester K. "Cursing." In *The Encyclopedia of Religion*, vol. 4, edited by Mircea Eliade. New York: Macmillan, 1987.

Longenecker, Richard N. *Galatians*. Word Biblical Commentary. Word Books: Dallas, 1990.

Lührmann, Dieter. *Galatians: A Continental Commentary*. Translated by O. C. Dean. Continental Commentary 48. Minneapolis: Fortress, 1992.

Malbon, Elizabeth Struthers, and Edgar V. McKnight, eds. *The New Literary Criticism and the New Testament*. Journal for the Study of the New Testament. Supplement Series 109. Sheffield: Sheffield Academic, 1994.

Martyn, J. Louis. *Galatians: A New Translation with Introduction and Commentary*. The Anchor Bible, 33A. New York: Doubleday, 1997.

Mburu, Elizabeth W. *African Hermeneutics*. Carlisle: HippoBooks, 2019.

McLean, B. Hudson. *The Cursed Christ: Mediterranean Expulsion Rituals and Pauline Soteriology*. Journal for the Study of the New Testament Supplement Series 126. Sheffield: Sheffield, 1996.

Mendenhall, George E. *Law and Covenant in Israel and the Ancient Near East*. Pittsburgh: Biblical Colloquium, 1955.

Mojola, A. O. "The Old Testament or Hebrew Bible in Africa: Challenges and Prospects for Interpretation and Translation." *Verbum et Ecclesia* 35, no. 3 (2014), Art. #1307. http://dx.doi. org/10.4102/ve.v35i3.1307.

Moo, Douglas J. *The Epistle to the Romans*. New International Commentary on the New Testament. Grand Rapids: W. B. Eerdmans, 1996.

Morland, Kjell Arne. *The Rhetoric of Curse in Galatians: Paul Confronts Another Gospel*. Emory Studies in Early Christianity 5. Atlanta: Scholars Press, 1995.

Ngewa, Samuel. *Galatians*. Africa Bible Commentary Series. Nairobi: WordAlive, 2010.

Pate, C. Marvin. *The Reverse of the Curse*. Tubingen: Mohr, 2000.

Perkins, Pheme. *Abraham's Divided Children: Galatians and the Politics of Faith*. The New Testament in Context. Harrisburg: Trinity Press International, 2001.

Pietersma, Albert, and Benjamin G. Wright. *A New English Translation of the Septuagint: And the Other Greek Translation Traditionally Included under That Title*. New York: Oxford University Press, 2007.

Rahlfs, Alfred, ed. *Septuaginta: Id Est Vetus Testamentum Graece Iuxta LXX Interpretes*. 9th ed. Stuttgart: Dt. Bibelstiftung, 1988.

Reed, Rodney L., ed. *Christianity and Suffering: African Perspectives*. Africa Society of Evangelical Theology Series. Carlisle: Langham Global Library, 2017.

Robbins, Vernon K. *Exploring the Texture of Texts: A Guide to Socio-Rhetorical Interpretation*. Harrisburg: Trinity Press International, 1996.

Robbins, Vernon K. "Socio-Rhetorical Criticism: Mary, Elizabeth, and the Magnificat as a Test Case." In *The New Literary Criticism and the New Testament*, Journal for the Study of the New Testament. Supplement Series 109, edited by Elizabeth Struthers Malbon and Edgar V. McKnight, 282–322. Sheffield: Sheffield Academic Press, 1994.

Roetzel, Calvin J. *Paul, a Jew on the Margins*. 1st ed. Louisville: Westminster John Knox Press, 2003.

Ryken, Leland, Jim Wilhoit, Tremper Longman, Colin Duriez, Douglas Penney, and Daniel G. Reid, eds. *Dictionary of Biblical Imagery*. Downers Grove: InterVarsity Press, 1998.

Schnabel, E. J. *Early Christian Missions*. 2 Vols. Downers Grove: InterVarsity Press, 2004.

Schreiner, Thomas R. *The Law and Its Fulfillment: A Pauline Theology of Law*. Grand Rapids: Baker Books, 1998.

Shreiner, Thomas R. *Galatians*. Zondervan Exegetical Commentary on the New Testament. Grand Rapids: Zondervan, 2010.

Schnelle, Udo. *Apostle Paul: His Life and Theology*. Translated by M. Eugene Boring. Grand Rapids: Baker Academic, 2005.

Silva, Moisés. *Interpreting Galatians: Explorations in Exegetical Method*. 2nd ed. Grand Rapids: Baker Academic, 2001.

Stanley, Christopher D. *Arguing with Scripture: The Rhetoric of Quotations in the Letters of Paul*. New York: T&T Clark International, 2004.

Stott, John R. W. *The Cross of Christ*. Leicester: InterVarsity Press, 2001.

Tate, W. Randolph. *Biblical Interpretation: An Integrated Approach*. 3rd ed. Peabody: Hendrickson, 2008.

Taylor, John V. *The Primal Vision, Christian Presence amid African Religion*. London, SCM, 1963.

Thielman, Frank. *Paul & the Law*. Downers Grove: InterVarsity Press, 1994.

Torrance, Thomas F., David W. Torrance, and T. H. L. Parker, eds. *The Epistles of Paul the Apostle to the Galatians, Ephesians, Philippians and Colossians*. Calvin's Commentaries. Grand Rapids: W. B. Eerdmans, 1965.

Travis, Stephen. *Christ and the Judgement of God: The Limits of Divine Retribution in New Testament Thought*. 2nd ed. Milton Keynes: Paternoster, 2009.

Versnel, H. S. "Beyond Cursing: The Appeal to Justice in Judicial Prayers." In *Magika Hiera: Ancient Greek Magic and Religion*, edited by Christopher A. Faraone and Dirk Obbink, 60–106. New York: Oxford University Press, 1997.

Wachege, P. N. *Curses and Cursing among the Agīkūyū: Socio-cultural and Religious Studies*. Department of Philosophy and Religious Studies. Nairobi: University of Nairobi, 2003.

Wakefield, Andrew Hollis. *Where to Live: The Hermeneutical Significance of Paul's Citations from Scripture in Galatians 3:1–14*. Society of Biblical Literature Academia Biblica, no. 14. Leiden: Brill, 2003.

Wallace, Daniel B. *The Basics of New Testament Syntax: An Intermediate Greek Grammar*. Grand Rapids: Zondervan, 2000.

Walton, John H. *Genesis*. The NIV Application Commentary. Grand Rapids: Zondervan, 2001.

Wenham, D. "Acts and the Pauline Corpus, II: The Evidence of Parallels." In *The Book of Acts in Its Ancient Literary Setting*, edited by B. W. Winter and A. D. Clarke, 215–58. Grand Rapids: Paternoster, 1993.

Wenham, Gordon J. *Genesis 1–15*. Word Biblical Commentary. Waco: Word Books, 1987.

Westermann, Claus, and John J. Scullion. *Genesis 1–11: A Continental Commentary*. Continental Commentary. Minneapolis: Fortress Press, 1984.

Williams, David John. *Paul's Metaphors: Their Context and Character*. Peabody: Hendrickson, 1999.

Wisdom, Jeffrey R. *Blessing for the Nations and the Curse of the Law: Paul's Citation of Genesis and Deuteronomy in Gal 3.8–10*. Wissenschaftliche Untersuchungen Zum Neuen Testament 133. Tübingen: Mohr Siebeck, 2001.

Witherington, Ben, III. *Grace in Galatia: A Commentary on St. Paul's Letter to the Galatians*. Grand Rapids: W. B. Eerdmans, 1998.

Wright, Christopher J. H. *The Mission of God's People: A Biblical Theology of the Church's Mission*. Grand Rapids: Zondervan, 2010.

Bibliography Information on Media Reporting on Cursing Practices in Marakwet

Kosgei Elvis. "Elders from West Pokot Conduct an Old Kalenjin Practice as a Last Resort to Cattle Rustling." Produced by Kenya Television Network. Aired 6 February 2019, on KTN News. https://www.standardmedia.co.ke/ktnnews/video/2000167346/elders-from-west-pokot-conduct-an-old-kalenjin-practice-as-a-last-resort-to-cattle-rustling

Rutto, Stephen. "Elders Turn to Curses to Help End Constant Bandit Attacks." *The Standard,* 5 February 2019. Accessed 7 March 2019. https://www.standardmedia.co.ke/article/2001312000/elders-turn-to-curses-to-help-end-constant-bandit-attack

Ancient Sources

Borret, M., *Origene: Contre Celse*. 5 vols.; Paris: Cerf, 1967.

Colson, F.H. and G.H. Whitaker (trans.), *Philo in Ten Volume*. LCL; Cambridge: Cambridge University Press, 1930.

Evans, E. (ed. and trans.) *Tertullian: Adversus Marcionem*. 2 vols.; Oxford: Clarendon Press, 1972.

Otto, J.C.T. (ed.), *Corpus Apologetorum Christianorum, III*. Jena: LibrariaRDufft, 1879.

Prigent, P. and R.A. Kraft, *Epitre de Barnabe*. Paris: Les Editions du Cerf, 1971.

Langham Literature, with its publishing work, is a ministry of Langham Partnership.

Langham Partnership is a global fellowship working in pursuit of the vision God entrusted to its founder John Stott –

> *to facilitate the growth of the church in maturity and Christ-likeness through raising the standards of biblical preaching and teaching.*

Our vision is to see churches in the Majority World equipped for mission and growing to maturity in Christ through the ministry of pastors and leaders who believe, teach and live by the word of God.

Our mission is to strengthen the ministry of the word of God through:
- nurturing national movements for biblical preaching
- fostering the creation and distribution of evangelical literature
- enhancing evangelical theological education

especially in countries where churches are under-resourced.

Our ministry

Langham Preaching partners with national leaders to nurture indigenous biblical preaching movements for pastors and lay preachers all around the world. With the support of a team of trainers from many countries, a multi-level programme of seminars provides practical training, and is followed by a programme for training local facilitators. Local preachers' groups and national and regional networks ensure continuity and ongoing development, seeking to build vigorous movements committed to Bible exposition.

Langham Literature provides Majority World preachers, scholars and seminary libraries with evangelical books and electronic resources through publishing and distribution, grants and discounts. The programme also fosters the creation of indigenous evangelical books in many languages, through writer's grants, strengthening local evangelical publishing houses, and investment in major regional literature projects, such as one volume Bible commentaries like the *Africa Bible Commentary* and the *South Asia Bible Commentary*.

Langham Scholars provides financial support for evangelical doctoral students from the Majority World so that, when they return home, they may train pastors and other Christian leaders with sound, biblical and theological teaching. This programme equips those who equip others. Langham Scholars also works in partnership with Majority World seminaries in strengthening evangelical theological education. A growing number of Langham Scholars study in high quality doctoral programmes in the Majority World itself. As well as teaching the next generation of pastors, graduated Langham Scholars exercise significant influence through their writing and leadership.

To learn more about Langham Partnership and the work we do visit **langham.org**

www.ingramcontent.com/pod-product-compliance
Lightning Source LLC
Chambersburg PA
CBHW070806230426
43665CB00017B/2504